Praise for *Cedric Maxwell*
and *If These Walls Could Talk: Boston Celtics*

"I'm grateful for my friendship with Max. I'll always be grateful for how he treated me initially, which probably started off our friendship, and it just grew from there. He's been loyal, and I think he's been a really good Celtic for all these years. I know we had a glitch in the middle, but I'm glad that he's back with us. Even with some of the things that he's had to endure throughout his career in Boston, I know the fans loved him. I really don't know any people that are not Cedric Maxwell fans."

**—Danny Ainge, Boston Celtics guard (1981–89),
president of basketball operations (2003–21)**

"Like the legendary Celtics Hall of Famer Sam Jones, Maxwell had been one of the sport's greatest big-game players. Besides the '81 MVP, he had turned in an epic performance in Game 7 of the 1984 championship, keying an epoch-making triumph over the Showtime Los Angeles Lakers of Magic Johnson, Kareem Abdul-Jabbar, and coach Pat Riley with 24 points, eight rebounds, and eight assists. As the video coordinator for the team in the 1980s, I watched the brilliant Maxwell add a vital element to a superstar-laden locker room. His hilarious exchanges with the moody legend Tiny Archibald were vital to the team's success. He gave newcomer Robert Parish the nickname 'Chief,' fitting and proper for a man who declined fanfare yet was a team protector. He brought the best out of the late Dennis Johnson, another legendary player."

**—Robert Schron, author of *The Bird Era: A History
of the Boston Celtics 1978–1988***

"We just really liked each other. It's funny. I talked with him and Danny [Ainge] in New York, and after two minutes, we're laughing our asses off at the same things we laughed at before. It's hilarious because we just go right back to where we were."

—Kevin McHale, Boston Celtics forward (1980–93)

"This book is long overdue. I covered the Celtics every day of Max's final three seasons here, and it's been a joy to have him as part of our local media team in the last couple of decades. Nobody who played in Boston was funnier or more clutch. Max and Mike Isenberg have brought it to life in these pages. Read it. You will learn and laugh."

**—Dan Shaughnessy, columnist, *The Boston Globe*
and author of *Wish It Lasted Forever: Life with the Larry Bird Celtics***

"Max's achievements on the court speak for themselves: NBA Finals MVP, two-time NBA champion, and a critical component on one of the most feared front lines in basketball history. Max played *big* in big games. But he also had fun. He always played energized and intense but would also laugh and crack a joke, never seeming to take himself too seriously on a team that rarely broke a smile. I got to know Cedric Maxwell the broadcaster, the legendary character that would draw a hush in the press room when entering. Dressed from head to tippy toe in custom suits, Max looked like an NBA legend. When he started telling stories, the press dining room followed his every word.

"Co-author Mike Isenberg navigates Maxwell's journey through racial tensions of growing up in the Jim Crow South, to his years as a professional basketball star in a city unfairly judged as racist, to his relationship with the 2008 championship team, to today's team in green. There isn't much Max missed when it comes to the last 40-plus years in Boston basketball. Mike and Max plow their way through the up and down relationship with Larry Bird, Red Auerbach, and the trade to the Los Angeles Clippers in 1985. They leave no stone unturned. Max is maybe the most visible mystery in Celtics recent history. Everyone always wondered what happened between Cedric and the Celtics way back in the golden decade of the NBA. Thanks to this book, you now can get a glimpse of the magic that is Cedric "Cornbread" Maxwell, the man who won a Finals MVP in 1981 and continued to change lives and make an indelible impact with everyone he met on and off the court."

—Nick Gelso, CEO, CLNS Media

"He got his number raised, which is always the way it should have been. And now we've had a second life as a Celtic—a symbolic Celtic, if you will—and a beloved figure in the community. It's all ended well, and I'm happy for that. He's just tremendously good guy to be around and he's got a lot to offer and that comes through."

—Bob Ryan, sport columnist emeritus, *The Boston Globe*

"He's funny and has a good heart. He cares about people. Basically, he sees things through the same lens I do. Cedric is cool…He's got a gift for talking, and I've listened to his commentating on games, and he's killing it."

—Robert Parish, Boston Celtics center (1980–1994)

"He's come back as a broadcaster, and everybody loves this guy. I think you have to understand about the fans in Boston: they're very knowledgeable, and a lot of them appreciate his contribution to the game."

—Don Chaney, Boston Celtics guard (1968–75, 1977–80)

"Cedric is a true friend. When he's on your side, you always know what you're going to get, it's going to be consistent. He's been adopted twice—biological adoption and sports adoption because the city of Boston has adopted Max. It's a two-way street. Max realized that Boston became his home. He's made a lot of friends there, and the city really, really, really cares about Max."

**—M.L. Carr, Boston Celtics guard/forward (1979–85),
head coach (1995–97)**

If These **WALLS** *Could* **TALK:**
BOSTON CELTICS

*Stories from the
Boston Celtics Sideline,
Locker Room, and Press Box*

Cedric Maxwell with Mike Isenberg

TRIUMPH
BOOKS

Library of Congress Cataloging-in-Publication Data

Names: Maxwell, Cedric, author. | Isenberg, Mike
Title: If these walls could talk: Boston Celtics : stories from the Boston Celtics sideline, locker room, and press box / Cedric Maxwell and Mike Isenberg.
Description: Chicago, Illinois : Triumph Books, 2021. | Summary: "This book includes stories from Cedric Maxwell's championship-playing days to the current era of Boston Celtics basketball"—Provided by publisher.
Identifiers: LCCN 2021019348 (print) | LCCN 2021019349 (ebook) | ISBN 9781629378831 (paperback) | ISBN 9781641257213 (epub)
Subjects: LCSH: Boston Celtics (Basketball team)—History. | Maxwell, Cedric. | Basketball players—United States—Biography.
Classification: LCC GV885.52.B67 M28 2021 (print) | LCC GV885.52.B67 (ebook) | DDC 796.323/640974461—dc23
LC record available at https://lccn.loc.gov/2021019348
LC ebook record available at https://lccn.loc.gov/2021019349

This book is available in quantity at special discounts for your group or organization. For further information, contact:

Triumph Books LLC
814 North Franklin Street
Chicago, Illinois 60610
(312) 337-0747
www.triumphbooks.com

Printed in U.S.A.
ISBN: 978-1-62937-883-1
Design by Nord Compo
Photos courtesy of AP Images unless otherwise indicated

CONTENTS

FOREWORD

The first time I met Cedric Maxwell was back in November of 1974 during the first of our two college matchups between my Centenary team and his squad from the University of North Carolina–Charlotte. We each won one of these games, but I don't remember much from those two contests except how great a player he was. His game was different than a lot of guys in that he had an unstoppable weapon—that deadly jump hook.

After those two games, I figured we'd play against each other in the pros but never could have imagined that we'd become lifelong friends. My NBA career began when I was drafted by the Golden State Warriors. Being younger than I, Cedric was picked in the following year by the Boston Celtics. But our fates would intertwine prior to the 1980 NBA Draft. Boston had the top pick; Golden State had the third. There were a lot of rumors that we were going to sign Cedric as a free agent and then draft Kevin McHale out of Minnesota. That would have given us a powerful front line of Maxwell, McHale, and myself.

Of course, Red Auerbach then pulled off one of the most lopsided trades in league history. He sent the No. 1 pick to the Warriors in exchange for the No. 3…and yours truly. He took McHale, and the Celtics now had Maxwell, McHale, and myself to go with a guy named Larry Bird. It's funny how one simple trade could change the course of history. Our "Big Four" ended up winning two championships and gaining enough memories for a lifetime. People know me as "Chief." That name came from Cedric, who compared me to the Native American character in *One Flew Over the Cuckoo's Nest* who went by the same name. Not only did I pick up a nickname that would follow me forever, but I had also gained a lifelong friend.

Bird, McHale, and myself were fortunate to be elected into the Basketball Hall of Fame. But let me tell you something: Cedric should absolutely be there with us. That era of Celtics basketball really started in the 1981 NBA Finals against the Houston Rockets. Cedric was—without doubt—the best player on the court, winning MVP and bringing the championship back to Boston. Then when we beat the Los Angeles Lakers in 1984, it was Cedric who told us to hop on his back. There's no way we win those two titles without him.

When Bird arrived in Boston, Cedric was coming off a season where he averaged 19 points per game. *He* was the big star. But instead of complaining and causing trouble, Cedric took on a less glamorous—but just as important—role, which allowed our success. The fact that he was willing to subjugate his ego for the greater good made all the difference. People ask why Cedric and I have been such good friends. After all, we seem quite different—he's never been shy about expressing his opinions while I tend to be a little more on the quieter side. But we're both about winning and being authentic. Cedric has a wicked sense of humor—as you'll read in his terrific insider's look into the Celtics—and we've always stood by each other through thick and thin.

When we don't speak for a period of time, it doesn't matter. We pick up like it was just yesterday. Cedric has a great heart; he cares about people. We see things through the same lens. So as much as I loved him as a teammate, I'm even more proud to call him my friend.

—Robert Parish
NBA Hall of Fame, Class of 2003

INTRODUCTIONS

As someone who has lived a public life, a lot of folks have approached me about writing a book. The obvious question is: why now?

When Mike Isenberg reached out to me on Twitter, I asked him the same question. He explained that I've been involved with the Boston Celtics—almost nonstop—from 1977 through today. I did have a detour with the Los Angeles Clippers and Houston Rockets, but I've always been a Celtic at heart. I played with John Havlicek, Pete Maravich, Larry Bird, Kevin McHale, and Robert Parish. As a broadcaster I survived the Rick Pitino experiment and have been around for the "new" Big Three of Kevin Garnett, Paul Pierce, and Ray Allen and now the Jayson Tatum and Jaylen Brown era.

I also wrote this to try and clear up some loose ends and tell people who I really am. So many people have predetermined ideas of Cedric Maxwell—he's funny, witty, and a sharp dresser. Some people think of me as a quitter, stemming from my knee injury in 1985 and someone who was basically exiled 12 months after leading my team to the 1984 NBA title.

My story has so many twists and turns—some that folks know about, others that they don't—and I want to be the one to tell them. My goal for you is to know who I am, what I stand for, and to hear it (or read it) from the horse's mouth.

I hope you enjoy the book!

—*Cedric Maxwell*

When I was growing up near Boston, a friend told me that I looked just like Cedric Maxwell. As a White Jewish kid from the suburbs, it was funny to hear that I was being compared to a 6'8" Black professional athlete from North Carolina. His point was that we were both all arms and legs, which was actually true.

I always liked Maxwell, but from that moment, he became "my guy." When I played basketball at Emerson College, I wore No. 31 in his honor. My email addresses all have 31 in them. Meeting him several years ago was very cool. But this is a whole different level. Maxwell and I conducted more than 20 interviews for this book and spoke several more times on a casual basis. To truly get to know the man behind "Cornbread" has been terrific, and you'll get that experience in these pages.

As we discussed the project, my only concern was how forthcoming he would be. At the time, we didn't know each other well enough for me to gauge it. Let's just say that it was not a problem at all. Maxwell is one of the most candid people I've met. Whenever he's made mistakes, he's always been accountable. The authenticity that we both share made our interviews seem more like conversations. It's always easy to talk about winning titles and the good times, but Maxwell was just as open about some really difficult topics. In my opinion, that's what makes this book different.

Cedric Maxwell is a man of the people. In this book you'll get a sense of that. People with such different personalities like Danny Ainge, Robert Parish, Kevin McHale, and Dan Shaughnessy found themselves drawn to him. I interviewed so many people for this book, and they could not have been more gracious with their time. And they all have one thing in common—they love Cedric. He has an incredible story, and I hope you enjoy reading about him and the Celtics franchise as much as we have enjoyed telling it.

—*Mike Isenberg*

CHAPTER 1
1984 FINALS:
LAKERS–CELTICS

The 1983–84 season was one of my favorites. The Boston Celtics had a new head coach and we were hyper-focused on winning the NBA championship—three years after our first as a group. The previous postseason we were swept out of the playoffs in the second round by the Milwaukee Bucks, and the team had basically quit on coach Bill Fitch. He was a hard-driving guy and after four years he'd hit his expiration date. So team president Red Auerbach fired Fitch and brought in Celtics legend K.C. Jones, whose easy manner was a desperately needed breath of fresh air.

The regular season was fun, as we won the Atlantic Division by 10 games over the defending champion Philadelphia 76ers. But that was the appetizer. All that mattered to us was winning another ring. We played with reckless abandon for Jones, for ourselves, and against Fitch.

We thought the biggest roadblock would once again be the 76ers, but they shockingly fell to the New Jersey Nets, who had a center Philly knew about…a guy named Darryl Dawkins, who they dumped to get Moses Malone.

In our first round, we had a tougher-than-expected series against the Washington Bullets but took care of business in four hard-fought games. Next up was the New York Knicks and the King. Bernard King was playing as well as anyone in the league. He averaged 43 points per game in an exciting first-round series win against the Detroit Pistons. King was truly a great player. I was supposed to play against him in college when he went to Tennessee, but he was suspended from the game. He battled substance abuse early in his pro career but had found a home in New York and finished second to Larry Bird for MVP. Everyone was building up King vs. Bird like it was a western showdown. The only problem with that was I was the person guarding King.

I was certainly impressed with the way he was playing. Who wouldn't be? But I made it clear I wasn't going to be intimidated. Before the series I was talking about how he always walked like he was on his way to the

O.K. Corral. That's when I officially lit the fire for the series, declaring, "Ain't no bitch who walks like this is going to score 40 on me."

Jones asked me why I thought that was a good idea to say. The media ran with it. I may not have read the paper, but King sure did. Before the first game, we were all shaking hands, and he just looked at mine…and I pulled it back. We won both games in Boston and held King to 26 and 13 points. This may have seemed pretty easy, but guarding King was anything but. He got his shot off so quickly that we couldn't double-team him. Heck, you couldn't even count to two before he released it. If he got you on his hip, he'd leverage you. The way I guarded him was to play circle defense and never let him lock me down on the post. His guards wouldn't throw him the ball those times. So it at least slowed him down.

We got to New York, and the "bitch" scored 24 points in a Game 3 win. The Knicks then won Game 4, and King put 43 on me. The Madison Square Garden crowd was just going crazy, knowing that I had no way to stop him. After the game King had instructed a reporter to give him the stat sheet. Man, was I pissed. In my mind I was like, *This motherfucker…I'm going to kill this guy!*

We blew them out in Game 5, but King still had 30. When we got back to New York, they won a close game, and King put another 44 on me. Game 7 was at Boston Garden. There was no way we were going to lose that one. Bird made sure of that with 39 points, and we won 121–104. King? He scored "only" 24, and I even blocked a shot of his. Years later at the end of my career, King and I were teammates on the Bullets. He told me I was really a pain in his ass during that series. At least I made "the bitch" work for it.

That win got us back to the Eastern Conference Finals against a familiar foe—the Milwaukee Bucks. This time we just kicked their ass. All of our frustration from the previous year came out. We were up 3–0 and were ready to sweep them. All of a sudden, Paul Mokeski—the same dude who averaged four points a game—erupted for 12 points, and they staved off elimination…until we closed them out in Game 5 back home. Beating the Bucks brought us to the main event.

There are certain rivalries that are worth waiting for: Red Sox–Yankees, Bruins–Canadiens, Michigan–Notre Dame. But there is nothing that equals Celtics vs. Lakers. This is what the NBA was dying for: East vs. West, Larry vs. Magic, the two winningest teams in league history.

You know how teams sometimes say they don't care about who they face in a playoff series? That was not the case for us. We *hated* the Los Angeles Lakers, and they hated us. Bird hated Magic Johnson, going back to losing the NCAA championship game to him. Make no mistake: this was who we wanted. The Lakers were so…West Coast. They had Laker Girls and Dancing Barry. They played in the "Fabulous Forum." We had the run-down Garden. They wore the beautiful purple and gold, and we had stone cold green. And you *know* we didn't have Jack Nicholson or Dyan Cannon at our games.

Aside from Bird and Magic, nobody was under more pressure than Robert Parish. He was going up against Kareem Abdul-Jabbar. "I always felt like Kevin and Worthy, that was going to be a wash," Parish said recently. "Magic and Larry, that was kind of going to be a wash. Where the Lakers had an edge was at the center position because Kareem was clearly better than I was ever going to be."

At that point in his career, Parish was an All-Star, but this was Abdul-Jabbar, arguably the best player in the history of college basketball. Already a three-time NBA champion, the guy ended up as the NBA's all-time leading scorer. Oh, and he was Parish's absolute favorite player. "I tried to make him earn everything he got," Parish said, "and tried to slow him down a little bit."

In Game 1 Abdul-Jabbar dominated the Chief, outscoring him 32–13, and the Lakers won 115–109. Parish played like he was playing against his idol, showing him too much respect. There were times when the Boston media would pile on Parish partly because he was so stoic. People didn't realize how great a player Parish was. He didn't have the sky hook like Abdul-Jabbar, but he had a nice little hook shot as well, and after Fitch got him in shape, he ran the floor better than any center. The bottom line is that we had given away home-court advantage. And things were about to get a lot worse.

Game 2 wasn't going our way. James Worthy went off with 29 points, and we were trailing 113–111 with fewer than 20 seconds remaining. We were in major trouble. If we lost this game, we'd go out to L.A. down 2–0 and on our way to a quick series loss. Jones put in Gerald Henderson and M.L. Carr to try and make something happen.

We also had another factor in our favor. As great a player as Worthy was, his Achilles heel was that he didn't want to go the free-throw line late in games. Worthy inbounded the ball to Magic, who gave it back to him. Worthy acted like it was a grenade; he couldn't get rid of it fast enough. I remember seeing him float the pass—and it seemed like it hung in the air for an hour. Henderson anticipated it, stole the ball, and laid it up over Worthy. L.A. was stunned. They still had 13 seconds to try and score, but Magic inexplicably dribbled the clock out, and we headed to overtime. That was when he earned the nickname "Tragic" Johnson.

We took care of business in OT and now we had a series tied at one game apiece before heading out west. After the game Henderson said he could hear legendary Boston radio announcer Johnny Most screaming: "Henderson stole the ball!" That play would go on as one of the most famous moments in NBA history similar to when John Havlicek stole a pass when the Sixers were trying to run out the clock. In his raspiest voice, Most shouted: "Havlicek stole the ball! Johnny Havlicek stole the ball!" Thanks to Henderson, there was a new classic in Celtics history. When I think about what might have happened, there was a very good chance if we lost that game, we would have gotten swept. Thank goodness for Henderson.

As serious and intense as this series was, we still were able to find some fun on the way to The Forum. Our hotel was at the airport, about eight blocks from the Lakers' home, so we took a bus to practice. We passed a car dealership that had a guy dressed as a gorilla in front, waving a sign to entice customers. Our assistant equipment manager, Wayne Lebeaux saw his opportunity. On our way back to the hotel, we passed the dealership again, and there was the gorilla wearing Quinn Buckner's uniform top. The bus literally almost tipped over because we were laughing so hard. Nobody enjoyed it more than Buckner. We actually made the driver do a U-turn, so we could see the gorilla again.

If anyone was worried about a Lakers hangover in Game 3, they quickly found out that wasn't the case. L.A. beat us like we committed a crime. L.A. ran free with 53 fast break points. We were never in this game. We trailed by 11 at half and 25 after three quarters. The final score was 137–104, and I don't know if it was even that close. Bird was the only person who played well. He scored 30, but it didn't matter. After the game he called us out. "We played like sissies. I can't believe a team like this would let L.A. come out and push us around like they did," Bird said. "We've just got to play more physical…We've just got to be a little more intense. The first two games were very intense. We played hard. Today, I don't think we played hard."

Nobody read anything else into Bird's comments. We didn't just play bad—we sucked. They did whatever they wanted. It was Showtime to the max, and they were laughing at us. We weren't going down like that. We were ready to play rollerball. Playing hard was not going to be an issue for Game 4.

We were down 2–1 in the series, but it felt a lot worse. I remember going to eat after Game 3, and some guy on the radio said the series wasn't over, but the fat lady was warming up. By all accounts, L.A. should have been up 3–0 and going for the sweep. Whatever we were doing wasn't working, and it was time for a change. We decided that there were not going to be any more layups. The Lakers looked like they were running a three-man drill in Game 3, and that needed to stop. We said we were going treat them like they killed your kids and raped our wives. Yep, it was that serious.

In practice it was obvious that our mind-set had changed, as guys were bouncing off each other. Even Kevin McHale, one of the most timid guys on the team, was knocking everyone around. When I saw that, I was like, *Okay, everyone is drinking the Kool-Aid. It's on now.* Danny Ainge noticed it, too. "After the meeting everyone was going, 'we've got to start fouling, like this is ridiculous,'" Ainge said. "I look at Kevin and say, 'Why don't you foul somebody one time? Why don't you take a hard foul once?' There was a lot of bickering. Our team was not happy after Game 3."

Ainge remembered one particular film session after Game 3 and how he then approached McHale. "It was basically a dunkfest in transition. They were just taking our missed shots and turnovers and coming in on a three-on-one fast break. It was embarrassing and humiliating," Ainge said. "We were going out to stretch, and I made a comment to him like, 'Why don't *you* take someone out?' I've been taking fouls on purpose and get booed in every arena in the NBA. Why don't you—one time—take someone out?' We had that kind of relationship."

Carr added gasoline to the fire. "If a kid goes to the store, runs as hard as he could to get to the store, and every time he gets to the store, he gets candy, he's gonna run right into the store," Carr said. "If he runs real, and there's a hornet's nest above the door when you go in, and every time it comes to get stung, he's not going to be so fast to get there. We've got to put the pressure on them physically. Well, Kevin, took it literally. And when that happened, we were like, *Oh, no, can't believe that—Kevin, of all people.* But we had already pumped him up with all this junk."

We were down 76–70 with about seven minutes left in the game. If we didn't come back, we'd be down 3–1 and just about cooked. McHale made sure that didn't happen. L.A. was on a break, and Kurt Rambis thought he had a layup. Instead, he got clotheslined by McHale, and all hell broke loose. "I was pissed," Rambis recalled on the ESPN 30 for 30 *Best of Frenemies*. "I thought it was a cheap shot and something you don't do."

If Worthy hadn't pushed him to the side, Rambis was heading toward our bench, ready to fight whoever was there. More than 30 years later, Worthy regrets holding his teammate off. "That was a nasty, dirty play, and I wish I had not been in the way of Kurt going to get Kevin," he said. "He deserved an ass-whooping for that."

Of course, there are two sides to every story. Just ask Bird all these years later. "Well, that's where all the flopping started," Bird said in the same documentary. "I don't think Kevin hit him that hard."

For his part, McHale apologized at the time...sort of. "I went to foul him, and when he skidded on the floor and bounced around," he said, "I didn't really care about hurting him that much, but I was like, *Oh, that might have been a little bit more than I anticipated.*"

We needed a jolt, and McHale definitely provided it, answering the challenge of his good friend, Ainge. "McHale did that, and it got us fired up," Ainge said. "And it wasn't Larry who did it. It was Kevin, and that got us geeked up. That was my favorite play that Kevin made in his whole career."

Even the mild-mannered Jones had gotten McHale fired up. "K.C. and everybody was yelling and screaming, how there would be no more layups. K.C. said, 'Next guy to get who gives up a layup comes over here on the bench,' which was not typical Case," McHale said. "I wish it had been Magic or Worthy or one of their top guys."

It could've been worse. The Pistons would do that and stand over you. McHale grabbed him and let him go. It, though, certainly shocked all of us. "As stunned as the fans and the Lakers were, Kevin's teammates were equally stunned because that is so unlike him," Parish said. "That was the furthest behavior to describe Kevin's personality as you could get. Kevin is not that type of player. I don't know where that came from."

If McHale committed a foul like that in today's NBA, he'd be suspended. For us it was the spark to a comeback. It emphasized what people were saying before the series: the Lakers were soft. It might have been harder than McHale had hoped, but he knew the result turned the game around. In the second half, Worthy missed a free throw, and I gave him the choke sign. Worthy had a rough series, and I know that he was thinking: *I can't make a free throw, and now I have to deal with this asshole.*

L.A. still had a five-point lead with less than a minute to go, but Magic turned Tragic again. First, he threw a bad pass that was picked off by Parish. Then after we tied it, he missed two huge free throws in overtime. One of the big moments in this series was when Jones switched Dennis Johnson onto Magic after I had guarded him the first few games. D.J. just hounded him from one end of the court to the other. That pressure definitely contributed to Magic making those mistakes. Later in overtime Bird hit a big jumper over Magic with 16 seconds left, and then Worthy had *another* pass picked off—this one by Carr—and somehow, some way, we were going home tied at two apiece.

This series was as much about mental toughness as what happened on the court. Red Auerbach was always in the opponents' head, and that was such a huge advantage. In Game 5 it was about one million degrees (actually 108) at Boston Garden, and, naturally, Lakers coach Pat Riley thought it was some dirty trick by us. The fact is that there was no air conditioning in the place, and both teams were sweltering. The difference was that we were used to it; they weren't.

When we saw 37-year-old Abdul-Jabbar sucking for air with an oxygen mask, we knew it was over; we were in their heads. These guys were used to 70 degrees in The Forum. But the stands of The Garden were full. Plus, there were fans smoking in the corridor; there was no escape. We had established residency right in their asses. To try and cool off, we had all the fans in our locker room. In fact, we actually changed into fresh uniforms at halftime. As a result, we were the roadrunners, and the Lakers were the coyotes. It was just great. This was like an old fashioned wrasslin' match. Bird had 34 points and 17 rebounds, and we were going back to L.A. with a chance to win the title.

When we returned to Los Angeles, let's just say we were in a much better place than our last trip. Instead of trying to figure out how to get back in the series, we were ready to close it out. Before the game a bunch of fans, calling themselves "The Rambis Youth," were giving us crap, telling me I couldn't guard their hero. So I went over there, took off their oversized glasses, and put them on. Then I started to throw the ball over the backboard. Yeah, we were a loose bunch. We lost Game 6, as Abdul-Jabbar went for 30 and 10, but the real problem was rookie Byron Scott. He went off, as they outscored us by 15 in the fourth quarter to even the series. I was doing a Celtics–Lakers game all these years later when Scott was the Lakers' head coach. Our broadcast position was right by the L.A. bench, and I said loud enough that he could hear, "And this guy cost us a chance to win a title here in L.A." Scott just turned around and smiled.

Sure, we were pissed that we didn't close things out, but we were still focused. In the middle of the game, I went up for a dunk on a fast break, and Worthy pushed me in the back. I came out like I was going to fight but then backed off. I said to myself, *I'm going to kick his fucking ass if we hook up again. I'm going to be right in his ass.*

* * *

When we came back to Boston for Game 7, I had a few things on my mind. Of course, we were one win away from winning another championship. But I was also getting ready for my wedding, too! Renee and I met when she was the nanny for Don Chaney's kids and I first came into the league. When I proposed we set the date for the one week after the last possible playoff game, which ended up being Game 7 of the Finals. Little did we know that we'd still be playing on that date. As you might imagine, I didn't sleep after Game 6 and the trip back from the West Coast. Some guys took a red-eye and got in at 5:00 AM. I flew with the team. We were disappointed but still very confident.

I drive under the basket past Kareem Abdul-Jabbar of the Los Angeles Lakers during our 111–102 victory in Game 7. I scored a team-high 24 points.

The day of Game 7, we had a morning shootaround, and then I followed my usual routine by taking a nap. My nephew Andre was with us, so I played with him for a couple of hours. Then I started to get antsy. By the time I got on Storrow Drive heading to the Garden, I was ready to kill someone. Shockingly, there was no traffic. If you're familiar with Boston, that's even more rare than a Game 7. On my way I picked up my traditional pregame meal: a Big Mac, large fries, and orange soda. The dinner of champions!

The locker room before a huge game is always an interesting place to be. Nowadays, guys will be into their phones or listening to music. On this day, Danny Ainge started prancing around with a stethoscope, checking everyone's heartbeat. When he came to me, he said, "Your heart rate isn't even up."

M.L. Carr described K.C. Jones' pregame speech, which was short, to the point, and had us fired up. "He walked up to the board and said, 'Men, you're the greatest team in the world. Go out and prove it,'" Carr said. "We were waiting for the rest of the speech, but that was it."

That's when I proclaimed, "You bitches get on my back. I'll carry you to this championship."

Talk about a scene-stopper. All the guys looked at me like "whoa." But Kevin McHale wasn't surprised. "That wasn't unusual for that team. We'd kind of have some fun," he said. "It was just a fun group of guys, but Max got it going. He said, 'Hey baby, let's go. I'm ready to roll.'"

It's like we were foaming at the mouth. "We were ready to tear the door down to get out there," Carr said. "I remember standing outside the Lakers locker room, telling James Worthy, 'If you win, you won't get out of here alive.'"

Besides me there was only one other player on our team who had been a Finals MVP, and that was Dennis Johnson, who won it with another team. I always thought I could raise my game from high school to the Final Four and, of course, winning it all that night in Houston during my first NBA championship in 1981. We'd talked enough noise. Some guys say they don't feel fear. I think they're full of crap. I always used it as a motivator.

The rest of the room was pretty quiet. Larry Bird wasn't really a trash talker at that point. That, of course, would change, but he wasn't at all during that time. Guys were getting their ankles taped or reading, just counting down the minutes until game time.

Early on, the big matchup was me vs. Kurt Rambis. You could have put cuffs on me for child abuse because I destroyed him that kid once and for all. The game was tied after the first, but we went up by six at halftime, 13 after three, and were on our way. "For a stretch of the game, it wasn't going to Kevin and Larry, who are first-ballot Hall of Famers. The ball was going to Max." Ainge said. "And it wasn't going to D.J., who was a multiple-time All-Star, a former Finals MVP. And it wasn't going to Parish, a top 50 player of all-time. The ball was going to Max."

For that game, *I* was the man, and the other guys were fine with it. "He got it going. He just started beating people off the dribble," McHale said. "Then he got in there and he was spinning and into his bag, getting more and more confidence. He just played great."

I was in the zone for the entire game. There was a play where I scored on Worthy, and I turned to Quinn Buckner and said, "That bitch can't guard me!" I knew I was in his head and was laughing my ass off.

It was so cool to be able to excel and elevate my game to that next level. Later in the game, I was on the free-throw line, and you can read my lips talking to Worthy, saying, "Bitch, you can't guard me." Worthy just lowered his head like he knew.

I ended up with 24 points, eight rebounds, and eight assists, Bird had 20 and 12 boards, and Parish had 14 and 16. This was a great team effort.

My only regret from that night was I wanted Jones to take me out in the last few minutes so I could get that ovation. But I played until the end. When Michael Cooper attempted the last three-pointer of the game, I ran back to try and block his shot. I was the first person off the floor. The buzzer sounded, and I was out. It was a good thing, too, after seeing Kareem Abdul-Jabbar elbow fans while trying to leave the floor and Bird having trouble getting to the locker room.

I take pride in being an X-factor in that game and the series. "It was inspiring," Ainge said. "We all knew Max could do it because it wasn't the first time he'd taken over games for a stretch. He just didn't get to do it a lot like he might have on another team because we had two of the most efficient scores in the history of the game in Bird and McHale, and so it wasn't shocking to any of us."

It was incredible to be the NBA Finals MVP back in 1981, but leading us to the promised land in Game 7 was even bigger for me. We were playing against the Los Angeles Lakers and we were on live TV (unlike the tape delay of '81 against the Houston Rockets). Magic Johnson had his boys, Mark Aguirre and Isiah Thomas, in the stands. I remember thinking how the entire world was locked in on that moment. How cool is that?

The locker room celebration was just awesome. I remember all of us jumping up and down, then huddling, and cheering each other on. We were like little kids. When they gave the trophy to Red Auerbach, he grabbed it, shook it, and said: "It feels great! Whatever happened to the Los Angeles dynasty? You guys are talking about a dynasty. Here's where it is, right here! That's the dynasty right here. We're the best team in the world right now!"

It was such a cool, iconic moment to see him so proud. I mean this was his 15th championship. I think the fact that he was used to winning every year and had been so far away from that recently made it even more meaningful. He won a couple with Jo Jo White, Dave Cowens, and John Havlicek in 1974 and 1976 and then went through the spell where the Celtics were one of the worst teams in the NBA. Now he was back on top.

Buckner came up to me after the game. He gave me a hug. "Hoss, without you," he said, "we wouldn't have won this thing."

That was such a compliment from a teammate. It was just a surreal moment. It's like the of the birth of your first child. I don't even remember leaving the arena. We were all just floating. Fans were chasing us in our cars. I lived in a gated community, and people were following me, but they had to stop at the gate. Even being the Finals MVP wasn't as great as that particular moment.

CHAPTER 2
GROWING UP IN KINSTON

The best way to describe me is happy-go-lucky. I've always been that way, always will be. My life has been one hell of a ride and filled with ups and downs, but I wouldn't trade it for anything in the world. Growing up, I always knew I was loved. My parents, Manny and Bessie Mae, ensured that. The sun shone on my ass all the time.

I grew up in Kinston, North Carolina, a small, sleepy southern town, which, as you can imagine, was steeped in segregation during the '50s and '60s. What you wouldn't imagine is that Kinston has turned out to be sort of an NBA breeding ground. In addition to yours truly, Kinston is the hometown of former players Jerry Stackhouse and Charles Shackleford, along with current guys in the league like Brandon Ingram and Reggie Bullock.

How does a town of around 20,000 produce athletes like this? Well, you might say Kinston is the "chosen" place. In January of 1961—in the middle of the Cold War—Kinston almost ceased to exist. There was an American B-52 in the air, and its wing snapped off, causing the plane to basically explode and fall to the ground. On board were two huge bombs with the power 250 times the strength of the one used in Hiroshima.

Incredibly, the bombs landed about 50 miles outside of Raleigh, North Carolina, but failed to detonate. The first one landed safely and was disarmed. The second, however, caused a huge crater, as its parachute failed to engage. Somehow, a nuclear disaster was averted. You might say that Kinston is a survivor, and that's how we became a basketball factory.

My hometown, though, was far from perfect. It was Segregated with a capital S. My father was in the military, so we spent my first to third grade years living in Hawaii with total integration. When we got home, things were different. Even though Kinston was about 52 percent Black, there was a clear division by color. We literally lived on the other side of the tracks and had separate restaurants, water fountains, etc. Kinston had some beautiful beaches, but White folks had the run of the land, and we were stuck with what was left over.

I played whichever sport was in season. If it was fall, that meant football, winter was basketball, and summer was for baseball. This wasn't like Pop Warner or AAU—nothing that organized—it was just me and my boys playing. Baseball always held a special place in my heart. We'd see the Kinston Eagles, our minor league team, whenever we had the chance. Going to see the Eagles was the one thing that Manny always gave us money for. Dad would give me $1, and that would get me admission into the game, a hot dog, Coke, and popcorn. If you were lucky, there might be a ticket in the popcorn to use for a free bat. I loved going to those games.

Basketball was in my blood. My mother, Bessie Mae, played at North Carolina Central, which Celtics fans know is the alma mater for Hall of Famer Sam Jones. So yes, I got my skills on the court from Mom. But that's not all I received.

* * *

About three years ago, one confusing situation turned into the biggest shock of my life. The night started innocently enough. I was hanging with some buddies, playing cards, when I got a text from this girl who went to UNC–Charlotte with me. I didn't think anything of it and went back to my game. The next morning this woman called and asked if I could talk. She told me that she had written me a letter 40 years ago, saying she had my child. She said, "That child has now found me, and I told her that you were the father."

I picked my jaw up from the floor and asked why she didn't tell me first? The whole thing seemed a little suspect, but I went along with it. We proceeded to take a paternity test, and it came back at 0.0 percent. I was disappointed because I actually wanted her to be my child. If it wasn't me, I was worried she'd never find her father. After the chaos died down, I had a conversation with my sister, Lisa, that really turned things upside down. I was explaining the situation and told her how I had taken the DNA test. Without hesitation she asked, "Oh, to find out who your father is?"

Excuse me?

When I pressed her, Lisa said she didn't know anything and basically took the fifth amendment. But the wheels in my mind were working overtime. Maybe I should have taken the hint from my daughter, Morgan. Back in 2013, she and a friend went to Africa and got a pretty big news flash. "We decided we were going to see a sangoma [essentially an African witch doctor]," Morgan said. "We found one and went into his hut. He had dried bats and animals, containers filled with all kinds of spices and liquids. It was like a movie. Then we saw a taller, dark-skinned Black man, and our translator said the doctor would give us a reading. We just had to pay him some money, and he'd throw out some trinkets, look at them, and talk to our ancestors.

"So he takes the trinkets—when I say trinkets, I'm talking like pieces of Legos, rocks, the most random things—and he throws them down and picks them up. Then he throws them down again and asked, 'What's your father's last name?' I told him 'Maxwell.' The sangoma repeated this twice more, then stared me in the face, and said, 'That's not your father's last name.' I said 'What?' He said, 'That's not your father's last name.'"

That's such a crazy anecdote, but I've always had a great memory involving my anecdotes. And when thinking about my childhood, I did remember when I was three or four years old, and Manny wasn't around. We moved to Jacksonville, North Carolina, because he was in the Marine Corps. Nobody ever told me anything, and Manny and my mom got married when I was four years old. Pieces were starting to come together.

About two years ago, I finally got the information out of Mom. She said my biological father was a man named Deford Small, and he was still alive. Oh, and I now had two brothers and a sister from his side. On New Year's Day of 2020, Morgan and I went to visit my new siblings in Greenville, South Carolina. It was just an incredible experience.

Mom had told me that Deford came from my hometown of Kinston, North Carolina. She said he didn't want to marry her, so she took her baby and kept me clean. From my new siblings, I learned that Deford's mother—my biological grandmother—lived in the projects in Kinston, the same projects I walked by every day growing up. Mom told me that I actually met Deford a few times, the last one being when I was 13, and my dad who raised me was in Vietnam. He came to our house, and I remember meeting people, but obviously had no idea of who he was.

With all of these new facts, there were so many things that began to make sense. For example, one of Deford's other children, my brother Reggie, is also 6'8" and played basketball for Furman University. My first college game at UNC–Charlotte was November 30, 1973, when we lost by eight points…at Furman!

Apparently, the only person who knew about all this besides my three parents was my younger half brother Timothy. One day he and his cousin were watching the Boston Celtics play on TV when his mother walked in and saw me on the screen. She then said, "I want to tell you something. See that guy? That's your dad's son!"

Unfortunately, I never got a chance to speak with Deford before he passed away, though I did write him a letter. Having said that, we did have one *very* close encounter. During my junior or senior year of college, someone came into the locker room and told me my father was there. I was like, "Manny is in Kinston." Turns out it very well could have been Deford. As I was starting to make a name for myself as one of the best players in college, he called my mother and asked if I was his son. She said I was. He then asked if she had thought about telling me about him. Mom replied, "Did you ever put any money in his pocket? Did you ever do anything for him?" The answer, of course, was no, and Miss Bessie said, "That's your damn answer, then!"

When I was around 50, DNA testing became pretty popular, and I remember telling the woman I was seeing that I didn't think Manny was my biological father. She said I should get a test, but that's not my way. I don't like to make waves.

Even when I was in my 20s, my grandfather told me he had met the man who got my mom pregnant, which led to her dropping out of college and having to leave the North Carolina Central team. I didn't really put two and two together. To be honest, I didn't really want to.

It's important to recognize both of my fathers. Obviously, I wouldn't be here without Deford Small, but I am the man I've become because of Manny Maxwell. His character and discipline were so important growing up.

Manny always tried to do the right thing and never sought glory for it. His lack of ego was on full display during the last conversation we ever had. He passed away in the spring of 2021 after a long battle with cancer. We were fortunate that Manny was with us at the end and we all had a chance to say good-bye. I used the opportunity to thank him for marrying my mom and taking me in as his son. The sacrifices he made allowed us to have the lives we've had. Even though I didn't know at the time that I was adopted, it didn't change the way I felt about him. As I finished telling him how much I appreciated him, how much I loved him, he had a typical Manny response: "Glad I could help out."

That sums up Manny. I poured my heart out, and he said, "Glad he could help out?" Those were the last words I heard from him. He was never looking for credit, always worrying about others.

My sister Lisa was very upset when she found out about Deford Small, telling me I shouldn't talk to him because he left Mom and this and that, but I told her it doesn't make any difference to me. It has nothing to do with me. I'm here because of their union. I don't get pissed off that he left her. It's all part of life. People get divorced, but you move on with your life and see your way out of it.

One of the funniest parts of the story is that I met my cousin who is named Lloyd Faulks. He's right in the middle of my mom and me. He's 10 years older than I and 10 years younger than she. He's the family historian and he told me, "I remember you with your snotty nose, and your name was Cedric Faulks!"

I was thrilled to learn that I have this whole other family, though it was disappointing that nobody filled me in about it until I was in my 60s. You'd think that you'd tell the child at some point between ages 13 and 18 and let them make the decision if they want to have a relationship with the rest of their family. This whole discovery did create a little angst, but there's no animosity. Still, it's one of the biggest regrets of my life that I never got to connect with Deford, knowing he was my biological father. I did speak with his wife but never with him.

CHAPTER 3
INAUSPICIOUS DEBUT

We've all heard the story about how Michael Jordan was once cut from his high school team. (Keep in mind, he did play junior varsity.) Well, I got cut from my team my junior year.

That was certainly a wake-up call.

For my freshman year, I was at a Black school called Adkin and I made the team. Our coach, Carl Miller, really believed I could play and moved me up to the JV team. But we were integrated during my sophomore year, and I twisted my ankle really bad during tryouts and didn't recover in time to make the team. I went out and got cut from the team my junior year. I was 6'3", skinny as a rail, and weighed 169 pounds. That could have been the end of the story.

As fate would have it, the summer after the season, I was taking a PE class, and the coach was just watching me for some reason. He pulled me aside and said, "Can you dunk?" I had never tried it before. He gave me the ball, and I dunked it with one hand. I was shocked. Then he asked if I could dunk with two hands, and I went up and did it. Our coach, Paul Jones came out and asked me if I was planning to try out, and I cackled, "No, you just cut me!"

He flatly said, "I wouldn't worry about that."

Putting to rest any questions about making the team was the fact that I had grown four inches to 6'7 ½" that summer. My senior year I averaged about 13 points, 16 rebounds, and five or six blocks.

After my senior season, my goal was to go to East Carolina University. It was only 25 to 30 minutes away from where I grew up, so it seemed like the perfect place. But the Pirates only offered half of a scholarship. I wasn't getting much attention—only from small schools like Lenoir-Rhyne. Even the dominant Black colleges like North Carolina A&T, North Carolina Central—where my mom went—weren't giving me offers.

There was a letter of interest from East Texas State, and I probably would have gone out for a visit, but UNC–Charlotte worked out to be the best school. It was about four hours from Kinston, North Carolina, and I really felt like if I stuck around, I'd get caught up in a small-town mind-set.

It wasn't like I'd done much research on UNCC, but probably the best thing that happened was when I visited. There were a bunch of recruits there, and the school took us to the NCAA Tournament, which was in town. Talk about an eye-opener! By the time we were done, I was convinced there was no way I could play Division I college basketball. We saw Maryland play Providence, which had future NBA Rookie of the Year Ernie DiGregorio and the incredible Marvin Barnes. Those guys were unreal.

UNCC convinced me to go there, but it wasn't like any big deal. Nobody paid any attention. I figured everything was set. I had a scholarship, I'm heading to Charlotte. I had completed all my classes and didn't realize that my transcript—all of it—would follow me to Charlotte. Big mistake! I was taking a math final, and the teacher told me we'd get five points just for putting our name on the test. I wrote my name, fell asleep, thinking it wouldn't matter because I was already locked in for college. Big mistake. As a result on June 7, 1973, my parents drove me to Charlotte for summer school, which is not the way you want to spend your last summer of freedom. After the first week or so, our assistant coach, Joe Kinnery asked me how I was doing, I told him I got an A. Yeah, I was going to be okay.

Tar Heel Footprint

In the summer after I graduated high school, I was the biggest kid on the east side of the state. That meant when we played the East-West All-Star Game, I had to guard a kid named Geoff Crompton, who would later play in the NBA. Crompton was a big dude, about 6'10", 280 pounds.

I chopped Big Geoff down to size, putting up 12 points and 12 rebounds. Apparently, legendary University of North Carolina coach Dean Smith was calling his assistant, Bill Guthridge, from Europe. The Hall of Famer asked how Crompton did since he had committed to the Tar Heels. Guthridge said he did okay, but there was a kid from Kinston, North Carolina, who tore him a new one.

When my UNC–Charlotte team later lost to Marquette in the NCAA Tournament, Dean Smith pulled me aside and said, "You're a great player." That was just mind blowing to me.

A couple of years later, I approached the Roy Williams, who was then an assistant to Smith before he eventually became the head coach, and began to introduce myself. Coach Williams stopped me in my tracks. "You don't have to introduce yourself. You're the reason we have the Cornbread Run." He explained that after seeing me play Smith stated that they'd always make to sure to keep an eye on any prospect in the state of North Carolina to ensure they never would overlook a local guy like me again. I was a type of mystery man since I didn't play until my senior season, and back then there were no AAU, no summer leagues. So nobody knew who I was. So even though I never set foot on the campus of Chapel Hill, apparently, I had an effect.

CHAPTER 4
49ERS AND
THE FINAL FOUR

Nowadays, when any college player worth a damn has a good season, everyone wants to know if they're leaving school and going to the NBA. Even as I started to make a name for myself, there was no way I was leaving UNC–Charlotte. I loved it there. None of us were big-time recruits, it was us against the world, and we all bought in. We were like the Rodney Dangerfield of college basketball. We'd play anyone, anywhere. When we got to UNCC, the school had around 9,500 students. Today, enrollment is more than 30,000. We were a big part of building that.

I taught at a basketball camp at East Carolina after my sophomore year, and David Thompson—*the David Thompson*—introduced himself. This guy was an all-time great after leading North Carolina State to the 1973 national championship. He was Michael Jordan before Michael Jordan. Well, I played well enough at the camp that East Carolina invited me back the next year (and asked if I would transfer to their school). By then we had gone to the NIT final, and I was making a name for myself. So I introduced myself to everyone, and people said "You're Cedric Maxwell! We *know* who you are!" Not that I was David Thompson, but I knew then that I was on my way to bigger and better things.

My four years in Charlotte were just awesome. We tangled with University of San Francisco All-American Bill Cartwright, and Oregon's Greg Ballard, and I put 30 points on both teams. We beat North Carolina State and lost to Kentucky, but I played well. The moment when I knew I could play in the NBA came my senior year when Walt Frazier tried to recruit me to his agency.

People sometimes ask if I ever received improper benefits. Well, sort of. I'm sure we got a free pizza here and there, but nobody knew about the big perk, and it had nothing to do with agents handing out cash. One day, the cafeteria got a shipment of 50 pounds of bacon. Well, we stole the whole delivery. My friend got 25 pounds, and we took the other 25 up to our room. That made us really popular. We had people just coming up to our room with nothing but bread, looking for some delicious bacon.

Between the basketball and campus life, it was just awesome in Charlotte. I loved the camaraderie with everyone. We lived in an 11-story building, and you could smell popcorn while roaming the halls. It was like honey for a bear. If nothing was going on in my room, I'd visit someone else. It was a great time for music with Marvin Gaye, the Ohio Players, the Isley Brothers, the Commodores, and, of course, James Brown. I wasn't the most studious person, but I still managed a 2.8 GPA.

We played Texas Tech, and the Red Raiders had this guy named Rick Bullock, a 6'9", 230-pound center who was pretty good and bullied my 190-pound ass around a bit. We won, but after the game, our coach, Lee Rose, wasn't happy when he shared his thoughts with us. He talked about how our forwards played well. He then asked: "Who's the center for UCLA?" We all answered. "Who's the center for North Carolina?" We answered again. "Well, nobody would know who the center is for UNC–Charlotte," Coach Rose said, "because he didn't do shit!"

I was the center and I was pissed. Wasn't this a team game? He berated me for about five minutes, though it seemed like hours. The tears welled up in my eyes. I was trying to hold it back, but he kept going and going. Coach then asked if anyone had something to say. Of course, me being me, I raised my hand. He asked what I had to say. I said, "I quit."

Our locker room was as quiet as a mouse pissing on cotton. The only thing we could hear was our sports information director typing away. Coach Rose deadpanned, "Well, I appreciate your offer. We're done with this meeting."

I walked out, still sobbing. Our assistant coaches came over to me and talked me down. As mad as I was, I must say his challenge motivated me and I never had another bad game under his tutelage.

As you can tell, Coach Rose was a no-nonsense kind of guy. He took over before my junior season, coming from maybe my favorite school in the country—Transylvania University in Lexington, Kentucky. Yes, Transylvania. I always crack up when I think about that.

One of the first things he told us was—just like the man himself—direct and to the point: "Gentlemen, if you can help me, I can help you."

With his silver hair, we used to call Coach "Silver Fox," and this dude was cold-blooded. He saw players who he didn't think could help us and told them he needed their scholarships. He offered to help them find other places to play, but they weren't going to be on his 49ers team.

After one game where we had pretty much put away our opponent. Coach's father-in-law was at the game, sitting behind our bench. There were about five minutes left, and Coach started to empty out the bench. His father-in-law was not pleased. "Leave the horses in!" he shouted. And, sure enough, we starters all got right off the bench and checked back in. We died laughing about that and we had a new saying: "Leave the horses in!"

I was never a good practice player, pretty lousy, to be honest. But when the lights were on, my team knew I'd deliver. Coach Rose knew this as well. Before one game everyone was running layup drills, shooting around, and I was just laying out in the middle of the floor, staring up at the ceiling. One of our assistants, Mike Pratt didn't approve and told Coach Rose that he wasn't going to take my shit: "Look at him out there! All the other guys are warming up. They're really getting a lather. I'm going to tell Maxwell myself!"

Coach Pratt took one step toward me, and Rose asked him, "Do you like your job?"

"I love my job," Pratt responded.

"Then I wouldn't do that," Rose answered. "Leave the horse alone. He's due for 30 points and 15 rebounds—and he's playing 40 minutes a game. Do you want him to warm up or do you want to win?"

Coach Pratt and I never had that discussion.

Under Coach Rose we reached the NIT Finals in New York City and really made a name for ourselves as one of the best independent teams in the nation. Then in August of 1976, the Sun Belt Conference was born with us, the University of New Orleans, South Alabama, Georgia State, Jacksonville, and Southern Florida. Vic Bubas, a long-time basketball coach at Duke, became our commissioner. Just as UNCC was gaining a reputation, I was proving that I was one of the best players in the country. Whoever we played, we usually beat, and nobody could stop me.

We came back to the New York City area for a big matchup with Seton Hall. Everyone was hyping it as a showdown between me and Glenn Mosley, who was their best player and averaging 20 points and 16 rebounds per game. The experts said whoever won the battle between us would catapult up the NBA draft boards. It really didn't turn out to be much of a fight. I had like 28 points and 15 rebounds, and Mosley finished with 10. While I ended up being the 12th pick, he went 20th and played 32 games in the NBA, averaging 3.1 points.

Coach Rose was very careful not to let us get too full of ourselves. When we played Wake Forest in Winston-Salem, North Carolina, my senior year, the oddsmakers had the nerve to make us two-point favorites, and he was furious. It ended up being a great game, and Wake Forest won by two in overtime. Coach's message was clear: we could play with anybody, but no win was a sure thing.

One of the big advantages of being in a conference was that the regular-season champion would get an automatic bid for the NCAA Tournament. I don't remember if the conference tournament winner got a bid as well, but it didn't matter because we won both. I was named regular-season MVP and then won the same award in the tournament, which was played in Charlotte. My teammates would always tease me, saying that they should just start engraving my name on all the trophies ahead of time. By the time the Big Dance arrived, people

33

around the college basketball world knew who we were and that we could play with anyone.

Our first trip to the NCAA Tournament was not going to be easy. We knew we belonged, but the committee put us in the same bracket as the top-ranked team in the country—the big, bad Michigan Wolverines. Also in our region was the University of Detroit. They had a coach you may have heard of: Dick Vitale. Dickie V had some terrific players, including future pros Terry Tyler, John Long, and my future teammate with the Boston Celtics, Terry Duerod. Tyler could jump out of the gym, and Long and Duerod were deadly scorers. Michigan defeated Vitale's team in the second round.

In the first round, we played a spunky Central Michigan team. In the first half, I already had like 14 or 15 points, and one of their subs came in. He was a 6'7" White guy. While I'm at the free-throw line, he told me: "I don't give a fuck what All-American team you're on."

You know I wasn't going to back down to anyone. So I responded, "After this fucking game, you will!"

They played us tough, but we got by 91–86 in overtime. I ended up going 11-of-15 from the field for 32 points and 18 rebounds. When we shook hands afterward, the same guy came up to me and said, "Good luck in the pros, Big Fella."

I love that story and always tell it to my friends.

In the second round, we played a really good Syracuse team. The Orangemen had future NBA player Louis Orr and a tough center in Roosevelt Bouie, who was 6'11" and averaged about 10 points and eight rebounds a game. I made him look pretty foolish when I scored 18 points (including 11-of-11 from the free-throw line) in an easy 81–59 win.

We faced the biggest test in our careers in our next game, taking on No. 1 Michigan. The Big Ten champions were led by center Phil Hubbard and point guard Rickey Green, who both averaged close to 20 points a game. Everyone focused on me, but we just had a good

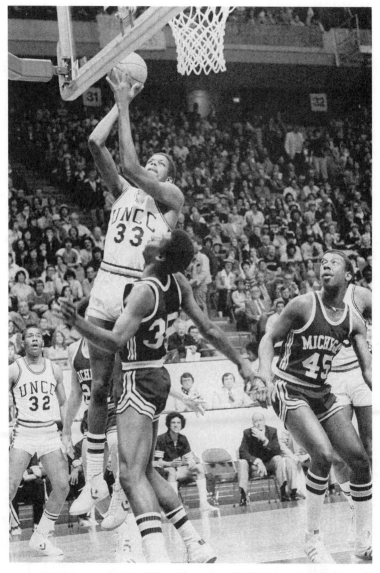

I score two of my game-high 25 points against Phil Hubbard and Michigan in 1977 to take UNC–Charlotte to its first Final Four in school history.

basketball team filled with guys who could play at a really high level. One of those guys was Lew Massey. He was the nephew of North Carolina great Walter Davis and could play. Against the Wolverines, Massey put 19 points and 11 rebounds, and I went for 25 and 13, and we rolled 75–68. Even today, I have UM fans come up to me and say how we stole their championship, but I just tell them they ran into a team that was destined to be there.

The Final Four that year took us to Atlanta, where we met Marquette and its legendary coach Al McGuire. The Warriors (now known as the Golden Eagles) were known for always having good teams but never being able to win the big one. We trailed most of the game but tied it at 49 with three seconds left. Marquette ran a play with a full-court pass, and Jerome Whitehead reached over me for the winning layup. I thought he fouled me and I wasn't the only one. After the game legendary UNC coach Dean Smith approached Coach Rose and said, "Your kid got fouled on that play."

I led the entire tournament field in scoring, but as you might imagine, we were really bummed after the loss to Marquette. I would actually give back an NBA title or Finals MVP just to get to the championship game against North Carolina.

They Call Me Cornbread

One of the questions I get the most is how did I get the nickname "Cornbread"?

Back in 1975, there was a movie called *Cornbread, Earl and Me* starring Jamaal Wilkes and Laurence Fishburne. In the film Cornbread (played by Wilkes, who was starring for the Golden State Warriors at the time) was an older basketball player, a mentor to some young kids. When he was running home in the rain, the police officers mistakenly killed him. In court Fishburne wailed, "They killed Cornbread!"

Jamaal was 6'6", and we had a similar build. My teammates used to call me "The Franchise." When we were in New York City at the NIT my junior year, they started busting my chops, calling me "Cornbread" after Wilkes' movie character. And that was that. Some people have speculated that I didn't like the nickname. Untrue! I would much rather have Cornbread than something like former NFL player Anthony "Booger" McFarland.

CHAPTER 5
MY EARLY YEARS WITH THE CELTICS

Once my college career was over, it was time to get ready for the NBA draft. Things weren't like they are now. There was no draft combine or pre-draft camps. But I did get a chance to play in the Aloha Tournament, which was a postseason game for seniors. It was an opportunity for a free trip and to put some money in our pockets. Our coach was C.M. Newton of Alabama, and I loved playing for that guy. Instead of cramming a bunch of practices in, he told us to go to the beach and enjoy ourselves. Our unique "preparation" paid off as we had a great time and won the tournament. I was on the All-Tournament team, and Tennessee's Ernie Grunfeld won MVP.

Another guy who played was some blond-haired 6'11" kid out of Illinois Wesleyan named Jack Sikma. Nobody was thinking of him as a future Hall of Famer back then. Guys thought he would be one of those players who went over to Europe. Nobody thought he'd be picked eighth overall (by the Seattle SuperSonics). When I look back at our draft class, we had some pretty good players. Kent Benson of Indiana was the first overall pick by the Milwaukee Bucks as expected. He had led the Hoosiers to college basketball's last perfect season the year before. Two minutes into his very first NBA game, Benson elbowed Kareem Abdul-Jabbar, who then broke Benson's jaw (and his own hand). It seemed like Benson never recovered. There were a few other names who made their mark in that year's draft. Oregon's Greg Ballard won a championship with the Washington Bullets while Bernard King out of Tennessee ended up in the Hall of Fame. North Carolina guard Walter Davis would have probably joined him if he didn't get caught up in drugs. Even the last pick in the first round did some big things. Norm Nixon won Rookie of the Year, was a two-time All-Star, and earned two titles with the Los Angeles Lakers.

There was no talk of me going to the Boston Celtics. In fact, the hot rumor was that Boston had its eyes on Grunfeld at the 12th pick. Me? I figured somewhere around pick 10 to 15 I'd be hearing my name. In fact, the only thing I knew about the Celtics was that Red Auerbach was at our big game against Seton Hall. When I finally spotted him in the stands, he was asleep. That was a classic Auerbach move—faking a lack of interest in a player to throw other teams off the scent. He might pretend he was sleeping or leave the game early, but he was never going to come out and say he liked someone.

One place I *knew* I wouldn't be going to was Milwaukee. Shortly after our Final Four run, Bucks coach Don Nelson and general manager Wayne Embry came to Charlotte to check me out. When I picked them up at the airport, I brought a buddy, who was playing ball in Europe at the time. Nelson and Embry said I was late in getting them and they were confused as to why I'd bring a friend. Anyway, I thought we had a good conversation and saw the Bucks as a possibility. The next morning I got a call from my agent, Ron Grinker, out of Cincinnati. He was panicked. Grinker said the Milwaukee brass thought I was a flake and didn't know how to dress. Additionally, they said I was trying to get my buddy a tryout. That part was untrue. But I did ask them what could they do for me if I was drafted by the Bucks. They were insulted so much so that not only were they unwilling to draft me, but they also told Boston not to pick me either. Nellie and Embry were both former Celtics, and I guess they told Auerbach to stay away from me.

The NBA draft was nothing like it is now. It wasn't televised, there was no big gala, or any of the hype. In fact, I spent the day at Grinker's office, waiting for the tickertape to let me know my new home. While he still thought I might become a Celtic, I really wanted no part of Boston. It wasn't about the city; although Boston has a terrible reputation for race relations, I didn't know anything about that. What I did know was that growing up I rooted for the Philadelphia 76ers, but guys like Bill Russell and John Havlicek always beat Philadelphia. The place I really wanted to go was Atlanta at pick No. 14. I figured it would be a cool story—"Cornbread" staying in the South, and it wasn't far for my parents to visit, so I was honed in on becoming a Hawk.

Once the Celtics picked me at No. 12, it was off to training camp at a place called Camp Millbrook, which is in Marshfield, Massachusetts. Auerbach had his summer camp there and he was so cheap that he always got his rookies to work as counselors pretty much for free. Skip Brown, who was the team's third-round pick, and I hung out in a cabin and met future Hall of Famer Jo Jo White, who spent some time talking with us about what the NBA was like. That was the beginning of a lifelong friendship.

Veteran guard Don Chaney became a mentor to me. As someone who spent 10 years wearing the green (over two stints in Boston), he explained what it meant to be a part of this organization. "It's something about being a Celtic—and I'm not I'm not bragging on the Celtics—they won championships and everything. But there's some truth to the fact of once you're Celtic, you have a certain responsibility that goes along with that," Chaney said. "They used to tell me that Red always selected players who were really into the game of basketball, not just as a player but mentally."

I may not have known anything about the racial tensions in Boston, but it had to better that what I experienced in Kinston, North Carolina. There was a huge busing controversy, where inner-city kids were sent out to the suburbs for their education because the schools in Boston were so bad. I saw stuff like that back home. There, though, were pretty obvious differences between the backwoods of North Carolina and a major city like Boston. When I went to find a place to live in Brookline, I was hit with an awful case of sticker shock. My first apartment was called the Brook House. Curtis Rowe and his wife lived there as did Dave Bing. My rent was like $839 a month. I came from Charlotte, where I bought a townhouse for $200 a month.

The worst thing about being on the team was my age. Aside from reserves Rob Bigelow and Tom Boswell—who were both two years older than I—nobody else was within four years of me, so I didn't have that comfort of a group of guys to hang with. Most guys were already married and had families. That made it tough for a guy like me, who's not going to go out and navigate the city. I just stayed in my bubble and hated the fact that it was such a small population for people of color.

The year before my arrival, the Celtics lost to the 76ers in the second round of the playoffs in seven games. I looked at the roster and figured they were loaded with future Hall of Famers like Havlicek, Dave Cowens, White, and Charlie Scott. Throw in former All-Stars Sidney Wicks and Rowe and a legendary coach like Tommy Heinsohn, and it was easy to see why expectations were still high.

As a rookie there were a lot of things I didn't know, but, apparently, I was doing the right things. "Very agile and a very bright basketball player," Chaney said, "the thing that really impressed me more than anything is that he really understood the game from the mental aspect. He knew his strengths and weaknesses and just played hard 100 percent of the time."

We got off to a really slow start, losing eight of our first nine. In our 10th game, we faced the Buffalo Braves, and Heinsohn had me replace Havlicek in the starting lineup, and I went for 21 points and nine rebounds, and we won. Hondo had come off the bench for some great Celtics teams, but to be replaced by a 21-year old kid, well, that was something. And in true Havlicek form, he could not have been nicer to me after the game. He was just such a classy man.

That opportunity to play confirmed to Chaney that his initial impressions were correct. "I didn't know exact height of his impact, but I knew he was going to impact the game," Chaney said. "He just had a knack of getting his hands on the ball, of scoring inside. He was fundamentally really sound."

Eventually, I went back to the bench. By the end of the season, I wasn't playing much at all. Guys were getting old quickly, and some of their skills had diminished. While my playing time dwindled, I was able to pick the brains of guys like Wicks and Rowe, whether it was learning specific footwork or learning about life as a pro. I tried to make the best of a bad situation. It was definitely an education, being around this group of characters.

Heinsohn got fired after we started 11–23 and was replaced by another Celtics legend, Tom "Satch" Sanders, who is one of the nicest men I've ever met. Satch was a really humble and polite man, but he would say it like it was. I remember how he used to always call us "Gentlemen." Of course, with the way we were playing, Satch would say, "Gentlemen, that effort you're giving…you've got to be shitting me!"

I so admire Satch, especially when I think about what he went through during his career. He and other Black players weren't even allowed to eat at certain restaurants. We all climbed on Satch's shoulders to get where we are today. Someone asked Satch if my game reminded him of his. "If I could do the things he does," Satch snapped back, "I'm not even in his shoes!"

That really boosted my confidence, getting that type of compliment from a Hall of Famer. Coaching in the NBA, though, wasn't a great match for Satch. He was much better working with college kids and in fact did coach at Harvard for a while.

Seeing Heinsohn get fired in my rookie year was crazy. I remember meeting him for the first time. I had just gotten into town, and my attorney hadn't arrived yet. So I went to Auerbach's office and could hear Heinsohn's barreling laugh from the hallway. I walked in there, and it's deadly silent.

In halftime of my first game, I smelled cigarette smoke. I walked around the corner, and White was smoking. So I went to tell Heinsohn… only to see him dragging on a butt, too. Heinsohn has always been a huge character. He did so much for my career. He told me, "I know they waited for you to develop at UNCC. We're not waiting!"

When Heinsohn got the axe, I wasn't expecting it. Maybe he had just done as much as he could with this group. Heinsohn passed away during the writing of this book, and his loss will definitely be felt for years to come. Although I'm glad to have had a brief chance to play for him, it certainly would have been even better to have a few more seasons with him on the bench. For a guy who was so gruff on the exterior, Heinsohn was really a cool guy. He had a love of art and painting but was a deep thinker, too. He wanted to challenge you in every way. Early in my broadcasting career, he asked me, "Why do all you Black people always vote Democrat?" I explained that the agenda of the party usually aligns with people of color. I think he knew the answer, but he was someone who loved to prick the bear.

* * *

That 1977–78 Celtics team may not have had a lot of wins, but what a group of guys it was.

The thing I remember about John Havlicek is that he never stopped running even as his career was winding down. Red Auerbach and Tommy Heinsohn would always let him come to training camp a week late. He'd miss the first few practices while he was fishing or hunting in Alaska. He'd come in and he was just like a cyborg running and running. I remember thinking, *How can I keep up with this guy?* Hondo was always a true gentleman. By the time I met him, he was like a nomad. He'd work out, play the games, but then we'd never see him again. He was off with his family.

To quote the late ESPN sportscaster Stuart Scott, Jo Jo White was cooler than the other side of the pillow. In his last season in Boston, he had bone spurs in his heels and said it was like having a nail at the bottom of his foot. He was The Celtic Way. Auerbach loved him, so trading him to the Golden State Warriors was so tough. Later in life we became very good friends. We both lived in a complex called Longfellow Place. His view was the Charles River. Mine was of the 7-Eleven.

What a character Dave Cowens was. I always wondered where he got his intensity from and then one day I found out. We were in the locker room, and Cowens broke out two ammonia tablets. He split them in half and stuck them up his nose. The next thing he did freaked me out. He pulled open his shirt and blew his nose on the inside of his uniform. Then he rubbed it all over his chest. On the court, he was a maniac, too. That's probably what made him so successful battling guys so much bigger than him like Kareem Abdul-Jabbar. He once was called for a questionable foul. The next time down the court, he tackled Mike Newlin and said, "Now that's a fucking foul!"

Heinsohn once came up with a bunch of new plays, and Cowens didn't understand them. That night he went to Heinsohn's hotel room and said he was confused. Heinsohn said not to worry because those plays were for everyone else. "You just keep kicking ass," he told him.

I liked to call Charlie Scott "The Mouth of The South." This dude never stopped talking. Scott was the same on and off the court. He probably talked in his sleep. But on and off the court, I am such a fan of this man. He was the first Black player at the University of North Carolina. I watched him growing up, and playing with him was a huge treat. Since the draft was eight rounds back then, we had a bunch of rookies at my first training camp. I was stretching with the other rookies, and Scott explained the reality of the situation. "I don't know why you guys are here," he started. "We have 13 guaranteed contracts." He then pointed to me. "And he's the 14th. If he's not too stupid, you other guys don't need to be here."

Not only was Dave Bing a great player, but this guy was a politician. His becoming mayor of Detroit was not surprising at all. He could always work a room, like a dog eating a neckbone. He was so smart and he'd know how to pit guys against each other. I always felt like we were playing checkers, and he was playing chess. Even at age 34, he could still play at a high level. But he came to Boston to try and win a title. He spent the previous two seasons with the Washington Bullets—only to see them win after he left. Bing was supposed to be a role player for us, but because we struggled so much, he ended up playing more than 28 minutes a game, which was just too much for him. He was one and done. I'm glad I had a chance to play with him. He told me, "Bread, I ain't coming back."

My rookie season was also Ernie DiGregorio's swan song. It was cool getting to play with him after watching him at Providence. He was Rookie of the Year with the Buffalo Braves and knew a ton about passing. But he had a knee injury that really slowed him down. He eventually became a celebrity host at Foxwoods Casino in Connecticut.

Kermit Washington was a veteran power forward who joined us after throwing one of the most famous punches in NBA history. In the previous season, his Los Angeles Lakers and the opposing Houston Rockets got into an on-court skirmish, and Washington just unloaded on Rudy Tomjanovich, nearly killing him. Rudy T broke like everything in his face, and Washington was suspended for the rest of the season. When I met him, I was petrified. After seeing the video, I wanted no part of him. I figured he must be a maniac. It couldn't have been further from the truth. He could not have been nicer. Even as he dealt with death threats, he taught me so much about the game. Washington was Karl "The Mailman" Malone before Malone existed. He couldn't run as fast, but in a time when the prevailing opinion was basketball players should avoid lifting weights, Washington did and looked the part.

Sidney Wicks and Curtis Rowe were two guys who have always been lumped together going back to their days at UCLA, but they were just different dudes. Rowe was a country boy, and Wicks was more city. Wicks was just a great, great player. He could shoot, pass, do it all. But his persona reminds me a lot of Kyrie Irving. Both had trouble getting along with teammates, and neither wanted to make that connection. Rowe used to tell me how I could become an All-Star. The key he said was just averaging four points per quarter. Throw in some rebounds and assists, and there you go. One thing was certain: neither guy was happy in Boston.

There was one road trip where the guys were partying, and I came to their room. I just wanted to play cards. Little did I know Wicks and Rowe (among others) were going to be doing cocaine. The vets offered some to me, which I refused. That was of no interest to me. They're about to start snorting, and some dude came in and literally blew their coke into the trash can. As you can imagine, Wicks and Rowe went crazy. One of the "intruders" came in with a rock—literally, a rock—and began to shave it off with a razor. Even though this was apparently an upgrade in product, Wicks and Rowe were pissed. They could have finished their original product before trying the new stuff.

Don Chaney was a longtime Celtic, winning two titles with the green and white before signing with the Lakers. He came back to Boston in the Washington trade. A shooting guard who really didn't shoot well, Duck was a terrific defender. We were friends, and one night I went to his house for dinner. I'm not sure if it was a setup or what, but he had a babysitter for his kids named Renee. "I was fond of him and I thought he was a good guy," Chaney said. "So I introduced them. I didn't know it was going to take that quickly, but they really got along well with each other. I thought they had similar personalities. She was like a daughter to me. So I wasn't gonna introduce her to just anybody."

She ended up becoming Mrs. Maxwell and the mother of my two children.

The Sports Landscape

It's hard to imagine now, but when I started my career, the Boston Celtics were pretty low on the totem pole of Boston sports. The Red Sox were No. 1. They had just been in the World Series back in 1975 and were (unknowingly) setting up for the famous collapse of '78. The Bruins were second and en route to the Stanley Cup Finals, and another loss to the Montreal Canadiens. What about the Patriots? Nobody cared about them in the pre-Tom Brady era back then, and we still ranked higher than them. Even though they were pretty good, those Patriots were about as dysfunctional as you can imagine and a long way from what they've become. "1978 was a scarring, defining moment, I think for any Boston sports fan," CNN *New Day* host John Berman, who grew up in Carlisle, Massachusetts, said. "It just made us feel hopeless and vulnerable like beyond hopeless about it. It just was this wound wouldn't heal."

Even around the country, interest in the NBA was perhaps at an all-time low. When we won our first championship, the clinching game in Houston was on tape delay! People thought the league had too many drugs and too many Black players. I remember talking with Bob McAdoo when he played in New York. The Knicks' unofficial nickname was the "New York Ni--erbockers." New Yorkers loved their team in the early '70s when they won two titles and had White stars like Dave DeBusschere and Bill Bradley to go along with Walt Frazier and Willis Reed. Things then changed. The 1977–78 team, for example, had two White players on the whole roster. That league in the '70s would be unrecognizable to today's players. In addition to guys smoking in the locker room, drugs were certainly all over the place.

Drugs weren't the only thing available to us. I was a young guy, coming from a small town. I never even realized we got per diem. I was like, *This is unbelievable! We get money for food—on top of our salary?* Guys also told me, "Rook, you're going to be in your room one day, and some girl you don't even know is going to call and want to come up to your room, begging you to have sex." So on one of our first road trips, I'm sitting in my room, minding my own business. Sure enough, the phone rings, and it's some woman I don't know. She came up to the room, and let's just say the NBA was fantastic! Fans really did love us.

CHAPTER 6
TINY ARCHIBALD
AND LARRY BIRD

One thing about the Boston Celtics—specifically, Red Auerbach—they were always on the lookout for undeveloped players or guys who were coming back from adversity. Back in 1965 Auerbach signed a guy rotting on the end of the Los Angeles Lakers' bench named Don Nelson. Nellie ended up playing a key role in five championships, including hitting a *huge* jumper against the Lakers to win one of them. His No. 19 hangs in the rafters of Boston Garden.

Years later, when Auerbach traded me to the Los Angeles Clippers, he got a broken-down Bill Walton, who fit in Boston like a glove for that one season, and the Celtics won their 16th title.

In August of 1978, Auerbach did it again. Nate "Tiny" Archibald is still the only player in NBA history to lead the league in scoring *and* assists in the same season. He'd blown out his Achilles tendon for the second time and sat out the previous season with the Clippers, who he'd been traded to the previous season. At age 30 there was certainly no guarantee that he'd play again—let alone at an All-Star level. That didn't deter Auerbach, who engineered a seven-player trade, including Kermit Washington and Sidney Wicks in exchange for Archibald, Marvin Barnes, and Billy Knight.

Archibald was still rehabbing and was more than 20 pounds over his normal playing weight. But boy, did he work his ass off! I remember getting to practice and seeing him in his sweatsuit, dripping with perspiration. He'd had all the accolades in his career, but now he just wanted a ring. It was a deal that not many folks paid attention to at the time but was critical to our future.

After my rookie season, the outlook for the Celtics was pretty bleak. We'd gone through two coaches, combining for a record of 32–50—12 games worse than the previous year. The extended playoff runs of years past were catching up with guys like Dave Cowens, John Havlicek, and Jo Jo White. Even as I kept improving, our future was uncertain at best. The 1978 NBA Draft featured a lot of guys who had good, solid careers.

Acquiring Nate "Tiny" Archibald, who drives around Randy Smith of the Cleveland Cavaliers in 1979, was another brilliant move by Red Auerbach.

The guys I saw at the NCAA Tournament from Dick Vitale's University of Detroit team—Terry Tyler and John Long—stayed home and were selected in the second round by the Detroit Pistons. First-round picks of note were guys like Reggie Theus (Chicago Bulls), Phil Ford (Kansas City Kings), and Micheal Ray Richardson (New York Knicks). Mychal Thompson was the first pick to the Portland Trail Blazers, but the best players taken were probably future Hall of Famer Maurice Cheeks (second round to the Philadelphia 76ers) and defensive stalwart Michael Cooper (third round to the Lakers). We had the sixth pick and could have definitely used some young legs. So while everyone expected him to zig, Auerbach pulled off one of the greatest zags in history. Instead of choosing a decent player who could help us right then, he utilized a little-known rule and secured one of the best players of all time.

Back then if a player's incoming college class had graduated, he was eligible for the draft even if he stayed in school. That included transfers, who usually have to sit out a year before playing at the new school. The drafting team would then have until the next year's NBA draft to sign the player. There was a kid who had gone to Indiana University but quickly left in his freshman year and later enrolled at Indiana State. It was a guy by the name of Larry Bird.

Many folks were surprised that Auerbach took the big swing at the future instead of helping us immediately, but he saw the potential for greatness in Bird and decided it was worth the wait. This was obviously big news for a struggling team. Bird showed up for one of our games during his senior season and got a huge ovation from his seat with Auerbach. I'm not going to lie; there was some definite animosity toward him. I mean, we're out there busting our ass, and nobody notices, but here's a guy who hasn't even put on a uniform, and the crowd was losing its mind.

There was a chance that Bird could re-enter the next season's draft, but Auerbach was going to do whatever it took to sign him. It ended up being a huge deal, which put a bull's-eye on Bird's back, but once he signed, he made an immediate impact. At our first practice, I did the slow clap, proclaiming, "Here he is: the Great White Hope." Bird came out as slow as Christmas. My immediate thought was: *This is the guy we have to depend on?*

We started to scrimmage, and Bird and I guarded each other. The first time he came down the court, he busted a 15-foot jumper in my face. *Swish.* The next time down, I pushed him out a few steps. *Swish.* Another couple of feet. *Another swish.* Now keep in mind, I was lighting him up at the other end of the court, but when we got done, I went up to one of my Black teammates and said, "This motherfucking White boy can play!"

The fact was that I'd never seen a White guy play like that. Yeah, we played against Rick Barry, and I was now teammates with Pete Maravich, but Bird was different. After playing against him, everything was transformed. Yeah, he was slow, but there was quickness in there. It was clear even at a young age that he knew how to play the game at a high level. Even a guy like Archibald, who'd seen a lot of great players come and go, knew Bird was different. "It became eye-opening to me," Archibald said, "He'd diagnose the game because he knew certain things."

Many think of Bird as just a shooter, bur Archibald and M.L. Carr knew otherwise. "His perception and court awareness were unparalleled," Carr said. "He made passes that shouldn't have been made. Man, it turns out perfect. He anticipated where players would be on the court."

The next year Robert Parish came to town, and seeing Bird day in and day out made quite the impression. "I had to reassess my opinion of Larry because I thought he was overhyped and overrated, but everything they were saying about Larry in terms of accolades on the basketball court? He exceeded them," Parish said. "That was a transcendent talent, especially for someone who was slow and couldn't jump. That's a generational talent. We may never see another Larry Bird."

Sure, Bird was on the horizon, but it didn't help us on the court. My second year was a lot like the first; we were not good. This time we only won 29 games, which was actually three fewer than the previous one. Tom "Satch" Sanders got fired after a 2–12 start. Coaching in the NBA was definitely not what Sanders was put on this Earth to do.

So who took over? Our starting center Dave Cowens.

That didn't work out so well either. Cowens played so hard that he'd call a timeout and then come over to the sidelines to draw up a play. Unfortunately, he was so out of breath that he couldn't even talk. Though we didn't have success under him, Cowens showed he belonged in coaching eventually became the head coach of the Charlotte Hornets and Golden State Warriors.

As disappointing as Year Two was for the team, I made a quantum leap. I was the first forward to lead the NBA in field-goal percentage (and did it again the next season, by the way). After coming off the bench for six games, I took off. Even when I put up a lot of points, Auerbach always made sure to let me know I hadn't arrived yet. There was one game where I dropped 27 on Scott Wedman and the Kings. Auerbach came in after the game, and he said "So, you scored 27, that's good. But you also gave up 20 to Wedman, so it's like you scored seven points."

I don't know if our team had character, but we definitely had some characters. One of the biggest ones was Rick Robey. He was the rare high draft pick who didn't last a full season with his team. Coming off a national championship at Kentucky, Robey was the third pick in the draft by the Indiana Pacers. But 43 games into his NBA career, he was heading to the Celtics. The Pacers had a chance to reacquire Knight, who starred for them in the old ABA. Robey was listed at 6'11", but we always referred to him as a seven-footer. That's how he became known as "Footer." He was never going to be a star in this league, but he had a nice little left-hand move. Quickness wasn't always his forte. One night we were playing in Houston against the Rockets, and Moses Malone was just killing him. Malone wasn't known as a big talker, but he came up to me and said, "That kid you have on me…if you don't get him off of me, I'm going to get 100 rebounds."

Footer would give everything he had, but he just wasn't athletic enough to hang with guys like Malone or Bob Lanier. Robey was a pretty smart guy on the court, but, man, could this cat party off of it. He hung out a lot with Bird. In fact when he was traded to the Phoenix Suns—in an all-time steal for Dennis Johnson—rumor was that it was because the Celts didn't want Bird partying with Robey too much.

I'll never forget spending New Year's Eve in Salt Lake City in 1983. Robey and Bird were having these little nips of vodka and grapefruit juice. That night we had the entire crew together, and we'd been drinking from 2:00 to 5:00 in the afternoon. We thought it was a good idea to grab something to eat and went to this place called "The Southern Plantation." I'm not really much of a drinker, so I got woozy pretty quickly. I actually pulled up two chairs next to each other and laid down—right in the middle of a full restaurant. As I was fading in and out of consciousness, I needed something to drink. There was some sweet tea, like we had down south. I took a huge swig of it…and it turned out it was pure vodka! I'll spare you the details, but let's just say I went out and fed the animals.

On New Year's Day, we had to get our stuff together for a game. I remember at shootaround that morning, seeing those purple and yellow lights beaming off the floor. I was about to die. We went back to the hotel and tried to sleep it off. Somehow, we won the game 127–112, but I was MIA, scoring nine points. Lesson learned. Don't challenge Bird to a drinking contest.

Chris Ford came over from Detroit and what a good guy he was. Probably because of some tough years with the Pistons, he hated losing. I remember seeing him play at Villanova, and this guy could shoot. It wasn't a thing of beauty, but his old-school set shot was cash money.

In fact, it was Ford—not Bird or anyone else—who hit the first three-pointer in NBA history.

Growing up in Absecon, New Jersey, Ford *loved* himself some Dr. J. Ford wasn't much of an athlete, so when he made a move, we jokingly called him "Doc." There weren't many smarter guys on the floor than Doc. He always knew how to get to his spots, always taking the right angles. He was a fierce competitor, like a little pit bull. When Bill Fitch yelled at him, Ford barked right back at him.

CHAPTER 7
BOSTON BOSSES

Most NBA owners back in the day kept a pretty low profile—but not our guy, the infamous John Y. Brown. He was better known than most of our players, and that's the way he liked it. Brown came from Lexington, Kentucky, so it's no surprise that he teamed with Colonel Harland Sanders, the founder of Kentucky Fried Chicken, to bring the restaurant to the nation during the 1960s. In 1970 he made his first foray into sports, buying the Kentucky Colonels of the American Basketball Association. His biggest accomplishment there was hiring a young assistant coach from the Milwaukee Bucks by the name of Hubie Brown, who ended up in the NBA Hall of Fame. He bought the Buffalo Braves in 1976 and made one splashy move after another—none bigger than what he did in 1977 when he and a man named Irv Levin traded *entire franchises.* He literally traded the Braves (who then became the San Diego Clippers) for the Boston Celtics!

As you might imagine, that didn't sit particularly well with Red Auerbach. When John Y. Brown later traded three first-round picks to the New York Knicks for Bob McAdoo, Auerbach was ready to leave and run the Knicks. Fortunately, on his taxi ride to the airport, his driver convinced him to stay in Boston. McAdoo, a former MVP and future Hall of Famer, is still one of my best friends today. Early in his career, the former University of North Carolina star came back to his hometown of Greensboro, North Carolina, for his summer league. I came back as well. So we'd party after the game and have been tight ever since. Even with me there, Mac wanted no part of coming to Boston to play for a lousy team. He was so pissed that he spent his three-month Celtics career sleeping on my couch.

Mac almost got me dealt to the Detroit Pistons. After the 1978–79 season, the Celtics signed M.L. Carr as what is now known as a restricted free agent. Back then, the team that lost a player could pick another from the signing team as compensation. The Pistons and their new coach Dick Vitale were debating whether to take Mac or myself as compensation. Thank goodness they chose Mac. He played one season in Detroit, had some off-the-court issues, and eventually ended up winning two NBA championships with the Los Angeles Lakers.

Brown, who eventually sold the team to Harry Mangurian in 1979, actually married the former Miss America, Phyllis George. In middle of their honeymoon, he announced he was running for governor of Kentucky. He won that election. You couldn't make this stuff up. I'm sure that if he had kept the team, those first couple of years would be even crazier.

Once after a huge loss to the Denver Nuggets, Brown came into our locker room and told us to get our heads in the game. Whether it was a young guy like myself—or a veteran—we were like, *Dude, you're the owner, not the coach.* Of course, we kept that to ourselves. After all, we did still want to be employed.

The Pistons nearly snagging me instead of McAdoo was not the only time I almost left Boston. The second came right after that second season, when I nearly joined the Indiana Pacers. Free agency back then was nothing like now, and I had no idea of the summer that was to come. Indiana had hired Jack McKinney, who was the ill-fated coach of the Lakers. The longtime college coach was hired to be Magic Johnson's first NBA coach. Unfortunately, 13 games into his first season, McKinney was in a major biking accident, suffering a near-fatal brain injury. Paul Westhead took over on the bench, and the Lakers won the title. Once he recovered, McKinney was hired by Indiana. Coach came down to Charlotte to visit and put me through a great workout. He told management that he loved me and wanted to make me the centerpiece of the team's future.

In the meantime, I was on a junket with Eastern Airlines, going from Charlotte to New York and Bermuda. My next stops were to visit friends in Dallas and Seattle. While in Bermuda, my agent Ron Grinker called me, telling me my vacation was over and that I had to fly to his Cincinnati office to sign the contract. So off I went. But the next day,

Grinker called me to say I was staying in Boston, and the deal was off. It turned out that Auerbach had scared off the Pacers, saying he'd gut their team as compensation if they signed me. I was pissed. We knew I was a valuable asset, but it was a case of being free, but not really free.

It worked out best for me, of course, that next year. I led the league in shooting percentage again and eventually won my two titles. That third season I sacrificed my offense a bit, dropping from 19 points to 16.9 per game. Playing with Larry Bird meant a change in roles, and I'd have to become more of a defender. Once again, some dumb luck and Auerbach's stubbornness worked out best for me.

* * *

We knew there was going to be a change on the bench for the 1979–80 season. Dave Cowens was burnt out trying to play and coach, so Red Auerbach hired Bill Fitch, who was a no-nonsense guy. He came over from Cleveland, where he was the first coach in Cavaliers history. In just six seasons, they made it all the way to the Eastern Conference Finals, losing in six games to the Boston Celtics. Three years after that run, the Cavs were struggling, and Fitch was out. It was something new for Auerbach to reach outside the family. From the time Auerbach retired to the front office, the only men to coach the Celts were former players; Bill Russell, Tom Heinsohn, Tom "Satch" Sanders, and Cowens. Fitch had no Boston ties.

My first experience with Fitch came up in the Catskills at the Maurice Stokes charity game. I had scored 35 points, but Fitch never even acknowledged me. He was all business. Once Fitch took over, Curtis Rowe showed up late to practice because his car had a flat tire. Fitch approached Rowe to ask why he was late. "Coach," Rowe explained, "You passed me on the road and didn't stop to offer me a ride!" Fitch cut his ass right there. Should Fitch have offered him a ride? Technically yes, but it shows how much of a screwup Rowe was that Fitch didn't care enough to help. He was looking for a reason to cut him. His message was clear: I am the dude. Rowe was pissed, but that was the new lay of the land.

Fitch made sure we all knew our roles. On his first day, he came up to me to fill me in. I had just scored 19 points a game and I figured that would continue. "You're a pretty smart guy," Fitch said. "So let me ask you a question: who do you think is going to be guarding the toughest forward every night?" I was sitting there thinking, *I'm a scorer, not a defender. This guy is off the chain.*

I had been the man on our team, and in came Larry Bird. I thought that he should have to prove to me that he was good enough for me to relinquish my role. But I wasn't stupid and I've always been a team player. (Plus, if I did cause trouble, Auerbach would trade my ass on the spot.) I realized that if I put my skillset with Bird's, we might have something. He was a great passer, and I was great down low. Bird was going to make my life a lot easier. "Let's face it: his career changed when Larry showed up, and that was the turning point. It actually made him play defense. He's the guy who had to guard Dr. J, among others," Bob Ryan, the legendary sportswriter for *The Boston Globe*, said. "And he was very happy and the beneficiary of Larry's great entry passes. He made the most of them, that's for sure."

Bird always said that Fitch was the best coach he'd ever played for. "I was very fortunate when I first came into the league," he told NBA TV. "We didn't really watch much tape at all in college. And he was ahead of the game really and watched a lot of tape. But he pushed us and made us better…Bill Fitch was very instrumental in making us better ballplayers."

Whether it was Bird or some other player, Fitch didn't coddle anyone; he was going to do it his way. A lot of people were uncomfortable with that but not me. I loved his coaching style and who he was. He didn't give a damn. He certainly wasn't concerned about hurting anyone's feelings, and it was all about winning. He certainly could be tough on us. "One time he jumped on my brother," Nate Archibald said, referring to me. "And I had to come to the defense because I didn't feel like he should be tearing certain guys down."

Being from New York City, Archibald wasn't intimidated by anyone despite his size. He always stuck up for us. "I've got a hard shell. So you can mess with me all the time, and one of these days or one of these nights, me and him might have to go to blows," he said. "Since I had the title of the quarterback or point person of the team, I didn't want you to mess with my guys."

Fitch wanted tough players, which is why he told Don Chaney to hold me all the time in practice. Elbows, body checks, he threw whatever he needed to slow me down. Fitch made sure Chaney and others never let up, which did make me a tougher player for sure. One of Danny Ainge's favorite stories came when we had struggled over a few games. We were in a team meeting, and Fitch said to me, "Max, you need to cheer for your teammates!"

"Well, if you didn't tell me I was the dumbest motherfucker you'd ever seen," I said, "then I could be a little more enthusiastic!"

Despite Fitch being so tough, the first year with him and Bird was the most fun I'd had in the NBA. We went from a lousy 29-win team to the Eastern Conference Finals. In addition to Fitch and Bird, we had some other interesting additions.

M.L. Carr came over from the Detroit Pistons as a free agent. He had been on the All-Defensive team the year before and brought great enthusiasm. The two of us became best friends. He became my road dog and he told me everything he knew about the game. Carr was from Wallace-Rose Hill, North Carolina, which is a country town near Kinston. We spent hours talking about the game. Both he and Duck Chaney brought me along. Carr, though, never saw a microphone he didn't like. I'm sure this guy talks in his sleep.

He's also the reason my No. 31 is hanging from the rafters. When I came to Boston, I wanted my college number of 33. Unfortunately, that belonged to Steve Kuberski. By the time he was cut, I ended up being No. 30. Carr came in and already had No. 30 jewelry, as he'd worn his entire career. He asked me to trade numbers, and that was that. I was just happy to be on the team. I didn't care.

The first time I met Gerald Henderson was my last game in college. We had gone 69–0 at home and wrapped up the season beating his Virginia Commonwealth squad. I dropped 35 on them. Once we became teammates, everyone referred to Henderson as "Sarge" because he had a shirt with that insignia on it. He was one of the coolest cats around, but my favorite story about him came in Salt Lake City. We beat the Utah Jazz and then headed to the club upstairs. Sarge was acting like he was all that and saw a hot blonde with wavy hair. Naturally, Gerald tapped the blonde on the shoulder and then realized it was a guy with a moustache. We got a lot of mileage out of that story.

I felt awful when Sarge got traded to the Seattle SuperSonics for a first-round pick, which became Len Bias, right after we won the title in 1984. Word leaked that he was out of shape, which was never true. Henderson was very bitter. The fact was that management wanted to make room for Ainge. They should have just said that. There was no reason to trash G on the way out.

No Celtics fan will ever forget Henderson's steal in Game 2 against the Los Angeles Lakers, which saved the series for us. We were about to go down 2–0 and would have to head out West. No doubt Sarge saved our ass.

We really had a great group. "It wasn't just Larry, it was Cedric, it was Kevin, it was Robert, it was M.L., it was Gerald, it was even [Eric] Fernsten, who didn't play that much," Archibald said. "We had a different camaraderie than guys have now. We can talk about the playing and stuff, but that doesn't include the stuff we did off the court, going to movies, eating dinner, and things like that."

The biggest new face on the team was "Pistol" Pete Maravich. I didn't know a ton about him from college, where he was one of the all-time most potent scorers. My attitude was that since Maravich was playing for his father, Press, at LSU, he always had the green light to shoot. Big deal. What really opened my eyes was watching him play with the New Orleans Jazz against the ABA's Carolina Cougars. I watched some of the things he was doing, and it was just magic.

By the time he came to Boston, he was chasing a ring but also wanted to experience playing for the Celtics. Fitch used to give him a hard time, but Maravich never changed stride. The Pistol epitomized cool. He was the first person I ever saw with some device where you could play music into headphones. It was called a Sony Walkman. Pistol had such a laid-back way about him. He was humble but knew he was special. He was just one of those guys who knew all types of random stuff, a true Renaissance man. At one point in a much-hyped showdown with Walt Frazier, who is a Hall of Famer and one of the best defenders in league history, Pistol tore his ass up for 68 points. In Boston he was well past his prime, but you'd see glimpses of just how great he was. I'm grateful to have seen firsthand what he could do.

One night Pistol threw the ball to Bird, who took an off-balance jumper with two guys draped on him. During the next huddle, Maravich told Bird he had to pass the ball when he was double-teamed. Without missing a beat, Bird said, "If you were any fucking good, they wouldn't double-team me."

When Maravich decided to retire in training camp of what would have been his second season with us, he told me on a plane the night before. Fitch really rode him hard, and as Maravich said, "The $400,000 they're paying me ain't going to change my bank account." It's such a shame that Pete died of a heart attack at just 40 years old while playing a pickup game. So tragic.

CHAPTER 8
OUR RIVAL, THE 76ERS

With Bill Fitch, Larry Bird, and M.L. Carr in tow, everything changed. For the first time in my career, we were actually a fully functional team. I first noticed the change when we played the Philadelphia 76ers during the preseason. It was obvious that we could hang with those guys. We were all buying into Coach, but none of it really mattered until the rubber hit the road of the regular season.

During my first season, we lost eight of our first nine games. The next year, it was six out of seven games. So you can imagine the feeling in Year Three when we won our first four games. This was the first time in my career we actually had a winning record *at any point*. Everyone loves a winner, and the fans were starting to come around. The way we played, people began to once again see basketball as a beautiful game. It wasn't about one-on-one play; it was about making the smart pass. We were a team.

Bird and I had something special going. His vision was incredible. He always knew where I wanted the ball. As far as my game goes, my confidence was at an all-time high. I knew how to get my shot off against anyone. There was a clock in my head. I had a formula: three seconds to shoot, and by then I'd already made my move. I studied the game and I played the angles, using my strength, quickness, and length. Even during my rookie season, Tommy Heinsohn would keep me after practice and have me practice boxing out again and again. If a shot hit a certain spot, eventually I knew exactly where the ball was coming.

Red Auerbach was such a smart coach. He always let his players play. In the front office, he was the same. He trusted Fitch to run the ship and hardly ever stuck his nose in where it didn't belong. That was really important. Sure, Fitch had a proven track record, but the pressure of working under the greatest coach in history could have been really uncomfortable.

We ended up improving by 32 games, which was the biggest single-season turnaround in league history at the time. It was only fitting that in the Eastern Conference Finals we faced the 76ers. They were in many ways our measuring stick in the preseason.

Philadelphia had some great players, but none more so than Julius Erving. Of course, everyone knew all about Dr. J. By this time he was 30 years old and would finish second to Kareem Abdul-Jabbar for league MVP. People now tend to forget just how bad a man this guy was in the ABA. In the five years before he came to the NBA, his *lowest* scoring average was 27.3 points per game, and that was in his rookie season. My first visit to the Good Doctor was memorable to both of us. Philly had a play where there would be four guys on one side of the court with Dr. J on the other. I remember seeing 18,000 fans rise to their feet in my peripheral vision. There was a good reason why. Dr. J set an NBA career high with 45 points. I was like a maître d' out there. Just for good measure, he put up nine rebounds, four assists, and four blocks. My line of 17 points, six rebounds, and five assists didn't feel so great.

Aside from Dr. J, the most entertaining Sixers player had to be Chocolate Thunder, Darryl Dawkins. He was one of the most prominent players who went straight from high school to the NBA. Dawkins was 6'11", 251 pounds, but he was one of those guys who seemed so much bigger. He had incredible athleticism and a huge personality. If he was a little more focused, Dawkins could have been Shaq before Shaq. One of the most famous dunks in NBA history was when Thunder dunked on Bill Robinzine of the Kansas City Kings to destroy the backboard and then issue a classic rap about it: "Chocolate-Thunder-Flying, Robinzine-Crying, Teeth-Shaking, Glass-Breaking, Rump-Roasting, Bun-Toasting, Wham-Bam-Glass-Breaker-I-Am Jam." He had it all. He could shoot, run, and put his big butt in the post. He was the opposite of the strong, silent Sixers, like Caldwell Jones, Maurice Cheeks, and Bobby Jones. Dawkins was so playful. We tangled during a playoff game, and he grabbed onto my arm and wouldn't let go. And he was laughing the whole time. I've often wondered what would happen if he had kept his focus, but I guess he wouldn't be Chocolate Thunder.

When Dr. J came to Philly, fans were expected multiple titles. Going into 1980–81, the total was still zero. He did a commercial proclaiming: "We owe you one." We didn't want to allow them any. Make no mistake, there was no love lost between our two franchises. The 76ers didn't like us, and we didn't like them. When we were in Knoxville, Tennessee, for a preseason game, we stayed in the same hotel. When both teams were in the restaurant, it was one of those deals where they'd see us and leave. And vice versa.

One of the most underrated players in the league at that time was Bobby Jones. I was pretty familiar with him, having watched him play at the University of North Carolina. He could run all day—it was really more like a gallop—and loved laying it in with that damn left hand. He was a great defender and deadly serious. He made the NBA All-Defense team 11 times. Most of the Sixers had the same all-business approach as Jones. They were the office guys, wearing plain white shirts. We were more like a carnival. We had some good ol' boys like Bird, Rick Robey, and myself.

Losing in five games in 1980 to those guys ended up serving us well in the long run. We were intimidated. We didn't know if we were good enough. We could compete with Philly, but we weren't sure if we could beat them. The moment was just too big for us. For us to climb the mountain, we needed to make some changes. When we looked at Philly's front line, they had two 6'11" guys—Dawkins and Caldwell Jones—along with Bobby Jones, who was 6'8" with arms that made him look like 7'8."

Boston had the top pick in the draft, and the big name was Purdue center Joe Barry Carroll. At 7'0" tall and 225 pounds, JBC was a good-looking prospect who led the Boilermakers to the Final Four. He had a nice hook shot, a jumper, and was a good passer. He wasn't the most rugged defender, but if we put him with Cowens and myself, that would have been a nice front line. JBC did have his detractors; his understated demeanor helped him get the nickname "Joe Barely Cares." Still, I think he could have done well in Boston. Auerbach had really hyped-up Carroll, so it seemed to be a done deal. In fact, not many people know this, but Carroll nearly ended up on the Celtics, and I was on my way to the Golden State Warriors. Golden State head coach Al Attles and one of his assistants flew into Charlotte to spend some time at my condo, laying out what now seems like a pretty wild scenario: they would draft Kevin McHale with the third pick and sign me to a free-agent offer sheet. That would have resulted in a front line of incumbent center Robert Parish, Kevin McHale, and yours truly. Coach Attles said this was a done deal.

So you can imagine my shock the next week when Auerbach announced the Celtics were sending the top overall pick (Carroll) and the 13th pick (which ended up being Rickey Brown, who never averaged even six points per game) in exchange for a 26-year old center, who just averaged 17 points and 11 rebounds a game (Parish) and McHale, a gangly 6'11" big man from the University of Minnesota. Nobody saw that coming, especially Parish. "I was so taken back when [Attles] told me that they were trading me," Parish said. "I was in the middle of negotiations for an extension on my contract, and then all of a sudden, they just went a totally different direction."

Auerbach traded Carroll and Brown for two Hall of Famers. Yup, he had done it again. I was stunned and thankful. Auerbach and Fitch both wanted to take credit for the deal. Fitch tried to say he thought more of Parish than Auerbach did.

Chief's reputation around the league was actually that of an underachiever. They should have asked me. I played against Parish twice in college when he played at Centenary. I knew how good he could be. Let me put it this way: in his senior season, Parish averaged 25 points and 18 rebounds per game.

I knew less about McHale. I had no idea what this guy was all about. He came to town as this gangly, awkward-looking White kid. He really didn't instill much confidence. People ask me if I feared that McHale's arrival was going to squeeze me out. Not at all. I was a borderline All-Star, and McHale wasn't even in my league at that time. He was raw but very talented. It wasn't like we had some crazy battles in practice either. We were both really good in the low post, but while I used my quickness, he used his size. In fact, when Fitch split up the teams for scrimmages, it was usually myself and McHale vs. Parish and Bird. He was a great student, and I spent a great deal of time with him working on interior moves. "I played a lot with Max. I played against Max a lot, too," McHale said. "Max really gets overlooked as really just how good he was. [He] was so gracious and helped me so much. I tell people all the time I just marveled at how those guys were so accepting."

Parish, on the other hand, got a rude awakening to Camp Fitch. "When I found out I was traded to the Celtics, I took the whole summer off from training. I started my workouts two weeks before camp," he said. "I'm leaving a bad situation for a better situation, so I was just in a celebratory mood for the summer, which was a paramount mistake."

It's hard to believe that the guy who played more games than anyone in NBA history wasn't ready for his first camp with us. "I learned a valuable lesson from that: there's no offseason for conditioning and nutrition," Parish said. "It was a whole different approach and mind-set to the offseason. Everybody came to camp in shape—except for me. The Warriors approach was that you come to camp and play your way into shape, but with the Celtics, everybody was in game shape except for me."

McHale was a key contributor in his rookie year. He brought energy and was a great shot blocker right away. There's no way we win the title that season without his contributions, especially against the Sixers. But if you look at that last game in the Finals against the Houston Rockets, McHale played a total of eight minutes. As we quickly discovered, getting Parish and McHale was the beginning of the most dominant four-man frontcourt in NBA history.

Sadly, Dave Cowens would not be a part of it. Over the past couple of years, the "old guard" of the Celtics became old. John Havlicek had retired in my first season, Jo Jo White's heel spurs led to him being traded, and Cowens was really the only one who still had some game left. Heck, his last season, he averaged 14 points and eight rebounds. When we were in Terre Haute, home of Indiana State University—and where Bird played—for a preseason game, Cowens got on the bus and just said "Guys, I just don't feel like I have it. The fire is gone."

We were all shocked. I mean this is a Hall of Famer we're talking about. Apparently, this didn't faze Carr, who said, "Great, now get off the bus, we have to go to work!"

Cowens was such a great player. His job was always the toughest on the team; at 6'8" he had to go up against the best players on the other team, and they always had a major size advantage, whether it was Elvin Hayes, Moses Malone, or, of course, Kareem Abdul-Jabbar. And he did it while averaging 13.6 rebounds over his career. In retrospect, Cowens retiring actually helped us grow as a team. You never want to lose an all-time great, but we had acquired Parish and McHale. If Cowens stuck around, Parish likely would have come off the bench.

Fitch was not shy about having us run in training camp. And run. And run some more. A few days into preseason, Parish must have thought we were in another world. We'd be coming back on defense while Parish was still lumbering down the court on the offensive end. He really put himself behind the 8-ball with his new team. It's funny to think that he built his Hall of Fame career by beating opposing centers up and down the court.

McHale, on the other hand, had worked his ass off. It wasn't easy to survive Fitch's boot camp, but he made it through. We could see that our frontcourt was going to be something special. Adding Parish and McHale along with myself in the frontcourt gave us three shot blockers. Back in the '70s and '80s, the prime real estate was in the paint. What made us so impossible to match up with was that our lineup was incredibly inter-changeable. Other teams would go smaller, and we'd just go bigger. We could have myself or Bird play guard. Try beating that. We used to tell our guards, "Just get the ball to the glass. We're good from there."

Hail to the Chief

I've accomplished a lot in my life, but one of the longest lasting things was naming Robert Parish "Chief." Over the years he's become my brother, but when he came to town, he wasn't exactly gregarious. Parish didn't say much—we actually thought he might be mute—but the one constant was that he'd ask everyone, "Hey, Chief, what's going on?"

One of my favorite movies is *One Flew Over the Cuckoo's Nest* with Jack Nicholson. There's a huge Native American character who never says anything. Parish is actually quite chatty, but it takes awhile to get him to trust you. What did he think of the nickname I created? "I didn't think much of it," Chief explained. "I'm a big fan of Jack Nicholson and was telling everyone that they had to go watch the movie. I was fascinated by it. Cedric obviously saw the movie and told me, 'You remind me of the Chief. You don't say a lot, but you've got everybody fooled like you can't talk or don't have much to say.'"

And so Chief was born. I was shocked that it got so much play. When we were at a James Taylor concert, everyone broke out in a chant for "Chiiiiieeeeef!" People are sometimes surprised to learn how close I am with Parish because from the outside we look like two total opposites. I'm gregarious, always talking to anyone, and he's the Chief, a man of few words. But the truth is: he's not like that at all. Parish is blunt, funny, and never hides his feelings.

Parish and I didn't get as much publicity as Larry Bird and Kevin McHale, but we didn't care. We just wanted to win. "We were all about wanting to win the championship," Parish said. "We didn't give a shit about who was doing the most damage as long as we win the game."

CHAPTER 9
THE 1981 POSTSEASON

After making the historic trade to get Robert Parish and Kevin McHale, we were ready. The Philadelphia 76ers had taken us out to the schoolyard and taught us a lesson. But Dr. J and company still hadn't won a title, losing to a rookie named Earvin "Magic" Johnson and the Los Angeles Lakers in six hard-fought games in 1980. While we were building something, they added yet another weapon, taking a lesser-known guard out of Louisiana Lafayette with the eighth pick in the draft. There weren't a lot of guys who earned their nicknames more than Andrew Toney, aka "The Boston Strangler." He averaged more than 23 points per game in college and he didn't slow down in the pros. Had he not retired at just 30 years old with bad feet, I believe in all my heart that "The Strangler" would be in the Hall of Fame. This cat was so strong. He could go to the basket or he could post up. Once he got it going, there was no stopping him. He was just fearless. I remember watching him in a nationally televised game in his second year and seeing him just torch all-world defender Michael Cooper for 46 points despite attempting (and missing) just one three-pointer all game.

In many ways the 76ers had a perfect backcourt. Toney was just a killer, and Maurice Cheeks had begun to come into his own. Cheeks was the classic old-school point guard. Never flashy or looking for his own shot, he just made sure Dr. J, Toney, and company got the ball in the right spots. His matchups vs. Nate "Tiny" Archibald were like watching a great chess match. On defense he was such a major pest that he made me want to get a bottle of Raid to spray on him. When Cheeks retired he was the league's all-time leader in steals and in the top five in assists.

When we played the Sixers in the Eastern Conference Finals, it was a classic backcourt matchup—the old pros of Archibald and Chris Ford against the young guns. We just wanted our guys to hold their own, and us frontcourt guys could take care of the rest.

To say Coach Fitch was a little bit extra tight whenever we hooked up with the Sixers would be an understatement. When we were practicing in Philly, he noticed a cleaning person up in the balconies. His radar went off. "The worker was so high up that I couldn't yell up to him and say, 'Hey, please get out of here. We've got a closed practice,'" said Jeff Twiss, the current vice president of media services and alumni relations, who was in his first year with the team back in 1981. "The only way to do it was walk all the way up there and ask the guy to leave."

Complicating things for Twiss was that the worker in the balcony did not have great command of the English language. "He had some type of headset on, probably listening to music. I said, 'You have to leave now.' And he shakes his head like smiling," Twiss said. "I could see Coach Fitch down on the court, thinking *What the hell is going on up there?* I just left; it wasn't like I could yell down to him. The players had a good time on that one."

Whenever we played the Sixers, it was different. McHale noticed that from his first regular-season game in Philly. "I really didn't know anything about them. I mean, I know they're good. I know the Celtics lost to them the year before in the conference finals but not much else," McHale said. "On the bus ride to the old Spectrum, it's always kind of quiet before the game, but guys would have some fun. Then we're walking down the hallway, and it's really quiet. We get to the locker room, and I'm looking at all these guys, and man, they've got a different look on their face."

In the 1981 Eastern Conference Finals, we split the first two games in Boston and then we got punched in the mouth, losing both in Philadelphia, falling behind three games to one once again. This couldn't happen two years in a row, could it? It was then that simple but straightforward words from Red Auerbach hit home. "He said, 'we're down 3–1, and you don't look to try and come back from 3–1,'" said M.L. Carr, repeating Auerbach's speech. "'They still have to beat you one more time. You're not going to let them do that—are you?'"

When a guy who has experienced everything like Auerbach speaks, everybody listens. Game 5 was a barnburner in Boston. Larry Bird went for 32 points, 11 rebounds, and five assists, Archibald had 16 points and seven assists, and I put up 23 and eight rebounds, as we held them off 111–109 despite four guys (Dr. J, Lionel Hollins, Darryl Dawkins, and Toney) all scoring at least 20 points.

Next up was Game 6…in our house of horrors, the Spectrum. Philly had beaten us 11 straight times there, and from the outside, there was no reason to think that Friday night would be different. Truth be told, we weren't confident, and it showed. We were down 13 after the first quarter. Early in the second, legendary Sixers public address announcer Dave Zinkoff announced that, "Tickets for the NBA Finals will be available immediately after tonight's game."

It was like someone put a lightning bolt into us. I call it, "balls to the wall basketball." This was for our collective lives. Shortly after the ticket announcement, Dawkins and I were battling for a loose ball, and he knocked me into the stands. As I headed back toward the court, a Philly fan told me to "Get back in the fucking game!"

I went after him with a flying forearm. Within seconds our whole team was in the stands. The rookie McHale didn't know what to make of it. "All of a sudden, [Maxwell] turned around and kind of just goes in there and starts fighting the fans," he said. "Usually, everybody's cursing each other out and yelling at each other. We're just yelling at all the fans and challenging them. I remember thinking, *Man, this is crazy. There's 18,000 of them and only 12 of us!*"

But on the Celtics, it was one for all and all for one. "Whoever was on the team, we represented them," Archibald said. "You can't do that to one of our guys. We might be friends in the summer, but you can't do that because we're competitive and we want to win."

It actually galvanized us. "It turned out to be a positive, even though nobody endorses going into the stands," Parish said. "It turned out to be a positive in terms of our attitude and approach for the series."

If you watch the video, you can see Parish asking me if I was okay. Clear as day, I respond, "Fuck that shit!"

From that point on, it was on like *Donkey Kong*. Bonding on the road and pulling out a huge win like that, I knew exactly what we had in store the next couple of years and what kind of balls we had. When we finally won in Philly, we were squealing like schoolgirls. We owe a lot of our big win to Bill Fitch. "We were down to Philadelphia 3–1, and he just kept telling us, 'We are not done. The series are not over. We can come back and beat these guys. We are better than they are,'" Parish said. "He just kept pushing it in practice, on the plane trip down to Philly, in meetings, always preaching the same message. He never allowed us to doubt for one second."

Fitch was the perfect guy at the time we needed him the most. This was the best coaching job. That concept of playing without expectations, just being free and easy, put us on the right path. Sure, there was still Game 7 to play, but we knew how that was going to end. Bird went for 23 and 11 boards, including the game-winning three-pointer (on a bank shot no less). I had 19 and six rebounds, and we were going to the Finals.

We couldn't have been more hated than we were in Philadelphia, and we still won. To think of it like a Philly legend: this was like a Rocky Balboa fight. We'd taken their best shot, and they'd taken ours. It felt like an out-of-body experience. Once we'd gotten our legs under us, it was just an epic battle. A couple of years ago, I spoke with Cheeks, and that series came up. He told me he still felt like they were the better team. The score said otherwise.

* * *

Larry Bird and I defend Philadelphia 76ers star Julius Erving during our Game 7 victory in the 1981 Eastern Conference Finals against our rivals.

As politically correct as we tried to be, everyone knew that who-ever won the Eastern Conference Finals was going to take home the championship. Thanks to some wild upsets in the playoffs, the Western Conference was clearly inferior. They were so bad that two 40–42 teams, the Houston Rockets and Kansas City Kings, were battling it out to go the NBA Finals.

The Rockets won the West in five games and they had the most dominant big man in the game back then, Moses Malone. At that time he was the best NBA player to ever go straight from high school to the pros. (Since then, obviously there have been guys like Kevin Garnett, Kobe Bryant, and LeBron James.) Malone was supposed to attend the University of Maryland but was lured to the Utah Stars of the ABA. By 1981 he was only 25 years old but in his seventh season. This guy aver-aged 28 points, 15 rebounds, and two blocks a game. He had already won the first of his three MVP awards. He was an absolute animal on the court. Malone never said much, instead letting his play do his talking. But when he did speak, it was usually pretty memorable. When I once was pleading my case to a referee, I said, "Everybody is trying to get paid."

Malone walked by without missing a beat and correctly stated, "Not everyone gets paid like me." At a time when most big-time players were getting deferred money to help the team's salary flow, Malone was the first player in league history to get paid a million dollars in cash.

That he was able to take a ragtag group to the Finals was really impressive. They'd do trick plays, like guys throwing it off the back-board and letting Malone put back the rebound. That's cute, but did they think they were really going to beat us that way? Houston actu-ally did have two other Hall of Famers: Calvin Murphy and Rudy Tomjanovich.

Murph was 5'8" and just so tough. By the time he got to the Finals, he was slowing down a bit—he'd retire after the next season—but in

Game 7 of their series against the San Antonio Spurs that year, he dropped 42 points on George Gervin and company. Murphy's hands were so strong. He was feisty, too, and not afraid to get down and dirty despite his short stature. There was a time where he tripped Mike Woodson coming down the court. Woody complained to the ref, who instructed him that he might not want to take on Murph.

Rudy T, of course, nearly died from a Kermit Washington punch in 1977. He came back and made the All-Star team again but understandably wasn't quite the same player. He eventually coached the Rockets to consecutive titles, earning him a place in the Hall of Fame. In the series against us, he wasn't a factor and then retired after the season.

The 1981 Finals weren't an artistic beauty. We definitely played down to the level of the competition. Sure, this was for the championship, but it was definitely a letdown after our high of the Sixers series. We held on to win 98–95 in a close Game 1 contest. Celtics fans will remember it for one specific play, where Larry Bird took a jumper at the top of the key, missed, then caught the rebound midair (with Bird's jumping ability, it was a short trip), switched hands, and put it in before hitting the ground. Malone struggled, going 4-of-17 from the floor and finishing with 13 points and 15 rebounds.

The guy who really gave us a hard time was Bobby Joe Reid, who had 27 points and eight rebounds. Reid was a good player, and at 6'8" he always gave Bird trouble. The Rockets stunned us in Game 2, as Malone bounced back with 31 points and 15 rebounds in a two-point win. Give them credit. These guys weren't in our class, but we were still heading to Houston tied at one game apiece.

Suffice it to say, the Rockets had awoken the bear. We crushed them 94–71 in Game 3. It was over by halftime. How bad was it? I had 19 points and 10 boards, leading six guys in double figures, and neither Bird nor Kevin McHale were among them. In this game Houston coach Del Harris decided to change their strategy. In the first two games, Billy

Paultz tried to guard me. The "Whopper" was a good player who had a nice career, but he was a slow, 6'11" White guy who had no chance against my quickness. So Harris decided to put Malone on me. Now remember, Mo didn't say much. But early in Game 3, he mumbled to me, "I've got you, you skinny motherfucker."

I answered by hitting my first shot. By the time I hit my second and third, Malone had changed his tune, saying simply "Good shot."

It was a heck of a matchup. "Max had one of those matchups where he was usually quicker. He was really long. They tried Billy Paultz and even Moses, but those guys just weren't quick enough to stop Max. He just went by them a lot," McHale said, "They would have been better off if they'd been guarding him with a smaller, quicker guy. Max just had it going."

With a 2–1 series lead against the Rockets, we honestly thought it was over. But again the scrappy Rockets didn't give up. This time Malone went for 24 and 22—*22 rebounds*—and we left Houston tied at two. Bird was struggling with his shot; he went 3-of-11 in both games. I kept us close with 24 and 14, but it wasn't enough.

At this point, some folks were concerned about Bird's shooting. We weren't. I've been asked if I felt like I had to pick up the slack. I was in such a rhythm it didn't matter who was guarding me, whether it was Paultz or Malone. I always loved big games. The bigger the stakes, the better I played. Fear was a huge motivator for me. Before there was "Big Game James" Worthy, there was me. Even now, I hate seeing guys who can talk the talk, but when it comes time to play, they're nowhere to be found. I would never compare myself to the great Muhammad Ali, but he would work himself into such a frenzy, getting fired up for a huge fight. I was kind of like that that—whether it was the NCAA Tournament or the NBA Finals.

We came back to Boston, knowing it was time to get serious and take control of things. This was one instance where Malone's mouth wrote a check his teammates couldn't cash. He was apparently unimpressed with us. "I could get four guys off the street in Petersburg [Virginia, his hometown] and beat them," Malone said.

We beat those boys like they did something wrong, rolling to a 29-point win at home. Even though Houston had the league's best rebounder, we pounded them on the boards to the tune of a 54–41 advantage. I personally had 15 of them to go with 28 points. Bird and Robert Parish also hit double digits in rebounds, and we were one game away. When I watch the tape of that game, I remember the crowd giving me a huge ovation when I checked out of the game

Celtics fans had to stay up late to watch us wrap up the title in Game 6 in Houston. That wasn't because of the time zone difference. It was because the game—the last game of the Finals—was on tape delay. We blew the game open in the third quarter. Bird erupted for 27, I had 19, and Parish scored 18. The Rockets came back, but we won 102–91. Rick Barry, who was working for CBS, came into the locker room and told me I'd been named MVP. "Cedric was the best player in that series. You think about all those guys—Larry, Kevin, myself, Tiny, Moses— Cedric was underrated. He catapulted us to that title," Parish said, "He spurred on the whole Celtics era of the '80s."

My best game was in Game 5 of the Finals when I had 28 points and 15 rebounds. "That's what earned him the MVP. He was at his Maxwell best. That's what I remember most. It was as simple as that," said Bob Ryan, the longtime sportswriter for *The Boston Globe*. "He wasn't unanimous, and people thought it was me because of my love for Larry, but I voted for Max."

That put me in a really exclusive club. Years later after I became a team broadcaster, I went into the Oklahoma City locker room to visit former Celtics big man Kendrick Perkins, who was then on Thunder, because I was due some cash from him. I went over to him and said, "You owe me some money!"

Perk turned around and playfully said, "I don't give a fuck if you're the Finals MVP!" Well, Kevin Durant and Russell Westbrook turned around so fast their heads almost spun off.

That Final MVP has given me street cred more than 30 years later. As a team broadcaster, I've gotten to know all of the Celtics who have come through. But they don't all know about my career. We had a guy named Jared Sullinger, a first-round pick out of Ohio State. He was a good player in his own right. He knew I had played in the league but wasn't aware that I was actually pretty good. One day we were playfully talking smack, and he made fun of my winning the Finals MVP, saying that the voters felt bad for me. It was all in good fun. The next year he came up to me and said he had a new respect for my game. He had worked a camp with Malone and John Lucas. My name came up, and Malone just said, "That motherfucker." In relaying the story to me, Sullinger said, "Man, you must have done some work!"

It's been a long-standing tradition that the NBA gives the MVP of the Finals some type of automobile. Unfortunately for me, this year was the exception. "He was rebounding like crazy with scoring inside. It was unbelievable. He put on a show," M.L. Carr said. "And the best part about this after watching all the MVPs get a truck or car, they gave Max a watch!"

How did the newest NBA champions celebrate? Since this was 1981, we had a *commercial* flight back to Boston—with a pit stop in Atlanta. So picture this: we win the title, enjoy some champagne, and then hop on a plane with everyday passengers. As we made our connection, we brought that trophy right through the airport. Times have certainly changed, but nothing changes when you win a championship.

The best part of the celebration was the championship parade in Boston. Bird never forgot anything, and it was time for him to answer Malone's claim that he could play with four guys from his hometown and beat us. When it was Bird's time to speak, he knew what the crowd was hungry for. "I guess this proves one thing…that Moses *does* eat shit!" Bird always had a way with words.

Red Auerbach had built the perfect team, and now we were champions, something we knew would happen once we finally took down the vaunted Sixers. "You had the talent of Bird, plus these amazing role players. Auerbach had put it together," CNN's John Berman said. "This is the part that I think I sometimes don't remember…it was the Sixers. You vanquished the Sixers. It wasn't about beating the Rockets in the Finals. It was about beating the Sixers on the way there."

CHAPTER 10
HEAVY IS THE HEAD
THAT WEARS THE CROWN

After spending the summer celebrating our title, we were really confident about becoming the first team since the Boston Celtics of 1967–69 to repeat as champions. Those teams had two all-time greats playing the last two seasons of their careers in Bill Russell and Sam Jones. We, on the other hand, were just entering our primes with myself, Larry Bird, Kevin McHale, and Robert Parish. The one area where we had some age on us was our backcourt of Tiny Archibald and Chris Ford. They were both still effective players, but we definitely had to get younger, especially with the Maurice Cheeks/Andrew Toney combo in Philadelphia.

Gerald Henderson was getting better and playing more minutes, but we still needed more. That's when Red Auerbach did it again. Our first two picks in that year's draft didn't really turn into much. Auerbach picked Charles Bradley, a physical defensive guard out of Wyoming with the last pick in the first round. Two selections later he chose Notre Dame's Tracy Jackson. Interestingly, two of the best picks in the whole draft came at No. 29 and No. 31. The Kansas City Kings selected Illinois' Eddie Johnson, a lethal guard who scored more than 19,000 points in his career, at No. 29. Then two picks later, Auerbach did it again.

There was no doubt that Danny Ainge was worthy of being a first-round pick. He averaged more than 21 points a game during his four years at Brigham Young and was best known for a length-of-the-floor, game-winning layup at the buzzer against Notre Dame. The only reason Ainge was available was because he was a highly-touted baseball player, who was already playing for the Toronto Blue Jays. He made it clear that he preferred baseball and wasn't looking for a two-sport career. But Auerbach had a hunch. Maybe it was because Ainge was overwhelmed by Major League Baseball pitching and batted only .187 over the 1981 season—or perhaps he just missed basketball. But Auerbach selected him at No. 31, hoping he could convince him to play for the Celtics.

One thing everyone knows about Ainge is that he's a smart guy. He quickly realized that hitting a jump shot was much easier than hitting a curveball and told Auerbach he wanted to give up baseball to join the world champions. There was a legal battle, but the Celtics paid the Blue Jays to extract him from his contract, and just like that, we had a young guard to grow with.

But success didn't happen instantly. There were certainly times when he struggled. I counted all of his misses out loud during practice, and Bill Fitch was particularly hard on him. Ainge later said his rookie season in Boston was the lowest he'd been athletically—and this was coming from a guy whose batting average didn't rise above .200 from May through the end of his last baseball season. He'd come in as hot shit, and we just rode him mercilessly.

Even while he shook the rust off, Ainge's skills were obvious. "I remember thinking, *man, this dude is a freakish athlete.* And I told him a couple times to just hang in there because I came in late [when I was a rookie] and I thought they were talking Spanish," McHale said. "But believe me: it didn't take long to realize that he was a really high-intelligent player and a great athlete."

I also tried to help the young man. I told him to throw me the ball, and the defense would automatically double-team me because the other team didn't think he could make the shot. We'd do this every day for 15 to 20 minutes after practice. He'd pass it down low and then spot up. I'd kick it out to him, and bang. The first time we tried it in an actual game, however, was a different story. "We're playing a game in New Jersey. And Max is working with me and my shooting because I just haven't been shooting the ball well, even though like I might only get five shots in a week." Ainge said, laughing at the memory. "I get in the game. And my first shot is from the baseline, and it hits the side of the backboard...Max's reaction was like his hands over his face, like *Oh, no, all that work I just put in.*"

I give him a lot of credit, though, he came out and had a great career. If he was on a lesser team, he would have put up better numbers, but he discovered his role and really helped us win two titles. He played so well that they eventually traded Henderson for the second pick in the 1986 NBA Draft. Unfortunately, that pick turned out to be Len Bias, who overdosed on cocaine the next night.

One of the highlights—or lowlights—of the season came the week of Christmas. We had a game in Kansas City on December 26. (You'd think as defending champions, we'd play on Christmas, but for some reason, that wasn't the case.) Much to our chagrin, Bill Fitch decided that we needed to fly out on Christmas day. Suffice it to say, we were not happy. On the flight—remember we were flying commercial back in those days—Bird, McHale, and a couple of other guys got the flight attendant to get all the alcohol that was supposed to be reserved for first class.

From there Bird turned into a bartender and mixed everything together, creating a concoction they called jungle juice. It was potent, and guys were feeling it pretty hard. Hey, it was Christmas. "The team was rebelling. So they were playing cards in the first-class section and getting all of those mixed drinks you get in those little bottles and pouring all of them into this pitcher," said Ainge, who doesn't drink. "Fitch was so furious from what he saw happening that he called for a late-night practice. We landed and went straight to the gym. We get our practice gear on and start out doing a three-man weave down the court, and if you drop the ball, then you have to run again. I'm in the same group with Kevin and Larry. I'd throw it to Kevin, and he'd drop it. Everyone started laughing, and Fitch is getting livid—and he's yelling at me! And I'm like the only sober guy that hasn't had one drink on the plane."

There was actually one other guy, our backup center Eric Fernsten, who didn't drink. He was a good guy, a hard-working 11th or 12th man who played five to six minutes every other game or so. But during this practice, he was on fire. When Fitch mercifully ended practice, Bird dropped an all-time great line. "I never thought Fernie was that good, and he just killed us," said Bird before turning to Fernsten. "Damn, Fernie, you turned into me!"

It was one of the worst practices I've ever seen. Bird and McHale didn't know which way they were running. They were throwing the ball all over the place. After about 10 minutes, Fitch finally said fuck it. We went back to the hotel and played the next night. The drinking clearly had no impact on Bird. He played 49 minutes, dropped 23 points, and grabbed 15 rebounds as we won in overtime, and McHale scored a big hoop late. "That was just kind of the DNA of the guys. A lot of teams would have just boycotted practice," McHale said. "We all went there and practiced, and you thought we're not going to play good but won the next day, and I just I think we all laughed about that."

The 1981–82 season went as scripted. We had the best record in the league, won the division by five games over the Philadelphia 76ers, and seemed destined to repeat. We had several guys nursing nagging injuries, but our confidence was sky high. For the third straight season, the Eastern Conference was us and the Sixers. After the first game, this didn't look like it would be much of a fight, as we put it on Philly 121–81. Bird had a triple-double, and the guy who played the second most minutes for us was M.L. Carr!

We lost Game 2 at home, as Toney did his Boston Strangler thing with 30 points in just 28 minutes. They took Game 3 in Philly by two points, and then Toney just crushed us with 39 points in 42 minutes, and for the third straight season, we trailed these guys 3–1 in the series.

Of course, after our historic comeback the previous year, we were still confident. Game 5 was at home, and it was another laugher for us, as Bird went for 20 points and 20 rebounds, Chief had 26 and 10, and we blew them out 114–85. Once again, we were down 3–2. Our fans were so emboldened that toward the end of the game they chanted: "See you Sunday! See you Sunday!" They meant we'd win in Philadelphia and return to Boston for Game 7.

Toney came out and laid an egg for Game 6. That's the only time I remember him doing poorly against us. He went 1-of-11 from the floor, and we rolled by 13. When we got home for Game 7, our fans didn't let up, chanting: "Today is Sunday! Today is Sunday!"

There was no chance we'd fail at home. We were the world champions and we were on the parquet floor. Our wins in the series were by 40, 29, and 15 points. The Sixers had to be fried mentally. Yep, Game 7 was just going to be a coronation of a much-anticipated Finals showdown with the Los Angeles Lakers. Oh, it was a blowout alright…a blowout for them. Toney had 34 points, Dr. J had 29, and they kicked our ass 120–106. There were fans literally dressed as the ghosts of series past, but Philly didn't care. You've got to give them credit: nobody thought they could overcome blowing another 3–1 lead.

We had a huge rebounding edge and crushed them on the backboard in six of the seven games. That's what you get, dealing with the best frontcourt of all time. But their guard play was just better. Archibald and Ford had slowed down, and Ainge was only a rookie.

The Boston fans showed their passion. Once it became clear that our season was ticking away, they began chanting "Beat L.A. Beat L.A." A lot of people ask me who did we hate more: the Lakers or the Sixers? I say we *learned* to hate L.A., but were *born* to hate Philly. They had Dr. J; we had Bird. The tradition was awesome. It was just combustible, and it didn't take much to ignite it.

CHAPTER 11
UNFULFILLED EXPECTATIONS

When things don't go as planned, there are usually consequences. We came up short in 1982 but had no idea of the implosion that lay ahead of us the following season. After losing to the Philadelphia 76ers in that shocking Game 7, Red Auerbach knew that we had to find an answer for Andrew Toney, aka "The Boston Strangler." We were at least even with Philly at the other positions but had no way of controlling Toney.

The next September it looked like Auerbach had struck magic again. He acquired defensive specialist Quinn Buckner from the Milwaukee Bucks in exchange for a guy who wasn't even on our roster—the retired Dave Cowens, who was making a comeback. Buckner was a big, thick, physical guard, who was named to the NBA's second team All-Defense four times. He was a winner, having led the University of Indiana to an undefeated season and the NCAA championship. On paper it seemed to be a perfect move.

But about a week later, the Sixers answered…with a boom.

They traded for two-time MVP (and Boston's good friend) Moses Malone. While many "experts" were already giving the Sixers the championship, we weren't intimidated. Of course, he was an upgrade on Caldwell Jones—who went to the Houston Rockets along with a first-round pick—but not as much as people thought. Jones was nowhere near the offensive player Malone was, but he was one of the best defenders in the league. Jones would keep his hands up all the time like a praying mantis.

Philly had also traded Darryl Dawkins to the New Jersey Nets a few weeks earlier for a first-round pick. Although Dawkins didn't always take the game seriously, he was one of the best talents in the league. The Sixers were clearly going to be better, but it didn't faze us. They came to town in the exhibition season during the fall of 1983 with their shiny new toy, Malone. But our boss wasn't going to let us get intimidated. Early in the game, Malone fouled me, and I still had the ball. He pushed me, so I threw it at his head. We tussled, and I don't know where I got the strength, but I was holding him up. That's when Toney came in from behind and grabbed me. I went flying over the stanchion. I ended up on the ground, and he started squeezing me like a boa constrictor! In the meantime Larry Bird and Marc Iavaroni got ejected for fighting. Benches cleared, and Auerbach came down to the floor—to take on Malone. He told him, "Hit me. Go ahead, I'm not big. Hit me."

Sixers coach Billy Cunningham got in Auerbach's face, and things got so heated that Auerbach's sports coat got split in half. It reminded me years later of the 2003 American League Championship Series between the Boston Red Sox and New York Yankees, when Don Zimmer came out, and Pedro Martinez threw him to the ground. Cooler heads did prevail, and there were a bunch of fines. "If Moses had hit Red, [Philadelphia owner] Harold Katz would be paying Red, not Moses," M.L. Carr said. "Moses' money would be referred instead of deferred."

In the regular season, we won 56 games—a good, but not great year—and finished nine games behind the Sixers, who were clearly on a mission. By the time they beat us in March, the division race was over—we were 11 games off the pace—and we had a four-game losing streak.

Bird had his typical great season, and Robert Parish stepped up for his best year in the league, averaging 19 points, 10 rebounds, and two blocks a game. The biggest note was that Kevin McHale was really coming on strong. This was the first time he played more minutes than me, and his scoring rose to 14 points a night.

You might think this would bother me, as my scoring dropped to fourth on the team, but it never did. I've always been a big believer that you can't fight city hall. When I was the best player on the team, Bird came in. Bill Fitch made it clear that my job was changing; I'd be guarding the best player on the other team. I could bitch and moan about it, but that wasn't going to change. McHale was a great player—one of the best low-post threats in NBA history—so he was going to get his touches. I never viewed McHale as a threat to my job. We were teammates and friends. Of the White guys, it was McHale and Ainge that I hung with. We were like the Three Amigos.

Even though things may have seemed all good from the outside, Dan Shaughnessy, the legendary columnist at *The Boston Globe* who came on the Celtics beat that year, knew something was amiss. "They weren't at their best in terms of the camaraderie. That was one of the rougher years for that group because it was Fitch's last year, and he'd kind of reached his expiration date," Shaughnessy said. "Max didn't talk the whole year, and Tiny was pouting, sulking the whole year, and Buckner—they thought he'd be better. Danny struggled that year, too. Fitch was hard on him, and he lost a lot of confidence, which was his trademark. So it was just a tough year."

And we *still* won 56 games! When the playoffs started, we were the third seed behind division winners Philadelphia and the Bucks. That meant a first-round matchup against Dominique Wilkins and the Atlanta Hawks. The Hawks were a pretty good team but not really in our class. We ended up winning the series 2–1, but that's not what everyone remembers. In the third and deciding game, we learned that perception sometimes outweighs reality. We won Game 3 by the score of 98–79, but the highlight was when Atlanta center Tree Rollins bit Ainge. My boy, Ainge was always a pest to other teams. Guys were always irritated at him; they said he was dirty. One time Sedale Threatt actually punched him. Bird, Parish, McHale, and I were like the big brothers, and Ainge was that little pain-in-the-ass guy that would piss everyone off. I gave him the nickname "Dennis" like Dennis the Menace because he was always getting into something. If someone hit him, he'd let one of us know, and we'd take care of it.

In this game Rollins and Ainge exchanged elbows, and then Rollins, who by the way was 7'1", 235 pounds, came after Ainge like a heat-seeking missile. Ainge went low to try and knock him over, and the fight was on. "We felt like Tree was being a little over-physical with his screen-setting,"

Ainge said. "He had knocked Quinn Buckner out. I was on the bench, and Quinn went in and got knocked unconscious for a second. When I came back in, he got me again, and the referees—they don't want to hear anything about it. So as we crossed each other in the open court, he was going to bump me, and I was going to bump him, and we sort of elbowed each other. Then he looked at me like he wanted to fight, and I had two choices: I could run or I could go for the legs. Then everybody was on the floor, and I was on the bottom of the pile with my finger in his mouth."

I was laughing so hard that I don't actually know if I came out on the court. Ainge emerged from the pile holding his finger, yelling, "He bit me! He bit me!" It was like watching pro wrestling.

Dennis the Menace was always into some kind of trouble. Years later, when he was playing on the Phoenix Suns, they were about to lose a playoff game to Houston, and Mario Elie made a shot, and Ainge fired the ball at him, nailing him in the head. Of course, Ainge denied doing it on purpose, but this guy was all about the mischief.

The funniest thing about the Rollins incident was that Ainge was the one who was bit by him, but because of his reputation, everyone blamed Ainge for it. It's safe to say we gave him a hard time on that. Ainge may have been the most hated player around the league, but he is a great guy. I gave him a hard time when he first came to town, but he has turned out to be one of my best friends.

In the second round, we faced Milwaukee, which was supposed to be a precursor to Celtics–Sixers IV. The only problem is we forgot to show up. The Bucks were a good team. They had future Hall of Famers Sidney Moncrief and Bob Lanier, along with Marques Johnson, Paul Pressey, and Junior Bridgeman. Having said that, they weren't better than us.

The whole series was a blur; before one game I was throwing up all day. In Game 2 Bird was sick and couldn't go. Ainge scored his ass off with 25 points. But it didn't matter what we did. They had the answer. You don't hear this often from a player, but we gave up on our coach.

I still believed in him, but we were just going through the motions, and we got swept. Even a newcomer to our beat like Shaughnessy could see what was happening. "It was hard for me because I hadn't been around them before, but I could see the potential for how great this team could be," Shaughnessy said. "But it would need a different coach. It would need Max to talk to the media, and all that happened in a year."

Bird summed it up best afterward. "This is sickening," he told *The Washington Post*. "It seems we played our worst basketball tonight. It was a pathetic thing to watch. I've never been this embarrassed in my entire career…and this is going to hurt for a long time because we didn't play to our potential. When we were backed against the wall and challenged, we were supposed to come through like the champions I thought we were and we didn't. We embarrassed ourselves, and I'll live with that the rest of my life."

Our team—with three guys voted to the NBA's top all-time 50 players—lost four straight, and only one was even close. We headed into the offseason unsure of our future. "In our entire run—from 1981 to 1988—that was the only year that we were funky going into the playoffs." McHale said. "You know what? We weren't as good. We just felt like there was something missing at that point. We were still good enough to beat most teams, but it just felt different than my first two years. This was a grind. It was like everything was really hard. It was odd because that was the only time I felt that and never felt like that again."

Bird vowed to come back the next season a new player, and the rest of us felt the same way. Losing a series is one thing, but getting humiliated was another.

Silence Is Not Golden

As miserable as the 1982–83 season was, there was one person you never heard a word from—me. As Dan Shaughnessy pointed out, perhaps the most talkative guy on the whole team—yours

CHAPTER 11: UNFULFILLED EXPECTATIONS

truly—never said a word to any reporters for the entire season. The reason was simple; I was disappointed that some of the media had gone into my personal life and was talking about the birth of my first child Shemeka, who was born before Renee and I got married. Then they started to go back and forth about how much money I was making and all that stuff. My personal life is personal. I have a private life, and it didn't seem like that stuff was newsworthy. Reporters were just shocked; I was one of the team's best interviews. Now there was nothing. Not even off-the-record talks.

Not to overstate the significance of my silence, but it definitely changed a dynamic we had. "For all Larry's great gifts, it's not exactly as if he was doing stand-up or Socrates or Cicero, not great philosophical musings. So a lot of the opportunities for personality and leadership fell in other players," CNN's John Berman said. "Max fell into that timeline. It was before Kevin McHale had a much bigger voice and before Danny Ainge. Max predated guys like them and postdated guys like Cowens and Havlicek."

Finally, the reporters cajoled me into talking the next year, and we were back to normal. Nowadays, of course, the league can fine you for not talking. But I wanted to prove my point, and I did.

CHAPTER 12
K.C. AND D.J.

Let me get this on the record: I liked playing for Bill Fitch. He helped me become a better player and get my first championship. But it wasn't easy. There's a reason Fitch is in the Hall of Fame. He was a smart, smart guy, really ahead of his time with a lot of things, including using video. Fitch's problem was probably his biggest strength: his intensity. "I will say this about Coach Fitch," Robert Parish said. "He was an asshole to everybody across the board. I respect that because he was like the father you could not please, and he didn't show preferential treatment to anyone. He was exactly what we needed because he instilled mental toughness in all of us."

When you ride guys like he did, there's a point where they stop listening. The exclamation point was getting swept by the Milwaukee Bucks, but there were signs before that.

We were watching video, and Fitch was pointing out that I wasn't guarding anyone. In the middle of the session, a chair leg broke, and smashed the video machine. Everyone started cheering, and Fitch was pissed.

If he'd just been able to take a step back, things would have been different for him. For example, he had a rule that when we were on the road, we'd stay overnight. (Remember, this was before charters.) If we were in a big city like New York, a lot of us would go out to dinner with our friends. Fitch had a rule mandating that even if we were meeting up with friends or family, we had to first take the bus back to the hotel. "We got on the bus, and he jumped on you," Nate Archibald said. "I was like, 'Hey, let's go outside.' I wanted to throw down with him because when you're messing with my teammates you're messing with me."

At the beginning things like this didn't bug us. We were young guys learning about the league. But by 1982 things had begun to erode. We were grown men, but Fitch was treating us like kids. We felt like we'd accomplished enough to earn his trust, but he felt otherwise. The league wasn't like it is now. Nobody was going to run to Red Auerbach to try and get Fitch to ease up. The only player who had that type of power was Larry Bird, but he'd do whatever Fitch asked. There were times that M.L. Carr and Parish barked at him, but the rest of us pretty much fell in line.

That's not to say there weren't exceptions. We had a game in Philadelphia, and I came out hot with 14 points in the first quarter. Fitch brought Kevin McHale in, and I went to the bench. But Fitch forgot about me. I ended up with 16 in the first half, and we lost. After the game he came into the locker room and said, "I'll take this one. Does anyone have something to say?"

Naturally, I raised my hand and said I did but would talk to him later. As the team filed onto the bus, Fitch came over to me and said he knew I wanted to play more. I told him we could discuss it later. The next day after practice, I went into his office. Fitch said I was playing well and I'm the guy who never complains about playing time. He explained: "You're that guy I know can take all the sticks and arrows. I might be mad at someone else, but I can go at you."

Our talk must have had some effect. I was horrible the next game, but he just kept cheering me on. On that night, at least, I could do no wrong. But overall Fitch had lost the team. "That would be my first taste of mutiny in terms of basketball," Parish said. "We wanted him out, and the only way to get him out was to be unsuccessful. As long as we won, he wasn't going anywhere."

The issues with Fitch were painfully obvious to those outside the locker room, too. "He lost everybody—everybody but Larry. They all turned on him," said Bob Ryan, the sportswriter for *The Boston Globe*. "The only guy that didn't quit on Bill Fitch that mattered was Larry. He didn't mind that kind of a hard coach. Larry respected authority always. Still the sweep by Milwaukee might have been better. Larry was sick and missed the second game. But believe me: they all had enough of Bill."

Fitch and Danny Ainge had their rough stretches, but by the end, they got along well. But even Ainge saw the writing on the wall. "I remember we were down," Ainge said. "And some of the players on the team were saying, 'Well, the good news is if we lose this series, we won't have to listen to him anymore.'…I think Kevin even made a comment in the papers about his free-agency status could be determined by whether Fitch was back or not."

Fitch was a hard coach, but even guys who hated him at the end will say that he was one of the best things to happen to them. Most of the time in pro sports, when a team fires its coach, the replacement has the opposite personality. If you fire a hard ass, the next guy is usually a players' coach. That was definitely the case in 1984. K.C. Jones was truly one of the nicest guys you'll ever meet. But make no mistake, this man was a winner: two NCAA championships and eight more in the NBA. He's in the Hall of Fame and has his number hanging from the rafters at Boston Garden.

Right after the sweep in Milwaukee, we had heard rumblings that Fitch was going to be fired, but I was still surprised when it happened. It seemed to make sense to give Jones a shot. "He's as opposite from Bill as almost anybody else in the business," Ryan said. "K.C. was all about relating to great players and getting the most from them and making them want to play for him. He's a wonderful human being and a guy who had a sense of winning and no interest or ability to develop young talent."

Jones was one of the first Black coaches in NBA history and led the Washington Bullets to the 1975 NBA Finals. Unfortunately, his heavily-favored Bullets were swept by Rick Barry and the Golden State Warriors. After winning 48 games the next season, he was fired. A lot of people didn't think he was really the coach; in Washington he caught all kinds of crap when a TV camera listened into a timeout, and Jones let his assistant run the huddle.

Jones, though, was a man who treated us like we were men. There's always a concern when an assistant gets promoted. Sure, it's only one seat over, but it's a huge move. As an assistant Jones was close with the players; he was our confidant while Fitch was driving us crazy. Fans think that a lot of coaches are supposed to be fire and brimstone, Knute Rockne style. That wasn't Jones. Sometimes he'd stutter a bit, but anyone could see that his basketball instincts were great. If anyone was expecting a Pat Riley, Chuck Daly type, we knew better.

"[Jones] was just always a gentleman, and there's no question he was the least knowledgeable guy about the league that there was," Ryan said. "I always said this: if you gave every coach in the league a yellow legal pad and say you have one minute to simply name as many players in the league as you can on the other teams, he would have finished last, and Fitch would have finished first...he barely knew who they were playing tomorrow."

The Boston Globe's Dan Shaughnessy added, "All the things that he wasn't, none of that mattered. What he was—he was secure enough in his own skin to just let them take it away. And he could be stern when it was necessary, but it was kind of a free reign and mutual respect he had built up...He was Red's guy; it gave Red new life to get rid of Fitch and have Case there."

It's not that he didn't have a personality. Jones had a terrific singing voice, and if a bar had a karaoke machine, you could be sure that K.C. the Crooner would take over. Here's the perfect story to illustrate the differences between Fitch and Jones. We were in the locker room after a tough game, and Fitch was just lighting us up. Everyone was sitting up at attention. You could hear a pin drop...except there was a non-stop cracking sound from the corner. Fitch lost his shit and screamed: "Who's eating fucking peanuts?" We all laughed...it was Jones.

Dennis Johnson, who had a reputation of being difficult but actually meshed perfectly on our Celtics teams, drives by Los Angeles Lakers star Magic Johnson in Game 1 of the 1984 NBA Finals.

The other big move that offseason was another Auerbach special, trading backup center Rick Robey to the Phoenix Suns for Dennis Johnson. We knew that D.J. was a great defender, but he'd earned a reputation as a head case. Coming in as a second-round pick by the Seattle SuperSonics, D.J. had to fight for everything in the league. Two years later he helped lead the Sonics to the NBA Finals against Washington. Then, on the biggest stage—Game 7—Johnson went 0-for-14—*0-for-14!*—from the floor, and the Bullets won the title.

You see a lot of guys struggle in big spots, and it ruins their careers. Not D.J. The next year he made his first All-Star team and brought the Sonics right back to the Finals against those same Bullets. This time D.J. took over, winning his first championship (in five games) and being named MVP in the process. When Seattle lost in the Western Conference Finals the following season, coach Lenny Wilkens labeled Dennis a "cancer," and he was traded to Phoenix for fellow All-Star Paul Westphal. In three years D.J. made two more All-Star teams but never got along with Suns coach John MacLeod either. Now he was coming to Boston with many doubting how he'd fit in. McHale, though, was among those who thought everything would be fine. "This is not a team where you worried about that," he said. "He's another guy that really knew how to play. This is a really high IQ player so he kind of just fit in pretty quickly."

Ainge made sure D.J. felt welcome on his very first day. "We were shooting in the gym, and I was having fun with D.J. and said, 'You know what? I'm going to call you 'chemo.' He asked why, and I said, 'because I don't want your cancer spreading.' And he just laughed, and D.J. and I hit it off pretty well. And he was another guy that was really fun," Ainge said. "He was really at the stage of his career where he was really open to just fitting in with our group."

Plus, if he couldn't get along with Jones, then we knew whose fault that would be. It was a good thing for D.J. that our team was so established. You weren't going to push around guys like Bird, Parish, or me. There was an incident that happened right when he arrived that really set the tone for how he would fit in. I don't remember the specifics, but he got into an argument with Jones. In this case D.J. was wrong. Usually, when a player gets pissed at his coach, he'll go to teammates, and they'll support him, no matter what. Not on this team.

D.J. came to two or three of us and vented what he was upset about. We told him in no uncertain terms that he was wrong. He was shocked, noting that players usually stick together, but we told him he needed to apologize. D.J. had been a wild stallion, but that day he became a great teammate and a versatile player. He could do it all: rebound, pass, defend. Also Jones could run us as much as he wanted, and D.J. would do it—maybe not as fast as you'd want, but he'd do it.

With a new coach and a new starter in the backcourt, we needed to begin the season well. We couldn't have a hangover from the sweep in Milwaukee. After losing our opener, we ripped off nine straight wins. We had a great team, but there was no question who was the leader. By this time, of course, Bird had established himself as one of—if not the best player in the game. But after getting swept in Milwaukee, he made a vow that he never wanted to feel like that again and would work his ass off that summer to become a better player.

Bird never lied.

When he came to camp, he was in the best shape he'd ever been. He was thinner and a step quicker. By the time we'd come out to practice, Bird would already be running the concourse of Boston Garden. Seeing that, we knew he'd dedicated himself.

The Philadelphia 76ers were the defending champions, and they still had Moses Malone, Dr. J, Andrew Toney, and Maurice Cheeks playing at a high level. Yeah, they tore up the league the previous season, but we weren't intimidated in the least. We always felt like we were just as good as them. It was like Muhammad Ali and Joe Frazier. Two of the greatest teams just happened to be playing in the same conference, the same division.

But we had Bird. He put up 24 points, 10 rebounds, and 6.6 assists per game while winning his first MVP award. Parish averaged at least 19 points for the third straight season, and McHale was at 18. D.J. fit like a glove, Gerald Henderson continued to improve, and I was steady with 12 points and six boards a night.

We were ready for the postseason.

CHAPTER 13
MY INJURY, THE RISE OF MCHALE, AND AN OVERDUE APOLOGY

June of 1984 was certainly a busy time. I'd just played the best game of my life in the biggest game of my life, and after winning the NBA Finals against the Los Angeles Lakers, we were champions again. Then Renee and I got married. Talk about surreal. It was almost like a fantasy. One of the biggest parts of any championship, of course, is the victory parade. I definitely remember our parade...even if I wasn't there.

My plan was to run down to city hall and get the marriage license. That's when I found out that being an NBA champion didn't carry the weight I thought it would. The woman there told me I had to fill out the paperwork for the license weeks before. Not like I was busy or anything. Renee and I were tired of all the travel during the playoffs. The last thing we wanted to do was spend all day in a parade; we decided to just fly out to the Bahamas to get away from everything. I was running around taking care of everything, and the day of the parade, I was in the barbershop, getting a haircut. It was hilarious. Everyone was looking at me and then looking at the TV, and saying, "Shouldn't you be there?"

We watched the guys celebrate at Government Center and saw all the signs that read: "Re-sign Max!" I was a free agent after all.

Thankful to get away from basketball and begin our official new life together, Renee and I headed on our trip. Who do I see at the hotel? Some 6'9" guy I had just left—Magic Johnson. After playing like "Tragic Johnson," I *know* I was the last person on Earth he wanted to run into. We saw each other from a distance but never talked.

* * *

I was a free agent in 1984. Unlike the last time—when the Indiana Pacers and Golden State Warriors came at me strong—nobody really showed any interest in signing me. The NBA was much different then. Teams that lost free agents received compensation, and everyone knew that Red Auerbach wasn't going to let me go. Auerbach had the hammer and he knew it. Getting paid by the Boston Celtics really depended on the situation. Larry Bird, of course, never had any issues. Gerald Henderson, on the other hand, didn't get a big money deal from the Celtics, and Robert Parish had to fight for his deal, too. Shortly after training camp had began, I ended up signing a four-year, $3.2 million deal with an option for a fifth year. Even though I didn't have many options, people started to get a little nervous when the team had a preseason game in Las Vegas and I wasn't there. They knew I loved Vegas and couldn't believe I'd miss that trip. Right after they came back, I signed.

The first thing you do when you come to camp is get checked out by the medical staff. Our team doctor was a man named Tom Silva. I, though, wouldn't say that our exams were exactly thorough. Doc would have you drop your pants and cough in order to check for a hernia. From there it was basically, "How was your summer?" And then a quick: "Okay, have a good year."

Looking back, I probably had torn cartilage in my knee at that time but never really thought anything about the soreness I was feeling. As basketball players we're always taught that it's not a big deal. You're going to feel the bumps and bruises and all of that as you get older. The season started, and we were playing like the champions we were, winning 15 of our first 16 games. I was kind of feeling my wind and getting into shape but averaging my normal 12 to 13 points per game. There were a couple of great games in there like when I dropped 30 on the Chicago Bulls and 27 vs. the Kansas City Kings.

Then we took our West Coast trip in February of 1985. On Valentine's Day we beat the SuperSonics in Seattle, and I scored 18 points in just 17 minutes of action. My knee was sore, but it wasn't something I was overly concerned about. The next night in Oakland, we beat Golden State, and I played 36 minutes, finishing with 17 points before fouling out. We had a day off in Los Angeles and then had our big showdown with the Lakers. We lost by six, and I had 12 points. That's when my knee just locked up. I hadn't felt pain like that before. So I was really concerned. I remember telling the doctors that there was a problem, but because the knee didn't swell up, nobody believed me. (It's funny, but over all these years, my knee never swelled until 2020 when I was on a cruise.)

Once we returned to Boston, they did an exam and found out I had torn cartilage in my right knee. Basically, the cartilage had wrapped around the bone. So when the flap got stuck, it essentially would tear on the inside of the knee. It was really painful, but again there wasn't really any swelling. My attorney, Ron Grinker, was quoted as saying the surgery was "probably done more for psychological reasons than anything else."

I heard that quote, but I think Grinker was just trying to make it sound like I wasn't hurt. There was a night in particular before the surgery when I was laying in bed and turned a certain way and then heard a scream. I turned over because I was by myself and didn't know who it came from. Then I realized it was me. That flap must have got caught or whatever, but it was a searing pain going throughout my body. So I knew something was wrong. I guess the difference now is that teams err on the side of the player. Back then it was on the side of the team.

When I had the surgery, they told me I'd be out for four weeks and then back to normal. That never happened. Whatever the training staff told me to do, I did. I went to therapy almost every day, but man, my leg was like spaghetti. Ice became my best friend. I remember putting an ice bag on my knee after working out, and you know that sound when you put ice on something really hot? It goes "fzzzzzz." That's what me knee sounded like. When I was icing, that's when it felt the best.

Once I got hurt, everything changed, especially my relationship with the team and my teammates. It was a really eye-opening experience for me. It all started from the top with Auerbach. He'd make comments about how he didn't think I was working hard enough to come back and how my motivation wasn't the same because I was making some money. This is the guy who drafted me and believed in me, so what he said hurt like hell. I was the Finals MVP—and a huge part of two NBA championships. I was also the first forward to lead the league in field goal percentage—twice. I earned my money. Anyone who really knew me also knew that I was as competitive as anyone on that team.

But I blame myself, too. Most people want to see you mope around when you're hurt. That's never been my personality, and I think a lot of people misconstrued my attitude as if I didn't care. There was one time where I made a comment like I just wish someone would cut my leg off. "Damn it—put it out there," Bird said. "And I'll just break it!"

He was kidding, but it was in a mean-spirited way. I knew he wanted me to come back, but he and some of my other teammates felt like I didn't want to come back. That really hurt me. Here's a guy I grew up with and won championships with. So, yeah, that stung. That was probably my lowest moment—just being hurt and people not understanding I was hurt.

Bird ripped my work ethic in well-known NBA writer Jackie MacMullan's book, *When the Game Was Ours*. "Max was out of shape when he came back. He didn't do the rehab the way they asked. I was so pissed at him because he was so good," Bird said. "He got his money and he quit. I like Max, but that's the bottom line."

The Boston Globe's Bob Ryan has a similar story from January of that year. "I am in French Lick, Indiana," Ryan wrote. "Larry called and began talking to Mom, and she told him I was there. They had a conversation, and I can hear these words in my head to this day as follows. 'Max doesn't want to play for us anymore. Period.' Larry, I don't know if he'll own up to it now or not. All I know is he said it, and that's all I can tell you…Now that said, he defends Max to the death today."

Not to let the facts get in the way of a good story, but neither one of these are true. I did *everything* the doctors asked of me. Again, maybe it was partly because of my attitude toward it or my not walking around all gloom and doom in the face. Remember Pig Pen, the kid from *Peanuts*, who always had a cloud of dirt following him? I was never like that. I was more like Peppermint Patty, always with a smile on my face, always happy. *"What's up, Chuck?"* That rubbed some people the wrong way. That attitude came from the way my father. Manny Maxwell raised me in a very military way: never let them see your whole cards and act like you're the same person. If you have something going on internally, let that demon stay internal.

It was incredible that this was the case less than 12 months after I'd carried everyone on my back to the promised land. Danny Ainge told me a story from his baseball days that put it in perspective. When Ainge was playing baseball, his teammate, John Mayberry, manned first base. Big John was a hell of a player and told Ainge, "Pup, if you bat .301 one year, that's great. The problem is that everyone is going to expect you to hit .302 the next season."

When I got hurt, Ainge would say that to me all the time, and we'd laugh. He had an interesting perspective about my injury. "I'm not judging Max," he said. "It was just his personality. The great part of Max is that he made everything loose, and that was a great quality. But he wasn't able to do that when it was stressful for him not being able to play and not being able to get healthy."

There were only a few people I thought felt compassion, but I also knew that it was about the people playing, and the players out there were trying to win another championship. So the focus had to be on those guys. I get that, but it just seemed like there were little whispers about me not wanting to give the effort and come back and play. Let me tell you: I busted my ass.

I do, however, want to formally apologize to my teammates for the way I acted during my rehabilitation from my surgery. A lot of guys—however, Auerbach, Bird among them—had an interpretation that I didn't care, that I'd gotten my contract, and that was it. That was the furthest thing from the truth, but I still want to apologize for my actions. Because I didn't mope around, guys perceived it in the wrong way.

At that point, I was in my eighth season, and other than my rookie year, I'd never missed more than four games. So being injured was a new experience for me, and I didn't handle it the way many other guys did. Looking back, it would have been better for me to explain that to them. I should've gone to Bird and said, "Dude, here's the deal: I am hurt, I want to play, but physically I can't." I wish I had emphasized that much more to the entire team, including K.C. Jones.

One of the things that actually made me think of this was Donald Trump. Just his inability to say, "Damn, you know what? I fucked up. It was me, my bad." I've always said that the true measure of a man is not how he acts in good times but how he acts in bad times. I missed the boat on this one.

For someone as old-school as Auerbach, this was tough to understand. "Red expected him to be more like one of his players in the '60s like Tommy [Heinsohn] or Satch [Sanders], who would play through anything and run through a wall for you," Jeff Twiss said. "Maybe that was the kind of connotation that Red had for Max being the veteran and the oldest leader on the team."

If I had to point out two guys that I did lean on, it would be M.L. Carr and Quinn Buckner. We kind of became our own little group away from the rest of the guys. At that point Jones didn't have any confidence in any of us. So there were times when one of us would get in, and the other two would just cheer like crazy.

We had one playoff game against the Detroit Pistons and we needed a three-pointer. Carr was the best three-point shooter off the bench so we told Jones to put him in. Lo and behold, he did. "I said, 'I guess you guys don't want to win the game. Why am I sitting on the bench? I should be in the game,'" Carr said.

They threw the ball over to Carr. "I caught the ball and I was out of bounds. So heading back to the bench, I knew what that was going to be like," Carr said. "It's been 38 years, and they still talk about it every time!"

When he got to the bench, we were laughing so hard about that out-of-bounds play. I said, "We need three points, not four!"

* * *

I knew my time in the starting lineup was gone when Kevin McHale was killing everyone he played against. Would I have been okay coming off the bench? Yes. But I think there was so much angst about my coming back at that point. Everyone could see how great McHale was becoming, and I became kind of the forgotten man. "Max has a lot of disrespect in his head at all times. It kind of motivates him," Dan Shaughnessy said. "But he was fairly unstoppable on the low block—almost as much as Kevin in that he could either get fouled or get an easy shot. Also, he could defend and he guarded Magic Johnson. People forget that."

McHale scored 56 points against the Detroit Pistons while I was rehabbing. I thought, *Well, that's probably gonna be the end of my starting here.* I wasn't mad; it was just a fact. But the next day, someone in the paper wrote that I'd gone from being an $800,000 starter to a $800,000 guy sitting on the bench.

The late Will McDonough was legendary for calling out players, and he was always writing little snippets about me. I know he was close with

Red Auerbach, too, so it was clear who was feeding him. I didn't really read the papers, but my friends would tell me what was being said about me. "It was just hard," McHale said. "I don't think it portrayed Max the way Max was—fun-loving. Hey, there were many, many nights that he had to guard the toughest guys, and Max would grind it out. He never backed away from a challenge."

It was interesting that years later when Larry Bird and McHale got hurt, nobody ever questioned whether they wanted to come back. I feel awful whenever I see McHale because he had a misdiagnosis of a broken foot during the 1987 season. He played through it, and they essentially had to fuse his ankle together. So now he walks around with a really bad limp. Boston does have a long history of racism, but I'm not going to say Bird and McHale were treated differently because they're White. The reason they were treated differently was more like green and red than Black and White. I mean green as in money, and Red Auerbach who was running the team. All I knew is I wanted to get the hell out of there.

McHale's emergence was definitely the biggest development while I was out. From the time he came into the league in 1980, everyone could see that he had the talent and drive to become a big-time player. He twice won the Sixth Man of the Year Award, and while I was on the bench, he took over the spot and never gave it back.

The highlight, of course, was that early March game against Detroit when he went for 56. Bird also had 30, and Robert Parish had 20. (Let's just say the Pistons weren't the defensive team they'd become yet.) Poor Kent Benson couldn't slow him down at all. The famous story, of course, is that McHale came out of the game for good in the fourth quarter, and Bird told him he should have scored more because he'd break McHale's record. McHale just laughed it off and actually scored 42 in the next game. But three games after that, Bird kept his word, and lit up the Atlanta Hawks for 60 points in a neutral

Kevin McHale drives against David Greenwood of the Chicago Bulls during his rookie season in 1980. Though he was still raw, he already was showing his potential.

site game played in New Orleans. By the way, Bird made one—*one*—three-pointer that whole game.

You could see the writing seemed on the wall regarding my future. "Maybe it was all working well for those two championships in '81 and '84, but maybe it was time where he had to start, and would Maxwell be happy coming off the bench after being the story all this year?" *The Boston Globe*'s Bob Ryan said. "I don't know. All I know is that it did deteriorate. I don't know about all the contract stuff, but it got to the point where they needed [him gone]. He needed to get out."

Let me clear a couple up a couple of misconceptions. First, I was not jealous of McHale. I couldn't have been happier for him. I took tremendous pride in his growth and to see him use some of the things I had taught him. McHale's development brought me back to a lesson I learned my rookie year. Tommy Heinsohn was trying to shake things up and started me in place of John Havlicek. I scored 21 points that night against the Buffalo Braves, and if anyone had the right to be pissed, it was Hondo. I mean, this guy was an all-time great, a no-brainer Hall of Famer. But after the game, the first person to congratulate me? Havlicek. It's the natural order of sports. I tried to do the same with McHale.

Especially when you're competing for a title, it's all about team. I couldn't do the job, and McHale stepped in and did. More power to him. In fact, I would have been fine basically changing roles with him. He was going to start regardless at that point because his talent was obvious. I could have come off the bench, done my thing, and helped us win another ring.

During this time McHale and I were totally cool. He knew it was his job and he was going to be a starter. We didn't have to go through everything. We just kept interacting like we always did. "That was 100 percent Max," McHale explained. "I remember being a little uncomfortable, but I can't tell you how gracious he was. As I started getting better, he would be my biggest fan. He was just so positive. What a credit to him."

McHale's ascension was not the reason I was ready to leave. It was the animosity and people questioning my integrity. *That* was the issue. Some people believe you can't lose your job in injury, but it happens all the time in sports. Here in Boston franchise quarterback Drew Bledsoe got hurt, and a guy named Tom Brady stepped in. He was pretty good.

Not So Brotherly Love

As the defending champions, we always got everyone's best shot, especially from the Philadelphia 76ers. In November of 1984, they came to Boston, and we kicked their ass. Larry Bird couldn't miss, making 17 of his 23 shots en route to 42 points. Dr. J struggled, going 3-for-13 and finishing with six points. But *that* wasn't the story.

By now everyone has seen the picture of Dr. J and Bird choking each other. We were coming down the court, and I could see in my peripheral Bird trying to hook Dr. J, who threw him to the floor. Referee Dick Bavetta called an offensive foul on Bird, and he was pissed. It was surprising—to say the least. "We did Converse commercials together. We did Spalding commercials together," Dr. J said on ESPN'S *Get Up*. "So we were kind of cool."

Unbeknownst to us, bar fights were right up Bird's alley. Charles Barkley grabbed his arms down, and Dr. J punched Bird three times in the face. Dr. J, though, remembers things a little bit differently. "I just extended my arm to hold him back, and it ended up sliding up to his neck. Then it was on. So it was really inadvertent," he said. "I didn't really mean to grab him by the neck. I pushed him in the chest, my hand slid up, go to his neck, he reached for my neck. Next thing I know, it's a melee."

> Intentional or not, it was on, and I ended up jumping on Barkley's neck. He went flying into the crowd. All these years later, it seems like a million people say they were at the game.
>
> Both Bird and Dr. J got fined $7,500, according to *The New York Times*, which was the second-highest fine in league history at that time.

* * *

There were two things I knew, heading into the playoffs: I could still play, and my time with the Boston Celtics was coming to an end. Whatever happened, I probably wasn't going to get a chance to repeat my heroics from the previous year. It was clear that K.C. Jones didn't trust me. After returning from injury, I only started one game and broke double figures just twice. My knee still wasn't 100 percent. In fact, I'd estimate it was 6 percent. Yes, 6 percent!

Once the playoffs tipped, we were again the top seed in the East. First up was the Cleveland Cavaliers, and they tested us. We survived in four games, but our wins were by: three points, two points, and two points. In the first two games, I played a combined 13 minutes. There wouldn't be any hopping on my back this time around.

An up-and-coming Detroit Pistons team was next, and in Game 1, I had my last big moment as a Celtic, scoring 16 points in 13 minutes. After the TV announcer interviewed me postgame, he said I was back. I remember thinking in my mind, *Uh, no, I'm not. Nope.* Instead, I just gave him a line about having a long way left to go, but it felt good to contribute.

In addition to the pain in my knee, the irregular minutes were hurting my game as well. I couldn't get anything going, make the moves I wanted, or find a rhythm. Jones decided to shorten the bench. So the only forwards getting serious time were Larry Bird, Kevin McHale, and Robert Parish. Scott Wedman and myself had to fight for scraps.

123

If you'd think that I might have earned a conversation telling me about this, you'd be wrong.

Fortunately, the Pistons weren't ready to be at our level, and we eliminated them in six games. Next up were the Philadelphia 76ers with all of the same names: Dr. J, Moses Malone, Mo Cheeks, and Andrew Toney, but they also added a rotund rookie named Charles Barkley. He wasn't a great player yet, and Dr. J and Malone had slowed down. I'll always remember how disrespectful Barkley was to me, especially when he blocked my shot. Barkley just had this smirk on his face. I put that one in the memory bank.

We blew them out in the first two games, but that's when trouble happened. Bird was in a bar fight and messed up his hand. Bird's index finger always had been grotesque after he had hurt it in a softball game, but the swelling got even worse. He told the media he injured it during Game 3 in Philadelphia, but everyone seemed to know the fight was two days earlier.

Reportedly, Bird got into it with a man named Mike Harlow. But Celtics management was standing by their man. "There were rumors that Larry had been in some kind of altercation," Dr. Tom Silva said. "I had examined Larry's finger, and there was no evidence of human bite marks or abrasions of the face or hand. And we know the condition of Larry's finger is such that he cannot make a fist."

Our general manager, Jan Volk, reiterated the company line. "As far as I know, nothing happened," Volk said. "It's a rumor. I know I saw him hurt it in that third game in Philadelphia."

Listen, I wasn't there, and Bird has never talked about it. But his late agent, Bob Woolf, said something that may have indicated the true cause. "All I will say is that an amicable agreement has been reached, and all parties are pleased with it," he said. "I do not want to comment anymore because all parties had a confidentiality agreement."

In fairness to Bird, he had a really good Game 3 in Philly after the alleged incident, making 11 of his 19 shots—including two three-pointers—en route to 26 points and an easy win. We were up three games to nothing. We ended up winning in five games, but Bird was just 10-of-33 from the field in the final two games.

After defeating Philly it was onto a championship rematch with the Los Angeles Lakers. Make no mistake, even though my role was diminished down to nothing, I desperately wanted us to win—if for no other reason that it would be another championship on my resume. It's incredible to think that just one year earlier I was L.A.'s worst nightmare. By that point, I could hardly move. There's nothing you can do when you're hurt. The knee would heal when it wanted to. It was just the darkest tunnel that I've been in.

Even the Lakers knew how lucky they were I wasn't playing. There was a game where Jones put rookie Greg Kite in the game instead of me. I heard Magic Johnson say that when he saw I wasn't playing that they knew they were going to beat us.

The thing I remember most about that series was when L.A. was up 3–2 in the series and came back to Boston. Kareem Abdul-Jabbar made a devastating sky hook and he was so excited that he pumped both fists. I'm sure he flashed back to 1984 when Boston Garden was so hot he had to ingest oxygen. Of course, I was disappointed that we lost, but Jabbar was a favorite player. Parish grew up idolizing him, too.

Game 6 really showed how far I'd fallen in Coach Jones' eyes. He only played seven players the entire game, and I wasn't one of them. "If he if he could have been even 90 percent of the player he was the year before, yeah, that would have been a weapon. And the notion that by Game 6 he's not even playing," said Dan Shaughnessy, pondering that concept. "And that was across the board. I mean M.L. Carr, Quinn Buckner, Carlos Clark, there were only seven guys who actually got off the bench."

In the locker room after the game, Carr, Buckner, and I went into the trainers' room, and we all cried. I was going to be traded, Buckner definitely wasn't going to be back, and Carr had already said he was going to retire. (He actually wanted to step away after we won the previous year, but Red Auerbach talked him into staying one more year.) We all knew that we'd never be playing with each other again, and I just wanted to put my clothes and get the hell out of there.

"It was a sad time because we've been through so much together," Carr said. "We've won championships together...We really cared about each other and we know that was coming to the end."

I knew everyone was going to be saying after the season that it was my fault because I didn't work hard enough to get back. That's so ridiculous to me. We had four Hall of Famers on our team (Bird, Parish, McHale, and Dennis Johnson), but *I'm* the reason we lost? Bird busted up his hand, and it's my fault?

CHAPTER 14
MOVING ON

Throughout the summer of 1985, I knew that I was going to be leaving Boston. I didn't know where I would be going, but there was no chance I'd be playing another game for the Boston Celtics. If this were going on today, I'd get a phone call from my agent, the team or I'd find out about a trade on ESPN's bottom line or social media. When I got traded, there was no Internet. I learned about my future…by reading *USA TODAY.*

Then, the mail came. Jan Volk, the Celtics general manager, wrote me a letter. It was basically how I should be proud of all the accomplishments during my time in Boston, blah, blah, blah. Oh, and sign this letter because you're officially traded to the Los Angeles Clippers in exchange for Bill Walton. The letter was polite but almost surgical—like a doctor saying, "We're going to amputate your leg. Oh, and by the way, you won't be walking much."

When I officially got the letter, I wasn't sad or mad. It was just a feeling of relief. I was like, *This is done. That should put that part of my life in the rear-view mirror.* My always colorful teammate, Robert Parish, had a different take. "Cedric got fucked," Parish said, "We tried to be supportive, encouraging, and positive about it, but you can't stop that outside noise. You can't stop Red getting in the way he's feeling. Then they tried to put all that unnecessary pressure on Cedric to come back before he was ready, which I thought was wrong, then they traded him, which made it more wrong. Like I said, Cedric got fucked and he was labeled as a quitter. And Cedric is not a quitter."

Another big difference between then and now is that there weren't all of the insiders who would break the story. When the trade was announced in September, I'd already been in L.A. for a month. There's no question that the Celtics have always been one of the premier organizations in the game. The Clippers? Well, they weren't. Having said that, my physical was a lot more detailed than in Boston, where the doctors basically just asked me how my summer was. Maybe it was because after signing Walton to a huge contract, the big man was constantly injured, missing two full seasons while playing 14 and 33 games in two others. Whatever the reason, the Clippers did a real physical... and I failed it.

For the trade to happen, I'd have to rehab for a month and get my knee right. As screwed up as this organization was, they didn't want to get burned again. Although a lot of players might dread playing for the Clippers, my desire to get the heck out of Boston was great. So it didn't matter to me. Plus, my old friend/teammate, Don Chaney, was the head coach and he called me to say the deal might be happening. Duck Chaney is even the guy who introduced me to his nanny, Renee, the woman who became my wife.

I spent more than a month out in L.A., proving that my knees were healthy. Chaney pushed GM Elgin Baylor to make the deal in the first place. "I definitely felt that what the Clippers really needed was a championship caliber-type player, and Max had proven he can win championships," Chaney said. "He could push his game up to another level and also set an example for the younger players who have not really had success at winning."

As much as the media made it sound like I got my money in Boston and then didn't care, I actually took a pay cut to make the trade work.

It was a different experience than Boston, where the fans are so intense. When I went to the mall, people would always stop me, ask for pictures and autographs, or just want to say hello. In Los Angeles nobody cared because *everyone* there was a star. The Lakers are always going to be the top dog in L.A. because they're the Lakers. Jack Nicholson and Denzel Washington ain't coming to see the Clippers. But it felt good to become a Clipper, even though they were second-class citizens in town. Whatever disrespect they received, they had earned. The Clips started as the Buffalo Braves and then moved to San Diego. They had a winning record their first year...then went more than a decade before doing it again. The weird thing was they had some good players. The problem was that they were mostly past their prime.

The biggest name was Marques Johnson, who was back home after a terrific career with the Milwaukee Bucks. Johnson was not only from nearby Crenshaw High School, but he won a national championship and was the Player of the Year at UCLA. He was a really witty guy, but it's a different type of wit. He definitely liked to curse. I liked Johnson, but he's one teammate I really wish I had gotten to know better. He was really guarded, and there were two reasons. First, playing in your hometown is never easy because people are always asking you for stuff, whether it's tickets (though that wasn't a problem for Clippers fans), access, or anything else. The other reason was that Johnson got into some trouble with drugs, which hastened his exit from Milwaukee.

My co-author reached out to Johnson for any good stories about me. He figured he'd share something about a big win on the court or something in that vain. Instead, Johnson pulled out an incident that told as much about the 1980s as it did about us.

We were a close bunch of guys and had no trouble making our own fun. As Johnson recalled, that included a mini-billiards tournament at the hotel. Keep in mind: this was a different time, where everyone wasn't so politically correct, and our language reflected that. "Max and Franklin are shooting pool, and I pass by," Johnson said. "Max asks if I play, and we start a game. I'm knocking 'em in left and right. Max starts talking trash to me and sees I'm getting rattled. He goes in full force, 'Okay, Cap, I see how you are. You're good playing 'White people pool,' all quiet, polite, and shit. We're playing n----- pool here, ghetto style. You don't like playing n----- pool, do ya?' I was laughing so hard and missing so many easy shots, which egged him on even more. I had to quit."

Our other former All-Star was ex-Los Angeles Lakers point guard Norm Nixon. He wasn't there when training camp started, as he was holding out for more money, but we became friends pretty quickly. One unique thing about Nixon: unlike most NBA players, he wasn't the most famous person in his own household. That distinction went to his wife, actress Debbie Allen, best known for starring in the movie *Fame*. Debbie had a party at the house for his birthday, and the cast of *A Different World*, which she executive produced, was all there. I ended up hanging with Norm and Grammy Award winner James Ingram. There was a piano in the house, so the two of us sang background, while Ingram played. Where else does that happen but L.A.?

On the court, Nixon and I were the guys with championship-winning experience (though Franklin Edwards did come off the bench for the 1983 Philadelphia 76ers). Our job was to try and bring that edge, and guys noticed. "He brought championship pedigree and he never let you forget it in a good way," Johnson said. "He and Norm would drone on and on about the NBA Finals being totally different than anything I experienced. I would mention UCLA and John Wooden, and Max would say it doesn't compare."

We had Junior Bridgeman coming off the bench. He was just a scorer plain and simple. Bridgeman was also really smart. He spent hours in the library, studying for his job in the NBA Players Association. You could just tell he was going to be successful after basketball, and he's made a fortune owning Wendy's franchises.

The other guy I was close with was Edwards. He spent the first few years of his career in Philadelphia, so we were certainly familiar with each other. Edwards and I were both huge Patti LaBelle fans, and we'd sit together, singing old soul songs. We had some great times. We had two pretty distinct groups on the team: those of us who were on the back nine of our careers and the young up-and-comers. I was the former group and brought wisdom. "Max was one of the most intelligent men I've ever known," Johnson said. "I used to bring this automated chess set on road trips, trying to improve my game. I would win on rare occasions. One day Max asks to see it. He beat the machine in less than five minutes!"

Johnson also appreciated my game as well. "I've never seen him miss a clutch free throw, and he shot a bunch," he said. "He had an amazing approach and he'd stand at the line all fidgety, talking shit to our opponents who tried to rattle him. He'd say, 'You can take that bullshit back to Cleveland. I ain't missing these bitches, am I Cap?' I didn't know whether to respond—I'd been taught to leave the free-throw shooter alone so he can concentrate. But with Max, the more chaos around, the more he thrived. He had amazing mental toughness. [He] wasn't anywhere near athletic as a lot of players, but he was the toughest guy mentally I ever played with along with Bob Lanier."

Lancaster Gordon had been the eighth overall pick in the NBA draft the previous year out of Louisville. The Clippers always picked pretty high because they lost so many games. Lancaster was a 6'3" shooting guard and he had some really good games but disappeared in the others.

And then there was Benoit Benjamin. This was supposed to be the franchise center L.A. was waiting for. To give you an idea of how much talent he had, look at the fact that Benjamin had a 15-year career in the NBA despite the fact he was as big a knucklehead as there was. "Benoit came to town right after we drafted him," Johnson said. "I got a call from [team president] Carl Scheer and was asked to come down to the Sports Arena to meet him. Norm was there also. Benoit said to me, 'Hey man, call Kareem and tell him I want to play him one-on-one today.' Kareem had just finished the NBA Finals."

One of his biggest issues was constant tardiness. There was one time when we had a shootaround, and he got there toward the end of it. He was sitting on the sidelines watching. Chaney was coaching us, and he called Benjamin over. Chaney said, "Back in the day, players would want to kick this guy's ass." Then he put his fists together and said, "You know what, I'm going to kick his ass!" And Chaney started walking up on him. We had to pull him back.

I lived close to Chaney, so I saw him later in the day and asked if he was okay. Chaney just walked around the house like nothing had happened. Regardless, the incident seemed to light a fire under Benjamin. He went out and had a huge game that night and for the next two-to-three weeks he was just a beast—and everything they had hoped for. Then he went back to normal.

Nobody knew what was going on in this guy's head. It's like he was in outer space. One time we were on the road, and he gets on the bus, talking about how the hotel left him a gift basket in his room and he'd eaten all the food and drank all the booze. What a life! He didn't realize that was the minibar and that he had to pay for everything. The way he spent money, well, let's just say he was no Bridgeman. He was buying *everything*. He was so proud that he could afford a Cadillac. One day while we were at practice, the car was repossessed. "No big deal," Benjamin said. "I'll just buy another one."

And of course, the most famous Benjamin story is when he showed up for a game with two left shoes. Imagine having to scour the town to find a place that sold size 18 or 19 shoes. Soon, he got involved in drugs and alcohol and he never came close to reaching his potential.

The centerpiece of the team, though, was a 24-year-old monster named Derek Smith. A former second-round pick, Smith was coming into his own. The previous year, his scoring average jumped from 10 points a game to 22, and he was just getting started. He was too big and strong for guards and too quick for power forwards. He was unstoppable. We got to be very close. He loved him some Cornbread. The first time we met, he said, "You know that little spot you like to score from? I own that spot."

And he was right. There weren't a lot of plays run for me, but it was fun watching a young guy like that develop into the player he was. Things started well, and we won our first five games. Then we lost eight in a row, and during that stretch, Smith shredded his knee. That was just devastating.

Overall, we were a relatively happy bunch of guys. If Smith had stayed healthy, we might have made the playoffs. Without him we finished 32–50. We still had fun, but I felt like we weren't really in the NBA anymore. We were just in the Lakers' shadow. Being a part of the Clippers was certainly different. With the Celtics every game was like a playoff game for our opponents. With L.A. there really weren't any big games. People got excited when we played the Lakers, but even our fans usually rooted for them.

I played pretty well for the Clippers, putting up 14 points and eight rebounds in 32 minutes a night. It was the most I'd played in three seasons. Even though my knee was never going to be the same, Chaney wanted me out there. "I wish he could have played every minute of every game," he said. "Even if he wasn't 100 percent all the time, having him on the floor gave me a chance to win just by his presence out there."

In 2014, of course, team owner Donald Sterling was forced to sell the Clippers after he was recorded saying some vile racist remarks. Naturally, I get asked all the time about my interactions with Sterling. People are generally disappointed in my response, which is I didn't deal with him much at all. The handful of times I met Mr. Sterling, he never showed any signs of being biased. Really, the only memory I have of him is when he came into our locker room with some friends and wanted to show off his players. See, the Clippers were really like a hobby for him, just a shiny toy to play with.

Seeing how everything blew up in his face was certainly a surprise to me, but it didn't stop CNN from interviewing me for about a full week straight. That experience taught me something as well. Back in 2007, I put my foot in my mouth on the air, criticizing Violet Palmer—the first female referee in NBA history—during a game. I made the comment that she should "go back to the kitchen and make me some bacon and eggs."

I was 100 percent in the wrong and truly sorry for my lapse in judgement. Palmer worked extremely hard to get to the league, and I never should have said that. Period. During one of my CNN interviews, I was on with host Fredricka Whitfield. As we were talking about Mr. Sterling, she called me out by bringing up the Palmer incident. I was pissed! First, it had nothing to do with what we were talking about, which were the racist views of the Clippers' owner. Second, my comments were seven years old! Lastly, I know she didn't hear me say those words and probably only knew about it from a producer telling her. Now I could have blown her up right on national TV. But I was respectful. I don't know Whitfield, but she's a Black woman who's worked her way up to the biggest news network in the country. I decided to take the high road. Sterling, on the other hand, did not. It's true that he had legendary cheapness, but when I was there, we actually had good players. We were just older and injured.

Late in the season, we still had a chance to catch the Sacramento Kings for the final playoff spot, but we needed to win our last five games against some good teams. Johnson was getting a little excited. I let him know the reality. "In the shower I was like, 'Max, if we really focus, we can do this,'" Johnson said. "Max was like, 'Cap, I'm calling my pool man tomorrow to tell him to get the pool ready. I'll be home soon.' Classic!"

Even though our team was losing, I enjoyed L.A. As someone who lived his whole life on the East Coast. There, though, were certainly adjustments. Coming from Boston the biggest thing difference was the weather. My body was so used to the cold, and now it was just warm every day. Having Thanksgiving and Christmas in the sun was certainly different. The whole vibe was a little strange to me. There were great restaurants, and these health food places that hadn't become really popular yet. Even buying a house was an experience. I learned that if you see a peacock in the backyard, you need to find another place because they make an awful honky noise. Everyone in California seemed so much healthier. Because they're showing skin 10 months out of the year, I think they take better care of themselves. Plus there's just so much to do. When I was with the Celtics, I'd go over to Beverly Hills on occasion, but that was about the extent of my sightseeing. When I was living there, I'd go to Pasadena, check out the Rose Bowl Parade, go to USC and UCLA. It was just a cool experience.

* * *

I had a sick feeling the first time we hosted the Boston Celtics, and it had nothing to do with the opponent. Two days before the Celtics came to L.A, we had a game in Seattle, which we won. But the game was secondary. I had a buddy in the area, and we went to grab dinner at a restaurant called Trader Vic's. So we're eating these chicken wings, and they tasted a little strange to me. Vic's was dimly lit, but I held one of the wings up to the candlelight, and the damn chicken was like half-cooked. You know how when you take a bite into chicken, and there's still that blood there? That's what this looked like. My stomach started flipping immediately. My buddy went through those wings like the Tasmanian Devil. Somehow, he ended up being totally fine.

When I got back to my room, I, on the other hand, could hardly stand up. I was sweating from a fever and couldn't stop. We had a 6:30 wake-up call for a 7:00 flight back home. I was throwing up all night. On the plane I talked myself into thinking that I'd be okay, even though I was still weak. As we started our descent, it was like someone lit a match on my body. I was sweating profusely and dry heaving. Some of my teammates were joking that I had the "[Larry] Bird flu."

I was so out of it the night of the game I don't even remember it. Somehow I played 31 minutes but only scored six points with 10 rebounds, and we lost by 22 points. It was definitely a night to forget.

The bigger deal was two months later when I made my return to Boston. I was pretty excited because I was coming back to a place where people love me. Every place we played that first year, I would get booed because I was former Celtics player Cedric Maxwell. Now, it was just the conquering hero coming home. When we got off the plane, there were cameras at the airport to document my arrival. We stayed at the Long Wharf Marriott hotel, and people were there just to catch a glimpse of me. It felt so strange. When I finally got to Boston Garden, it was the first time I'd realized how small the visitors' locker room was.

I was so jazzed up that I didn't even come out to shootaround. If I didn't know these hoops by then, that would be a problem. When we took the floor for warmups, the crowd started going crazy, taking pictures and screaming my name. I was the first person announced for our starting lineup and got a huge ovation. I looked down to the other bench, and Dennis Johnson, Bird, Kevin McHale, Robert Parish, and the rest of the team were all clapping. It was one of the coolest moments I had in sports. Just surreal.

Oh yeah, there *was* a game as well. My defensive assignment went back and forth between Bird and McHale. There was one time where Bird got me up in the air on a head fake, and as soon as I jumped, I could hear a voice in my head screaming, "Nooooooo!" He scored, and all I could do was giggle. I mean, I thought I'd seen every possible move these guys could do after battling in practice all these years. I even chuckle about it now.

The only other thing I really remember from the game was I made a steal and was going in for a layup, and Danny Ainge banged into me. It really should have been an and-one play, but instead I was called for the charge. When I turned to Ainge, he was laughing.

There wasn't much trash talking, though there was one funny line. We used to tease Parish because he had trouble pronouncing the letter S. During one break in the action, D.J. came up to me, telling me they were going *straight* toward me. "We're going *squait* at you!" That was funny.

CHAPTER 15
REUNITED WITH FITCH

I'm sure some of the fans missed me while I was gone—along with some of my teammates. But if they did, it certainly didn't show on the court. Bill Walton was the perfect fit in Boston. Even though he was a California guy, the tradition, the mystique was right up his alley. Everyone knew how great Walton was when he led the Portland Trail Blazers to their only championship. But everyone also knew that he could not stay healthy. In fact, in his last season with the Los Angeles Clippers, Walton set a career high in games played, and it was only 67.

Walton knew this was his last chance. He was such a great student of the game and he really loved the chance to be around guys like Larry Bird, Robert Parish, and Kevin McHale. Knowing how special the team was, Walton basically sold his soul to the devil to play with the Celtics. Whatever he did, it worked, as he amazingly played in 80 games.

With the Hall of Fame front line of Bird, Parish, McHale, and Walton, the Celtics rolled to a 67–15 record and the franchise's 16th championship. I was happy for my friends, but there was definitely a little jealousy about what was going on in Boston. It was hard to hear everyone talk about how great "the Big 3" was and how great it was to have Walton come off the bench. I'd have been fine playing behind McHale, but it didn't work out that way. The Celtics defeated the Houston Rockets in the NBA Finals to cap their 1985–86 season. Little did I know that I would be joining that team soon.

* * *

Even as the Los Angeles Clippers struggled, we had some pretty good players, including future NBA head coaches Larry Drew and Mike Woodson. You could see even back then that they knew the game. Woody and I became pretty close. We started the season 3–3. Then came the tsunami—a 12-game losing streak. If we thought things couldn't get worse, we were wrong. We snapped that skid with a win against the Seattle SuperSonics…and then lost 16 straight!

When we were in Oakland, a couple of games after finally winning a game, to play the Golden State Warriors, I read in the paper that the Houston Rockets' backcourt—Mitchell Wiggins and Lewis Lloyd—had been suspended for using drugs. That day Woody and I were playing cards in his room and laughing that he was probably going to be traded to the Rockets.

We finished, and I went back to my room. The next thing I know, I get a call from my attorney, Ron Grinker, asking if I want to get traded. I had no idea that was even possible. I asked where, and he said Houston. He told me that Bill Fitch, my former Boston Celtics coach and the current Rockets one, wanted a veteran guy to go with Hakeem Olajuwon and Ralph Sampson. After losing to the Celtics in six tough games the previous season, they were middling along at 18–18. I asked Grinker how serious this was, and he told me if I wanted out, it would be done by the end of the day. *Did I want out? We were 5–31!* Half an hour later, I was a Rocket. Woodson was so pissed off. He was like, "You're not leaving me here!" Two years later, though, Woody signed with Houston as a free agent.

The NBA was different than today, when players essentially have to give permission to be traded. The only reason Grinker was asking me was because of my big contract. As I learned later, in reality my contract actually got bigger with the trade, as there was no state income tax in Texas. Another funny thing was that the Rockets were on the road, so I had to fly to meet them—in Boston.

When Fitch got fired in Boston, I sure never thought I'd be playing for him again. The Rockets may have been struggling, but they had still had a good team. Olajuwon was just coming into his own, Sampson was an All-Star, and Rodney McCray was another really good young player. McCray was skeptical when I came into the locker room. I believe he was in his contract year, and he thought I was coming in to take his job. Hey, I was toward the end of my career. I wasn't looking for anyone's job. If I could help provide some veteran leadership and win another ring, that was good enough for me. I was always a good interior passer, and my job was to get the ball to Olajuwon inside. I think what eased McCray's mind was my line to the media that "I'm coming to be the horse, not the jockey."

Olajuwon was the top pick in the 1984 NBA Draft ahead of some guy who went third named Michael Jordan. Sampson had been the top pick in 1983. They were known as the "Twin Towers." Even though he was only in his fourth season, you could see Olajuwon was going to be great. One of his biggest skills was that he could mimic any move. Since he was a soccer player growing up in Lagos, Nigeria, he was still learning basketball. He saw my jump hook in practice and told me he liked it. "Maxie, I'm going to have that jump hook," he said.

I explained that it took me years to master it. This wasn't something that was going to happen overnight. Sure enough, in our next game, he nailed a jump hook. Dream was so cool that he looked over at the bench and winked at me. That ability to quickly master things is why I say that he was the best player I've ever played with or against. He just dominated both ends of the floor. His footwork was fantastic, tracing back to the soccer field. At that time his work ethic wasn't there. He'd be the last one to practice and the first to leave. But Clyde Drexler told me that Moses Malone spent a summer with him and showed him how to work on his game. Early in his career, it was all athleticism for Dream. As he got older, he got smarter.

I was really fortunate to play with two guys who had some of the best footwork the league has ever seen in Olajuwon and Kevin McHale. Nobody could stop either one, but they were so different. Dream was like watching Michael Jackson. He was graceful like a ballerina. He was so quick with such great anticipation that he was always making steals. In fact, he's one of the only guys in league history who recorded a quadruple-double. McHale was more cumbersome. He always looked like a guy who was ready to fall apart. He always had the ball up high and never got blocked. They were two guys who had incredible moves.

The other "tower" was Sampson. There haven't been many college basketball players who received more hype than he did. He had way more skill than you'd think for anyone like that who was 7'4". He was a three-time National Player of the Year. The rumor was that he might leave college after his freshman year. That was the draft where Boston had the No. 1 pick, and Red Auerbach wanted Sampson badly. Our front line would have been Sampson, Larry Bird, and me. Management wanted me and M.L. Carr to fly down to see Sampson at the University of Virginia to convince him he should turn professional and come to Boston. I told them there was no way I was going to go beg some kid to become a millionaire.

Sampson was much-maligned for never winning an NCAA championship, but teams were tanking to try and draft him. When Houston lost to the Celtics in the previous year's Finals, Sampson got into a fight with Jerry Sichting who stood 6'1". It seemed like no matter what Ralph did, people wanted more. His biggest problem was that despite his size, Sampson was a jump shooter and didn't have much of a base. In practice I could move him off the blocks without any problem, even though he was half a foot taller.

Whenever Olajuwon did something great, Sampson was expected to do the same. When the Rockets drafted both of them, the thought was they'd revolutionize the game. But as Sampson's knees began to go, so did his game, and he was never the same player. They were both good guys dealing with great expectations. Olajuwon and I didn't hang out off the court, but all of us got along really well. We had guys like Jim Petersen, Buck Johnson, Bobby Joe Reid, Lester Conner, and eventually

World B. Free. One day in practice, Reid said something about a girl to Olajuwon, and Dream just slapped the snot out of him. It was quickly over, but lesson learned: don't piss off the big guy.

It had been several years since Fitch's film machine had broken, resulting in cheers from our team. He'd taken over a Rockets team that had won 14 games the year before (in part because it lost on purpose to be able to draft Sampson) and three years later had them in the Finals. Though still intense, Fitch definitely had mellowed with age. It's like when you're the oldest kid in a family. You're treated one way. Then when your younger sibling grows up, there's a much more lenient set of rules. We had one game where we were up big in the fourth quarter. Fitch called me in and said, "Go get Hakeem before he gets hurt." I was thinking, *What? So* he *doesn't get hurt?*

The next day at practice, I pulled Fitch aside and told him I didn't appreciate that. We both laughed. We'd been through the wars together, won a title together. So my understanding of Fitch was different than any other player's on the team.

Those Rockets teams were really fortunate, as we had two Hall of Fame coaches on our squad. Fitch's assistant was Rudy Tomjanovich, who later led Houston to two NBA titles. Tomjanovich was just one cool dude. Everyone loved Rudy T. He was one of the Rockets' all-time great players so he'd been there and done that. But, of course, everyone knows him for "The Punch." I liked Tomjanovich a lot, but, honestly, every time I looked at him, I saw my old friend, Kermit Washington, crushing Tomjanovich's face with a single punch. Rudy T came very close to dying that night and at one point he said was tasting something like metal. It was spinal fluid.

It's impossible to give Rudy T enough credit for having the guts to come back after that, but by the time we beat Houston in the 1981 Finals, he was at the end of his career. I remember him trying to guard me and thinking, *This old dude has no chance.* He was still a great guy, and

I'm glad for all of his success. He definitely took the hard route to the Hall of Fame.

Overall, I was pretty happy in Houston. No, I wasn't the same player I'd been, but we had a great group of guys on the bench, and I was cool backing up Petersen. Little did I know that on March 31, 1988, there would be a highlight I'd never accomplished before.

We were playing the Indiana Pacers at Market Square Arena. Since I wasn't starting, I'd often have the ballboy get me a Coke and drink it right on the bench. There was time since Fitch wasn't calling my number until late in the first or early in the second quarter.

Not this night.

Petersen picked up three fouls in like two minutes trying to stop Wayman Tisdale. It was Max Time, and I was like, *Damn, you couldn't even let me finish my Coke?* I ended up going 42 minutes with 23 points, 15 rebounds, and 10 assists for my first and only triple-double in my career. Yeah, I could still play, just not every night.

* * *

That triple-double came during my second year with the Houston Rockets when we won 46 games but lost in the first round of the play-offs. Bill Fitch was fired, and our new coach was my old pal Don Chaney, the guy who introduced me to his nanny, Renee, who became my wife. Weirdly enough, he had just left my previous team after getting fired as coach of the Los Angeles Clippers and was now following me to Houston.

Little did I know that this move would become the first step of my marriage coming to an end. We were living in Charlotte, and Renee's brother, Dane, and I planned on driving out to Houston for training camp before my third season in Houston—or so I thought.

Hearing about Chaney's arrival was cool. He and his wife, Jackie, were like second parents to Renee and me. We figured it would be a great reunion. We began our journey, enjoying the ride. This was when there weren't any cell phones. So I'd call home on occasion. We stopped overnight in Louisiana and we pulled into Houston about five in the afternoon. As we settled in, I got a call from Chaney, who said he had some bad news, which scared the crap out of me. *Had something happened back at home? Was my family okay?* Everyone was fine, Chaney said, but I was traded to the Washington Bullets. I believe it was the first time a player had been traded for salary cap room.

Since I'd been traded a couple of years earlier, this wasn't nearly as big a deal. I still had about two years left on my contract. So it made sense financially. I went to call Renee, knowing she'd be heartbroken that there wasn't going to be a reunion with the Chaneys. What I didn't know was the bombshell that was about to land. I got on the phone, and Renee answered. "I've got bad news," I started.

"You've been traded," Renee interjected.

"What?" I screamed.

"I knew you were going to be traded before you left the house. I didn't tell you," she calmly answered.

You could probably figure out the next question was asking how did she know. This was the time where Renee had better come up with a hell of an answer because we're talking about our marriage right now. "I didn't tell you because I didn't want to get Jackie in trouble," she explained.

Well, I guess we knew which team she was on. This was the beginning of the end of our marriage. I was just blown away that she was so cavalier about such a huge deal to our family. Needless to say, this was one of the most pissed off times I've ever been because she showed me no respect and no loyalty.

I didn't really have a choice about going to Washington; today guys can just say they're not reporting. I wasn't going to do that anyways. I had money still coming to me. The Bullets (who became the Wizards) were a mediocre team but had one of my old rivals on the squad—Bernard King. It had been four years since I declared "the Bitch" wasn't going to get 40 on me, and he did. It was cool getting to know him a little bit. It's so much different when you're on the same team.

Probably the funniest moment I had as a Bullets player was when John Williams (nicknamed "Hot Plate" because of his weight problems) told me he used to watch me play when while he was in college at LSU. "It's been burning me since I was in college. We were watching the Celtics and Lakers in the Finals," he said. "I told someone what you said to James Worthy on the free-throw line. They said you didn't. What did you say?"

"I told him, 'You can't guard me, Bitch,'" I explained.

Williams was so happy. It was like he discovered the biggest secret ever.

I didn't know it at the time, but Washington just wanted to take my salary; the team didn't want me. They weren't going to cut me right away like teams do now. That camp was about the worst I've ever been through. They wanted to work the shit out of me so I'd quit. The coach, Hall of Famer Wes Unseld, worked us nonstop. He put up this rope and had us jumping over it again and again. My knees were just hobbling to make it over.

I didn't play the whole preseason. Then in a game against the Philadelphia 76ers and Charles Barkley, Unseld called my number. Barkley came down and scored on me, and then I answered at the other end. And that was it. I played like two minutes and I was done. The next day at practice, the trainer came over to me and said, "Corns, coach wants to talk to you."

I went into Unseld's office, and he said, "Corns, I think the world of you, but we just had to release you." I got up, and he started to explain.

I said, "No, let *me* explain. I have two years left on my deal. Let me get out of here before you change your mind."

When I returned home after the Bullets' training camp, my daughter was waiting for me at the airport dressed up like a lion. It was so cool—like welcome to regular life. My NBA career was over, and shortly thereafter, so was my basketball career. I took a shot and went to play in Italy for a hot minute. It seemed like an easy way to make a quick buck. I think they were going to pay me something like $10,000 if it worked out. No harm, no foul, I figured.

It was so miserable. All I did was go to practice and then back to my hotel. I spent like $500 on phone bills calling home because it was so lonely. The team wanted to play a running style, and they thought they were getting the guy who went 24-8-8 in Game 7 of the NBA Finals. That guy was gone. I'd wake up at three in the morning just to watch CBS evening news so I could hear somebody speak English. One thing I'll say is that the food there was great, but it was time to go home, so I did.

A couple of weeks later, my attorney, Ron Grinker, asked if I wanted to play with Philly. The Sixers had some interest, but I told him I was good. Physically and emotionally, I was done with NBA basketball. I was only 32 years old, but you know what, I wouldn't have changed a thing about my career: the struggles of my first two years, leading the league in field-goal percentage twice (the first forward to do that in history), being a two-time NBA champion and a Finals MVP. There's nothing in my career I wish could have gone differently—even getting traded from the Boston Celtics or getting hurt—because I feel like my whole career was just meant to be.

CHAPTER 16
LARRY BIRD'S RETIREMENT

It wasn't long after I retired that Larry Bird and Kevin McHale started to break down. I knew this was going to happen with Bird. He played 100 miles an hour 100 percent of the time. It didn't matter if we played the Little Sisters of the Poor; he was going all out. Bird wouldn't take any shortcuts. If there was a loose ball that he couldn't get, he would just fling his body out there and throw himself into the crowd to make sure he gave his best effort. The fans loved it, especially a blue-collar crowd like in Boston, but he paid for it with the battle scars he had.

That was a big difference between the two of us. He'd be going 110 mph, and I'd be cruising along at 80. In the playoffs he'd still be going the same speed, and I'd be driving about 130. He just didn't understand the idea of pacing like I did. There were times when I didn't think he had another gear because he was always in fifth gear already. I always took pride that my guys knew when the lights were the brightest that they were going to get the best out of me.

McHale didn't always look like he was giving it his all, but he was. In 1987 he played the whole postseason with a broken foot that I believe was misdiagnosed. Seeing him drag it around now just kills me. By the time he retired, he had nothing left.

The Lord is funny. I came to Boston as a prejudiced guy. I didn't think White guys could play basketball. Even in college when my coaches would give me a scouting report, I'd always ask if the guy was White or Black. They didn't find that funny. So to play with—not one but—two of the greatest players in the history at the same time, and they were both White? Throw in Danny Ainge as a White kid who could really play the game. Yep, God is funny.

The strangest thing to me was that while Bird and McHale broke down, Robert Parish, who is three years older than Bird and four years older than McHale, just kept going like the Energizer Bunny. Of course, I was surprised at how long he lasted, but I saw firsthand how he took care of his body. He was one of the first guys who changed his diet.

Chief was into martial arts, so naturally, we called him Bruce Lee. He did all kinds of stretching and workouts, which elongated his career. There's a reason why he's played more games than any player in the history of the NBA.

* * *

Like a lot of guys, I wasn't really sure what my plan was going to be in retirement. Money wasn't going to be a problem. I had two years left on my contract and then was scheduled to make $200,000 for a few years from deferred payments. I briefly did some coaching after the Boston Celtics recommended me for a job in the old United States Basketball League with the Long Island Surf. Former NBA star Kiki VanDeWeghe's sister, Tauna, was the general manager, and we'd have all different types of fans come to the game, including former New York Knicks coach Jeff Van Gundy.

My biggest concern was that I'd get a player like me, who was great when he wanted to be but not at other times. The USBL was full of guys who thought they were NBA-bound. I was like, *If you were as good as you think you are, you'd already be in the NBA.* We had this one player whose name I forgot. He was pretty decent but wouldn't stop running his mouth, telling me what to do. So I told him to shut the fuck up one day. That night we lost by a single point, and I came into the locker room and told the guys, "I'll take this one."

I'd made some mistakes, and the team needed to see me be take some accountability. As I was addressing the guys, this guy was busy getting undressed. I asked him to wait a minute, and he told me to fuck off and how I disrespected him. We both knew where this was heading.

I cleared everyone out of the room. They thought I was going to fight him, which wasn't the plan. I just wanted to talk to him one on one and see if we could move past it. Since he already had a chair in his hands,

I guess the answer was no. I got on him so fast, just punching nonstop, that the other coaches had to break it up.

I was talked out of quitting and got ready for practice the next day. I apologized to the team and explained that stuff like this happens to a family. I said I wasn't going to quit, we were going to get better, all that stuff. So after practice he came up to me and said, "Hey, Coach, I'd feel much better if you and I just went out there in the grass and just fought."

I wasn't sure what he was expecting my response would be, but I looked him dead in the eyes, and told him, "You know what? I feel the same way you do." His eyes got big really quickly. "But let me explain something to you," I began. "I'm going back to the Celtics as a broadcaster. Whatever happens, I win. If you beat my ass, which is probably not going to happen, they're not going to have you in the NBA because you beat a coach's ass. If I beat your ass, your boys are going to clown you like hell again. So why don't you pick what we should do. If you want to go out there and fight, I'm game. But if you're smart—like I think you are—you'll just let this shit go."

The postscript is that we had a game two days later in Massachusetts. My broadcast partner at the time, Spencer Ross, came to the game. That former player of mine got in the game and scored. As soon as he did, he turned to me and said, "I knew you shouldn't have taken me out!" After the game Ross told me that guy was crazy. We ended up going 14–13 that season but got hot in the playoffs. Eventually, we lost to Portland in the quarterfinals by one point at the buzzer. That was it for my coaching career.

* * *

Without going to practice or preparing for the next game, I was kind of lost after retiring. I dabbled in a bunch of things, including promoting some theater shows and concerts in Charlotte. I quickly decided that wasn't for me because to be really successful at it you had to be cantankerous, and that wasn't me.

I did some analyst work on TV and was terrible, but I began to have the broadcasting bug. I knew I had things to say. So I started working with Mark Packer on his radio show. We spoke with NFL Hall of Famer Reggie White about why so many players try to hold on until the very last drop of their careers. I played 11 seasons in the NBA. Other than my knees, I still felt pretty good. "Corns, there's a reason why: because if you want to go play basketball right now, you can do that," he said in his deep, well-recognizable voice. "Once you retire from tackle football, you can never go back and say, 'Hey, let's go back and play some tackle football.'" Such wise words he offered. I was devastated when he passed away a couple years later.

When Renee was flying out of town, I had my daughters Morgan and Madison at my place. Renee and I were separated. So it was just us three of us. The kids used to always laugh when they came over. They'd look at each other and say, "Dad's cooking…I guess that means we're having Shake 'n Bake."

I saw Morgan taking the braids out of her hair. Her mom was supposed to be back that night, so she could fix her hair. But I had warned her that Mom might not be back. Morgan, though, didn't listen. When we got word that she was still out of town, there was no other choice than for me to become a beautician. I put her hair in a ponytail and was going to just put in a barrette and send her to school. That's when Morgan checked herself out in the mirror—and started bawling. Being Mr. Mom wasn't so easy.

At this time I had no relationship with the Boston Celtics. There was still a lot of animosity about how I was treated. Trades are going to happen, but they went out of their way to trash me on my way out, saying how I wasn't in shape, how I didn't work hard. Outwardly, I tried not to let it affect me because I've never been a moper. When Larry Bird was injured, he'd just shut down. Me? I could be in a cardboard box and I'd be happy to be alive. But sometimes teams hit you on the way out instead of just admitting what their real reasoning is. Like when they traded Gerald Henderson, they said he wasn't in shape. I can tell you there was never a day that Sarge wasn't one of the best conditioned athletes in the NBA.

The Celtics questioned if I was really hurt, questioned my heart. Yet they never said anything about me for eight years. They didn't say anything when I took on a lesser role. And they sure as hell didn't say anything when I said, "You bitches hop on my back, and I'm going to win this championship." It wasn't like I walked around every day bitter, but the Celtics part of my life was just over. Or so I thought.

Bird retired following his participation on the 1992 Dream Team. He was still a great player, but he just couldn't stay on the court. So the Celtics decided that on February 4, 1993, they'd retire his number. It was going to be different than a lot of retirement ceremonies that are squeezed into halftime or postgame. This would be an entire night at Boston Garden. General manager Jan Volk, the guy who'd written me a letter telling me I was being traded, asked me to come back for the ceremony. After all, I played eight years with Bird, and they wanted to have as many of his old teammates there as possible for his special night.

Whether to come was a tough decision. I'd almost promised myself that I'd never see Boston again. The woman I was dating, Maurice Stark, convinced me that maybe it was time to go back. Finally, I decided to return. To be honest, I was kind of dreading it, but I wanted to honor Bird. He was a great teammate, and even though we weren't best of friends, we did win two championships together. He deserved to have this night.

Coming back for that night changed my life. It was like all the hard feelings went away, at least temporarily. Even with the titles, the Finals MVP, this might have been the best moment of my career. The expression of love was unreal. Bob Costas was the emcee. And when he introduced me, he asked, "How's it feel to be back in the Garden for the first time?"

The crowd went nuts and gave me a standing ovation. So did my ex-teammates, guys like Bird, Kevin McHale, and Nate Archibald. It was just a surreal moment. The team asked me to present Bird with a gift, representing all of us. I said yes, even though I didn't know what it was.

I talked about how I was the first guy Bird challenged in the NBA and how he'd drop three-pointers on me in practice, leaving me thinking, *this White guy can really play.* Then, as always, I spoke more truth. I didn't know what the gift actually was. "Larry, it's my honor to present you with this…um…what the hell is this thing?" I said. "A commemorative coin, looks like a gold-plated coin that's very expensive."

The crowd loved it. When I left Boston Garden that night, I don't even know if my feet hit the ground, I was floating from the emotion. Adding to this momentous occasion, I was walking to the back after the festivities, and Volk said, "We'd like to offer you a broadcasting job." I was blown away. There *was* one condition, however; I had to apologize to Red Auerbach. Apologize for what? For helping to win two championships? For putting my body on the line for eight seasons? Volk explained, "The father never apologizes to the son."

We made the arrangements, and I said I'd prefer to come to Auerbach's home in Washington, D.C. His wife answered the door, and there was Auerbach. I don't know that I've ever been more nervous for a meeting. He took me to his back room and said, "When you're young, you don't do smart things…I forgive you."

Again, I didn't have anything to apologize for, but the voice in the back of my head told me to shut up. I graciously thanked him. One thing I've always been able to do is look at the situation and know how to play it. On this day, I needed to just shut up. "Time heals a lot of wounds," Jeff Twiss said. "Max understood a little bit better, and I think Red understood it from input from a lot of other people…And I think they came to some reconciliation that they had a good resolution to what they stood for."

The fact that I was coming back to town was certainly a shocker for everyone, not the least of whom was me. Given the way my exit was handled, the last thing you'd expect was to hear me doing Celtics games on the radio. After the 1984 season—at the height of my powers—I told the media they'd never hear from me after I was done playing. "That was one of his funnier lines," *The Boston Globe*'s Dan Shaughnessy said. "I thought that's it."

CHAPTER 17
THE M.L. CARR AND ANTOINE WALKER ERA

While the 1980s signaled the rebirth of the Boston Celtics, the 1990s were…a step back. Larry Bird retired in 1992 after his career had been cut short by chronic back problems. Then real tragedy hit. The guy who was supposed to take over, Reggie Lewis, died after collapsing from a heart issue. The first sign of trouble for the team's captain came against the Charlotte Hornets in the very first post-Bird playoff game. Lewis came out hot, scoring 17 points in the first 13 minutes and then collapsed due to a cardiac abnormality. He missed the rest of the series, and a medical battle ensued about whether he was fit to play. A medical battle ensued about whether he was fit to play. Right after he was cleared, Lewis died during a workout in July.

That playoff series against the Hornets also marked the end for Kevin McHale. I actually went to his last game in Charlotte and came into the locker room afterward. McHale acknowledged me, saying, "Max, this is my dude right here." We've had such a great relationship, especially for someone who, as people like to say, took my job. There were a lot of things I ended up teaching him, and he was always appreciative.

That left Robert Parish as the last man standing. He played one more year in Boston and averaged 11.7 points and seven rebounds a game at 39 years old. Incredibly, he went two more years in Charlotte and capped it off with another ring with the Chicago Bulls. He ended up playing more games than anyone in the history of the NBA. Not bad for a guy who was out of shape when he joined us.

In the 1994–95 season, there was a new man in charge of the Celtics— none other than my former teammate, M.L. Carr. It was a pretty quick rise for Carr, who was working in community affairs. I wasn't shocked, though, because Red Auerbach loved him, and Carr loved Auerbach. Carr always had Auerbach's ear and also took over as head coach. Carr gets a lot of crap because the team lost so much. (He went 48–116 in his two years on the bench.) But he knew what his job was: to get the team in the best position for the future. The organization was tanking, and the Celtics had a loyal soldier to fall on the sword.

Even though it was obvious what they were doing, it was still tough to watch those Celtics teams struggle. Carr was my buddy, and Dennis Johnson—one of my closest friends—was his assistant. There were guys coming on and off the roster that you've never heard of. Hell, a lot of those guys, I had never heard of! But I think the coaching staff all knew the marching orders and handled it well—except for one night against the New York Knicks.

Celtics guard (and Boston College product) Dana Barros had the NBA record for most consecutive games with a three-pointer at 89. (To show how much the game has changed, Steph Curry now holds the record with 157 straight games!) Anyway, we were on our way to another loss, and Carr was doing everything he could to get Barros a three-pointer. Don Nelson coached the Knicks for half of that year and he was determined to snap the streak. Nellie was double-teaming Barros even when he didn't have the ball. There were a few occasions when that double-team led to an open layup, but Nelson didn't care. In the last minute of the game, Barros threw up five three-pointers and missed them all. The streak was over. That was really the only time I thought Carr lost perspective.

Even with all of the losses, he was still a smart guy. One time he actually listened to me.

Our broadcast position was right next to the Celtics bench, and Carr decided to put Marty Conlon into the game to try and guard Denver Nuggets forward Antonio McDyess. (Remember it's not like there were a lot of better choices.) So I pointed out that, "This might not look good with the high-flying Antonio McDyess against the slow-running Marty Conlon." Carr overheard me, and quickly took Conlon out of the game.

There were certainly some interesting players on the roster during those lean years. One of my favorite guys was "Never Nervous" Pervis Ellison, who had led Louisville to the national championship as a freshman. He eventually became the top pick in the draft by the Sacramento Kings. He was a great talent who just couldn't stay healthy. As he got older, he had a reputation for being soft since he was always hurt, and I think that was unfair. This dude just had that injury albatross around his neck. One time he broke his toe and told the team it occurred while he was helping a teammate move. What really happened was that he was playing cards and slammed something down. When he did that, a vase fell down and broke his toe.

He didn't have much better luck in love either. I remember spending an hour outside my apartment building, talking with him about the breakup with his wife. He had been chatting with her, and a call clicked in on her end. She switched over—or so she thought—and said, "I'm busy talking to this asshole." That obviously didn't sit well with Ellison. But the worst story for them was when Ellison was coming back from Foxwoods Casino in Connecticut, and for some reason, he looks on the other side of the road, and there's his Range Rover driving in the opposite direction. His wife was behind the wheel, and the guy she was having an affair with was in the front seat. Ellison was ready to go all Rambo and chase them down, but fortunately he didn't.

Ricky Davis was part of those teams as well. In fact, I still have a bobblehead of him. Davis was a guy who was just destined not to have money because he spent it nonstop. We used to play a card game called Boo-Ray, and you could win some serious cash. I had a hot streak, and Paul Pierce actually owed (and paid) me $25,000. So I beat Davis, and he owed me $4,000. That sounds like a lot of money, but considering he was making a couple of million, it was no big deal...or so I thought. Davis came in one day and gave me a check for the $4,000 but told me to hold off on cashing it. I eventually went to the bank and asked one of the tellers if he had enough money to cover it. She laughed and said, "He has like $200!" What a funny dude.

Vin Baker was a hell of a good player, a four-time All-Star early in his career. But by the time he came home to Boston, the former

University of Hartford star was on his last legs. He had some serious alcohol issues and hadn't won the battle yet. There were times his breath would smell like Scope because he was trying to mask the booze. I'd always call him "Mr. Baker," and he'd call me "Mr. Maxwell." We still do the same thing even now. In his contract the Celtics acquired from the Seattle SuperSonics, he was guaranteed a suite on the road. So there were times where Baker, who wasn't even playing 20 minutes a night, had a better room than the coaches! I'd have loved for us to have had Baker in his prime. He could post you up and had some nice moves inside. He was a really good dude, who had some tough times. I'm so proud to see him working as an assistant coach with the Milwaukee Bucks now.

David Wesley is the type of success story you don't see too much of in the NBA. He was a six-foot combo guard who went undrafted out of Baylor, and his goal was just to make the league. When he retired 14 years later, he'd scored more than 11,000 points and was beloved everywhere he played. He's such a mindful, thoughtful guy. When he played for Charlotte, he told me the story of his teammate and close friend, Bobby Phills. One day after practice, they were racing their Porsches, and he saw Phills' car spin out and crash. Wesley rushed to the wreckage and literally saw the life drain out of his buddy. Phills had broken his neck and was dead at the age of 30. As devastating as that was to witness, Wesley played another seven years in the league. He was always hard-charging on the court and just a really cool guy.

Most us didn't know it, but there was a future Hall of Famer on these losing Celtics teams. Dino Radja only played four years in the NBA but was inducted due to his play overseas. Radja was from Croatia. Like a lot of European players, he smoked like a chimney and definitely enjoyed his beer. But he could rebound, run the floor, and had that typical overseas game. Nowadays, everyone in the league does the Eurostep, which is basically a traveling crossover that doesn't get called. Radja was the first player I actually saw do it.

The most heralded and talented player of the Carr era was Antoine Walker. He came to Boston after winning the national championship at Kentucky and he strut into town like he was in the Kentucky Derby, and his name was Secretariat. Walker was a great guy, one of the nicest around. The problem was, he was *too* nice. He just could not say no. Like a lot of players, Walker had his entourage, and those guys just about milked him dry. When I was at the barbershop, Walker walked in with his boys. This was when cell phones first became popular, and these four guys walked in and were all on the phone *talking to each other.*

I sat behind him one night at Foxwoods Casino in this private room reserved for big rollers and watched Walker play blackjack for $5,000 a hand, and he's playing three hands at once. He gets dealt 6–5, 7–4, and 8–3. The dealer has 4 showing, so Walker doubled down. He ended up getting three face cards, and the dealer busted out. My guy ended up winning something like $65,000 in a matter of minutes. They actually had to go get more chips. But if he did lose at cards when he was playing against me, he wasn't like Davis. Walker would show up with a saddlebag full of cash to pay off his debts.

It was certainly no surprise after his career when he had well-documented financial issues. That stems from his inability to say no. When we were on the road, he'd make sure his boys flew separate from the team and had nice rooms. They'd order everything and charge it to the room, including expensive watches, room service, etc. On another night at the casino, Walker rolled in with Michael Jordan. Next thing you know, they're down more than $50,000. Jordan said not to worry and that the cards would change. And you know what? They did. Jordan and Walker walked out up $150,000.

I'm sad that he had so many money problems, but I don't feel sorry for him, and here's why. He lived a lifestyle that 99 percent of all people will never experience. He tried to do the right thing like when he bought up a bunch of buildings in the projects of his hometown of Chicago, but

Antoine Walker dunks in January of 2003, a year he averaged 20.1 points, 7.2 rebounds, and made the All-Star team.

something bad always happened. Once he was on Michigan Avenue in his Bentley, and someone stole his jewelry. Walker was a flashy dude, that's for sure.

On the court, what a player he was. Walker was 6'8" and could do it all. He'd rebound, bring the ball up, make great passes, and had some terrific inside moves. Believe it or not, Walker reminded me more of Magic Johnson than anyone else. He'd put the ball in his left hand and just gallop down the court. He was amazing. Boston fans fell in love with him, and that Adidas commercial for "Employee No. 8" just made him a local legend. As I like to say, he fell in love with the three-point shot before it loved him back. In today's game with everyone shooting from downtown nonstop, he'd have fit right in. But when he did it, the crowd would groan.

Even when Paul Pierce came to town, Walker was cool about it, but it did overshadow him and probably affected him a little more than he'd want to admit. I love that late in his career Walker got a ring as a key reserve on the Miami Heat's first championship team. Seeing him with some lousy teams in Boston and then hooking up with Pat Riley and his system with Miami, that was awesome. On the other hand, watching him do his Antoine Wiggle while hanging on in Puerto Rico was just sad. Early in his career, he stayed in shape, but now he's gotten so big, and it's hard to see him like that.

Max at the Mic

You may have thought I'd be a natural working in the media, but let me tell you: it wasn't easy. When I first started with Raycom Sports, I was bad but worked to get better. I figured talk radio would be easy. I mean, I can talk in my sleep. But one of the biggest challenges in radio is that you need to be articulate, insightful, and smart...all in about four seconds. It's hard to do. Once you get it, though, it almost becomes second nature. I've got a ton of stories, but on radio you just don't get the time, especially when you remember where I came from and had a slower, southern dialect. For me to be successful, it was time to go back to school.

I worked with a professor at Brandeis University who was a speech therapist. He told me I could be really good and had some great insights. The problem was, however, that if only 5 percent of people understood what I said, it wouldn't matter. I had to learn how to both elongate my words and be concise at the same time. That allowed me to come up with some catchphrases. Like when someone makes a great play, I'm going to go "quack, quack, quack." I might say something like "sandwiches" or "big girls in the paint."

CHAPTER 18
THE RICK PITINO ERROR

Even as the losses piled up, M.L. Carr always had his eyes on the prize. And that prize was attending Wake Forest University. His name was Tim Duncan. Carr doesn't get the credit, but he did his job. The Celtics had two lottery picks and were under the salary cap. Plus, they had some good players in David Wesley and Rick Fox. With the second worst record in the league and two picks in the lottery, they had the best odds to get Duncan. It seemed like a sure thing. Unfortunately, the San Antonio Spurs, who won five more games than us, landed the No. 1 overall pick and thus Duncan.

One guy who definitely thought that Duncan would be headed to Boston was Rick Pitino, the supposed savior of the franchise. When Pitino came to town, it was like a damned coronation. He certainly had the credentials, having taken Providence College to the Final Four and then having a successful run with the New York Knicks. He'd turned down many offers to return to the NBA, but the prestige of coaching the Celtics—and a 10-year, $70 million contract—was too irresistible to reject. Now he was going to save the Celtics. It meant Antoine Walker would be coached by his college coach. "Because I was one of the guys left off the team that won 15 games, I was super excited," Walker said. "He was going to get it right, make us better. So the excitement was there. I was ecstatic to play for my college coach again, who I had so much success for and won a championship with. I do remember that excitement."

Pitino was hired on May 6, 1997, and one of his first acts really set the stage for what was about to come. He demoted Red Auerbach from team president to some type of consultant. Whatever differences I may have had with Auerbach, there's no denying that he *was* the Boston Celtics. It was a move that alienated many. "Red was having some health issues, and I went down to see him in D.C.," Carr said. "And his daughter said how upset her mother was, going to her grave, seeing that Pitino had stripped Red's title of president."

Carr assured her that he'd take care of things. He came back to Boston and set up an interview with Lenny Megliola, who was a longtime columnist for *The MetroWest Daily News.* The only condition was that he had to quote Carr verbatim. "I told him that as long as Red Auerbach was alive, there would only be one president of the Boston Celtics. That making him vice chairman was like giving him a dishonorable discharge," Carr said. "And I said that it's a disgrace that we would treat the guy who built this organization that none of us would be in if it weren't for him."

A couple of days later, he got a phone call from team owner Paul Gaston. "He said he'd read the article and was a little bothered. He said that I couldn't say those things publicly. He then told me that this was my last day as a Celtic," Carr said. "I said, 'You're wrong about that. I'm going to be a Celtic for life. You're going to be a Celtic as long as you own the team. If you ever sell the team, you won't be a Celtic. My story has already been written in Celtics folklore, so I'm going to be a Celtic for life.'"

Pitino seemed to make smart moves early on. After missing out on Duncan, he drafted Colorado guard Chauncey Billups and Kentucky swingman Ron Mercer. But then he put his foot on the gas and made two of the worst signings you'll ever see. In July he inked a seven-year, $22 million deal with Los Angeles Lakers backup center Travis Knight. I'm not saying this was ridiculous, but Knight was drafted in the first round the year before by the Chicago Bulls...and released less than a month later! Nobody in the league could believe the deal, but Pitino defended it, saying that Knight had averaged more offensive rebounds per 36 minutes than just about everyone in the NBA. First, he was playing 16 minutes a game, not 36. Second, he was getting garbage time boards because the other team spent all its energy on L.A.'s starting center, some guy named Shaquille O'Neal.

The next month Pitino signed forward Chris Mills away from the Cleveland Cavaliers with a seven-year, $33.6 million deal. Mills was a pretty good player, but that price seemed to be steep. Do you not remember Mills playing for the Celtics? There's a reason for that. It became apparent during training camp that Mills wasn't going to be cool with Pitino barking at him all the time. So Pitino traded him to New York—before the first game. To give you even more of an idea of Pitino's patience level, Knight was back in L.A. after just one season. Making matters worse: to make salary cap room for Knight and Mills, the Celtics had to renounce their rights to two of their best players, Fox and Wesley.

Pitino's impatience when it came to correcting mistakes he made in free agency was nothing compared to how he dealt with rookies. Billups came to Boston as the third overall pick. He was raw, having only played two seasons at Colorado. There was no doubt that he had talent, but his game was just so green. He could hit floaters, but he was lacking on defense. Being a point guard in the NBA is tough enough. Doing it in a frazzled, frantic system was darn near impossible for a 21-year-old kid. Whatever confidence Billups came in with, Pitino just beat it right out of him. Fifty-one games into the season, Pitino traded Billups to the Toronto Raptors. In fairness to the trade, Billups did bounce around a bit before settling down in Detroit and leading the Pistons to the title. But between a lot of early injuries and Pitino crushing his psyche, the fact that it took him a bit to develop is understandable. Now "Mr. Big Shot" is, at least in my mind, a future Hall of Famer.

Mercer was a really talented kid as well. He'd won a championship at Kentucky with Walker and Pitino, so Pitino knew what he was getting: a really good athlete with a very solid midrange game. Like Billups, he was really quiet. Mercer was averaging 17 points a game in his second year when Pitino traded him to the Denver Nuggets. When Michael Jordan and Scottie Pippen left the Bulls, Chicago had all kinds of salary cap space. They ended up signing Mercer but just about no one else. He was out of the game at age 28.

As it would turn out, Pitino's manner of communicating wasn't going to work in the NBA. "It was one of those things that was hard to explain because he was a guy that's a screamer and yeller, but he also gets the maximum effort and gets the maximum ability out of you to make you the best player that you possibly can be," Walker said. "That's the hard part about it and that's what makes him so special. He was before his time. I think that style of coaching worked at the collegiate level. It wasn't going to work at the NBA level because those guys got paid so much money."

Too bad. Pitino could have had a really nice nucleus with Billups, Mercer, and Walker, but he couldn't wait for it to happen. Once the Pitino Celtics made it out of training camp (minus Mills), they had quite the test to start the season—a home game against the two-time defending champion Bulls. It was a crazy game. Chicago led by 20 after the first quarter, but Boston was up 10 after the third. Walker had 31 points, and both rookies scored in double figures (15 points for Billups and 11 for Mercer), and we shocked the champs 92–85. After all the pomp and circumstance of Pitino coming to Boston and now a stunning win against Michael Jordan, everyone was walking on clouds. Little did any of us know that this would be the high point of Pitino's Boston career.

As Celtics fans all over New England were plotting the championship parade, reality came crashing down on them, as the Celts lost their next five games. Pitino's full-court pressing was great in college. When he was with the Knicks, it worked to a degree because he had Patrick Ewing stationed at the end of the press. Having Knight there wasn't quite the same.

Early in his tenure, we were in Milwaukee, and Pitino took all the writers and broadcasters out for dinner. I didn't really want to go, but my broadcast partner at the time, Howard David, convinced me to go. We figured maybe we'd pick up some of Pitino's thoughts so we could apply them during the broadcast. We showed up at the restaurant, which I will forever refer to as "Chez White" because I was the only brother in the whole place. You could tell they hadn't seen a lot of Black folks because they acted like I was from *Roots*. And instead of learning basketball theories from a great coach, it was all about Pitino—where he got his clothes made, how successful he was, etc. We realized then that this could be a long season. No, there wasn't a championship for Pitino and his group, but they did improve by 21 games. You could feel like they were making progress. Then they got an absolute gift as Paul Pierce landed in their lap.

Probably the best-known moment of Pitino's time coaching the Celtics happened in March of 2000. Vince Carter had won the game at the buzzer, and Pitino wasn't pleased. "Larry Bird is not walking through that door, fans," Pitino began saying, as he was getting more upset by the second. "Kevin McHale is not walking through that door, and Robert Parish is not walking through that door. And if you expect them to walk through that door, they're going to be gray and old...There are young guys in that room playing their asses off. I wish we had $90 million under the salary cap. I wish we could buy the world. We can't; the only thing we can do is work hard, and all the negativity in this town sucks."

Well, he was right about Bird, McHale, and Parish not coming through the door, but regarding salary cap space, maybe he shouldn't have signed Knight and Mills? Pitino's message was a good one: he was trying to stand up and protect his players. But the way he went about it was not so good. It probably wasn't a smart idea to step on the toes of the guys.

Pitino's first year in Boston was his high-water mark, and he finished with 36 wins. There was a lockout the next season, and the Celtics went 19–31. They won 35 his third season, but with all the constant personnel moves, players were looking over their shoulders and stopped believing in their coach.

As much as some of his players hated their coach, I only had one run-in with Pitino, but it was memorable. The team was mired in some losing streak, and right after the final horn, my job was to go to the locker room and get sound for the postgame show. On this night it was pretty quiet in there, so I started my question. "Antoine and Paul got their numbers," I began, and then Pitino just blew up. "Numbers are for fucking losers!"

That went over the air live. He apologized after, and I explained that he hadn't let me get the full question in.

One of the best lines during the down times came from forward Danny Fortson. The team traded him to Toronto, and on his way out, he said, "The ship be sinking." As funny as that was, the even more hilarious part was that the trade was rescinded, and Fortson had to come back and face his coaches and teammates.

Forton was right though. The team was flailing. Stuart Layne, a vice president of marketing and sales, came up to David and I one night in Miami. He told us it was our fault that things were falling apart because we hadn't pumped up Pitino and the team enough. After that loss to the Miami Heat, Pitino resigned as head coach and president of the Celtics. His hiring was a great idea at the time because there's no question that he's a great coaching mind. It's just that he's better suited for college, where it's about your system, and you can impose your will. There haven't been a lot of college coaches who've succeeded in the pros in recent years. Brad Stevens sure was one, though, who did succeed. Pitino was even a damn good NBA coach, but his arrogance and impatience did him in during his time in Boston.

On the night Pitino quit, Auerbach tried to praise him, which was generous since Pitino stripped him of his presidency. "I like him, I really do," Auerbach told Dan Shaughnessy of *The Boston Globe*. "He worked hard. But you never know with these players. Those things happen. Sometimes you outlast 'em and can do something; sometimes you can't." Then Auerbach added a classic zinger, "How much can you take losing? If I lost as much as he did, I might be jumping off a building."

CHAPTER 19
THE TRUTH: PAUL PIERCE

Paul Pierce thought he might go No. 2 in the 1998 NBA Draft. There were some really good players that went early: Antawn Jamison, Vince Carter, Dirk Nowitzki. But the top pick—of course made by the Los Angeles Clippers—was Michael Olowokandi. For whatever reason Pierce slipped and slipped and slipped all the way down to the Boston Celtics at No. 10. Did I see the guy who was going to become an all-time Celtic? No, but you could tell he was special. I remember sitting in the practice facility, and as we're talking, he's just drilling three-pointer after three-pointer. He made like 20 in a row. He told me, "I can do this all day long."

He was not some fantastic athlete, but he was so fundamentally sound and had great footwork. He wasn't as good as Kobe Bryant, but when it came to the midgame, they were carbon copies. Pierce had just enough quickness that he could beat you to the elbow and make that jumper. Pierce is my favorite player I've covered. Hell, he's all of my kids' favorites. He might have grown up in Inglewood, California, but he was a country boy through and through. When he came to Boston he was a horrible card player, but he became better.

Just before his third season, Pierce was stabbed repeatedly at a nightclub. Keep in mind that the organization had lost star draft pick Len Bias to a cocaine overdose in 1986 and Reggie Lewis to a heart issue seven years later. Everyone was terrified. I went to see him at the hospital but didn't get to speak with him. Not only did he survive, but he also played in all 82 games that season.

Early in his career, after a dominating performance against the Los Angeles Lakers, Shaquille O'Neal said, "That guy is the M-Fing truth." That's how the Truth nickname was born. When the Truth came to Boston, Antoine Walker instantly became like last year's Christmas present. But they always got along and played well together.

* * *

Paul Pierce, who reacts after hitting a three-pointer against the Charlotte Bobcats in 2006, was a favorite player of mine and my kids.

Once Rick Pitino left town, his longtime assistant Jimmy O'Brien took over. He inherited the same team and took them to unexpected heights. As talkative and charismatic as Pitino could be, that's how reserved O'Brien was. As the team started to blossom, there was quite a bit of hype about O'Brien being the NBA Coach of the Year. I was on a talk show and actually supported my old teammate Rick Carlisle, who was doing a great job with the Detroit Pistons. Although he didn't like the spotlight, O'Brien wanted to know what was going on.

Before one game I was out there talking with some folks, and Celtics assistant Lester Conner came out and said Coach O'Brien wanted to see me. I walked into O'Brien's office, and he said, "I just want to see what side you're on."

I explained that both he and Carlisle did a great job, but I felt like Carlisle's team had less talent than the Celtics. O'Brien looked at me and said, "Yeah, I agree with that."

And that was the end of the conversation. I think he was challenging my loyalty toward the team and just wanted an explanation behind what I said. It was weird. There was another interesting conversation I had with the coach. The Celtics had won one of those low-scoring games, and he and I were the first two people on our team charter. I said, "Boy, Coach, that was ugly."

He looked at me and said, "That's where you and I disagree."

I looked at him like, *it's just you and me up here. What could we disagree on?* It was like I had challenged him. But I held my tongue and just said okay and walked away.

The Celtics went 49–33 in O'Brien's first full season, a 13-game improvement. The team's first-round draft pick was Joe Johnson, a big guard out of Arkansas. But much like Pitino did with Chauncey Billups, general manager Chris Wallace traded "Iso Joe" after just 48 games in green, dealing him to the Phoenix Suns in exchange for Rodney Rogers and Tony Delk, two veterans brought in to help during the postseason. It's too bad because Johnson ended up having a hell of a career, playing 17 years, and making seven All-Star Games. He had this herky-jerky way of shooting, and it made him tough to cover. Playing against his old team years later, he laid this crossover on Paul Pierce that left the Celtics captain on his knees. But at the time, the team was trying to become relevant again, and it's like they sold their soul to the devil—giving up a piece of the future for immediate need. It was kind of like when they traded me for one great year of Bill Walton, which resulted in championship No. 16. But sometimes those things happen when you're trying to win in the short term. I always joke with Johnson that it's great that they retired our number, as he wore No. 31 just like me.

Don't get me wrong: Rogers was a good player, and Delk had some moments as well. Add them to Pierce, Antoine Walker, Tony Battie, Eric Williams, and Kenny Anderson and you had some guys who you could compete with. Rogers played a big role in the series win against the Philadelphia 76ers, as O'Brien played him at center. Because he could shoot the ball, Rogers hung out at the three-point line, and Dikembe Mutombo just wouldn't come out that far to guard him.

After a quick series against the Detroit Pistons, the Celtics ran into the New Jersey Nets in the Eastern Conference Finals. Jason Kidd had breathed life into a terrible franchise, and this may have been the best Nets team since the ABA days of Dr. J. They dispatched the Celtics in six games, but the one everybody remembers was Game 3. For the first three quarters, it wasn't even competitive. New Jersey led by 15 points after the first, 20 at halftime, and built the lead up to 26 points in the third. That's when Walker showed some leadership skills that people didn't realize he had. Our radio broadcast position at that time was right next to the Celtics bench, and we heard everything going on during a timeout. "We ain't losing to these motherfuckers!" Walker yelled at his teammates. As much as this was Pierce's team, Walker had always been the mental leader. "They ain't that good! They're assholes!"

And this was all on Walker, as the coaches were off to the side trying to figure out what to do. Whatever Walker was selling, Pierce was buying. The Truth outscored the Nets—by himself—in the fourth quarter 19–16, and the Celtics pulled off a comeback for the ages. The Garden fans were incredible; I don't think I've ever heard them that loud. As a broadcaster this game was probably the most fun for me other than when they destroyed the Los Angeles Lakers to win the title in 2008.

* * *

Boston Celtics owners Wyc Grousbeck and Steve Paluca approached me before a game in 2003 and told me they'd like to retire my uniform number. They'd gotten approval from Red Auerbach, and any negative feelings were washed away.

Shortly before the December ceremony, I was at the Boys & Girls Club. They presented me, and I talked about how big an honor it's going to be to get my number raised to the rafters. Then without telling anyone, I decided to auction off the opportunity to help me raise my banner. Apparently, someone had some money to burn because the bidding started at $1,000 and ended up at something like $21,000! I was laughing for a few reasons, one of which is that at my moment of Celtics immortality I'd have some White kid standing by my side. My son had this look like, *what are you doing? I'm your flesh and blood!* But any chance to raise money for a worthwhile charity is always good.

The ceremony was at halftime of a game against the Minnesota Timberwolves, who were up by 19 when the festivities began. Kevin McHale and Robert Parish were in attendance, but Larry Bird was not. He said the reason he skipped was because he didn't want to overshadow the ceremony. Truth be told, I was disappointed since I'd gone to his, but I was okay. After the way things ended for me in Boston, I'm sure

I laugh with my former teammate Kevin McHale during my jersey retirement ceremony in December of 2003.

Auerbach didn't ever envision himself speaking at my number retirement, but there he was. He got up and said I was a pretty good player, a pretty good rebounder. He then added, "I'm not sure why we're giving him all these gifts!"

We were all in a festive mood, so when I got up, I said, "Red, let me tell you why...because it's *about damn time!*

Seeing all the people who love me was a cool experience. As I left the court, the first person to come over and greet me was Kevin Garnett. KG giving me props is something I'll always remember. That meant so much. The whole night—after everything I'd gone through—meant so much. "He got his number raised, which is always the way it should be," said Bob Ryan of *The Boston Globe.* "Not rehashing the stormy and messy exit."

Here's what some of my former teammates said:

M.L. Carr: "It's about time because he absolutely was one of the best—not just in 1981 or '84. All throughout his time in Boston, he was just a great player."

Don Chaney: "I was so happy for him because I thought he deserved it...You're talking about the Celtics. There's some great players over the year, and Cedric was just a great player who didn't get to eat like the Birds or other players on those particular teams. I was just happy to see that somebody appreciated his contribution to the game."

Danny Ainge: "That was awesome to me because he deserved it. Sure, he could have managed things differently and maybe Red could manage things differently, and Max would have played a few more years with the Celtics. But in hindsight I'm glad they were able to make up and I'm glad Max got the recognition he deserves."

CHAPTER 20
THE DOC IS IN

Ahead of the 2004–05 season, the Boston Celtics hired Doc Rivers as head coach. While I didn't know Rivers well, he always liked to remind me that his school, Marquette, knocked me out of the NCAA Tournament in the Final Four (though he was not a student there yet). Rivers is one of the most charismatic people that I've met. He was the modern-day P.T. Barnum. This guy could sell anything to anybody. And he made everyone feel like they were the most important person in the room. It didn't matter if you were the guy who swept the floor or the general manager of the team. Rivers treated everyone the same, which is a great gift, especially as a head coach.

During his 14-year career, he was a good, sometimes great player. He was a different style but comparable to Danny Ainge. After he retired he was immensely popular as a San Antonio Spurs broadcaster and then with ABC. He got the coaching bug and landed his first job with the Orlando Magic, replacing the retired Chuck Daly. That Magic team was a bunch of anonymous players, but Rivers pushed them to a shocking 41–41 record and won NBA Coach of the Year honors. Orlando seemed like such a franchise on the rise that it was able to lure free agents Tracy McGrady and Grant Hill. T-Mac was as advertised, but in that first year, Hill only played four games because of ankle problems, followed by 14 games, 29, and then zero. Remarkably, Rivers still led the Magic to the playoffs all three seasons. When he started the next year 1–10, he was fired.

What always impressed me about Rivers was the way he wrung every ounce of effort out of his teams. I was thrilled to have him come to town because his players would run through a brick wall for him, which is the best attribute any coach can have. The best example was an unknown point guard from Fayetteville State University named Darrell Armstrong. FSU is a small Black school that had never had a player in the NBA (and hasn't since, by the way). Armstrong wasn't the best shooter or defender, but he used his quickness for whatever Rivers and the team needed. He went from being undrafted to winning the NBA's Most Improved Player and Sixth Man of the Year awards.

It was a similar story for Bo Outlaw. He was another undrafted guy, who spent some time with the Los Angeles Clippers before coming to Orlando. To say he was limited offensively would be understating the word *limited*. I'm not sure that he could score 10 points if he was locked in the gym by himself all day. But he would run through a damn brick wall for Rivers. And if Outlaw was guarding you, you were going to earn anything you got. He'd take charges, do whatever he had to. Our team had much more talent than Orlando, so I thought hiring Rivers would be the perfect move. But it wasn't without some bumps in the road.

By the time Rivers joined the Celtics bench, Paul Pierce had been in the NBA for six seasons, and the team was in the playoffs for the past three. But Rivers would be Pierce's fourth head coach—John Carroll finished up after O'Brien resigned in January of 2004—and Pierce longed for stability. In a moment that will never be forgotten, Pierce addressed the media after a playoff loss to the Indiana Pacers with an ace bandage wrapped around his head, protesting how much he was getting beat up. Rivers would have his work cut out for him.

For a head coach to be truly successful, he needs his best players to buy in. It happened with Bill Fitch and Larry Bird just as it had in San Antonio with Gregg Popovich and Tim Duncan. Rivers was a tough, demanding coach and, though he wanted to have Pierce on his side, the Truth would have to reach Rivers' expectations—not the other way around. With our broadcast position, we literally had a front-row seat to the interaction between the two.

Late in one close game, Rivers was on him about getting back on defense. So Pierce took a shot and jogged back up court. True to his word, Rivers yanked his ass out and put him on the bench. Pierce sat and huffed and puffed because he was pissed. The game got tighter, and he wanted to check back in. Rivers came up to him and said, "You want to go back in the game? Well, you want to go back in the fucking game and play the right way? Then go." He did, and the Celtics won the game. I talked to Pierce later about what had happened, and he said he and Rivers spoke about it and that they were all good. So in that one instance, Rivers established an important precedent; he was the coach, and Pierce had to do what he said. Period.

The lesson may have been learned, but there were still bumps in the road. After a strong first season, the Celts fell to 33 wins in Year Two and then a measly 24 in 2006–07. That year featured an 18—*yes, 18*—game losing streak. There were plenty of rumblings that Rivers might not be long for Boston. You'd never know it from talking to him. Don't get me wrong: Rivers was frustrated, but you'd never know it from his positive attitude. He never changed who he was for a second. Even as a player, Rivers was always friendly, but you knew there was a mean streak in there. Still, he was exactly the same guy, win or lose. He'd compete like hell for 48 minutes, but when the game was over, he was done with it. That's the mentality you want in your head coach.

After another loss a group of fans put bags over their heads in embarrassment. One of our owners, Wyc Grousbeck, came over to talk to the group. "You know what? If you keep doing this, I'm going to give Doc a five-year contract," he said.

That told me there was no way Doc was getting canned. Ainge and Rivers had built a relationship and they were heading in the right direction. They had the right coach for the job. The next step was to get the right pieces.

* * *

As a player Doc Rivers was a scrapper, true to his Chicago roots. Those were the type of guys he wanted on the Boston Celtics. So Danny Ainge went out on a mission: to get players who were good and tough.

In the 2003 NBA Draft, Ainge acquired Kendrick Perkins, a 6'10", 270-pound high school player out of Beaumont, Texas. If you looked up country in the dictionary, you'd see a picture of Perk. He was so raw that they basically had to teach him how to run. He used to take little baby steps, and they taught him how to elongate his stride. His running was really more like plodding, and they wanted him to be more like a stallion. That never happened, but at least he was able to be a trotter.

I like to say Perk is country smart. You might not be able to pull words out of him, but he would know the concept and he'd break it down in his own country way. He was someone that was really impacted by the trade for Kevin Garnett a few years later. I remember him telling me that he thought he was getting to practice early by coming 90 minutes beforehand. When KG joined the team, Perk would find Garnett there by that time, already working and sweating. So Perk started coming two hours early. He had to pick up his game. Perk has always been a very honest guy. We got along since we were both from the country. He used to tease me about how he was going to break my field-goal percentage record (which still stands today, by the way). One year he got close, and when he missed a shot, I was hooting and hollering. We had a lot of fun with that.

We were in Denver on a gloomy day in 2011, when Ainge traded Perk to the Oklahoma City Thunder. Garnett was pissed because he felt like Perk was his soulmate. Both of them were enforcers and brothers. KG got on the bus and said how bummed out he was. Perk fell into KG's arms. Both guys bawled. That was their relationship and how vulnerable both men were.

The year after adding Perkins, Ainge selected three more tough guys: Al Jefferson, a 6'10", 290-pound center from Prentiss, Mississippi, and two tough, physical guards, Tony Allen out of Oklahoma State and Delonte West from St. Joseph's.

Here's all you need to know about Allen: Kobe Bryant always said he was one of the toughest defenders he faced. Allen likes to say that he went to the Paul Pierce Boot Camp because going into practice every day and having Pierce give him the business made him ready to guard any player out there. He'd study Pierce before practice, trying to find ways to beat him on that day. It was kind of crazy, but it's what Allen brought to the table.

West had just helped lead St. Joe's to an undefeated regular season. Despite standing only 6'4", he didn't fear anyone. What's happened to West is so sad. Obviously, nobody could predict he'd battle mental illness, but you could always tell something wasn't right with him. I heard rumors about stuff he was doing in Black areas like Roxbury and Dorchester, Massachusetts. There was one time where he was talking to a young lady and had pulled over his Mercedes. The police told him he'd have to move, but he just kept saying, "Give me a minute!" It looked he might be soliciting, so he was lucky he didn't get arrested. On the court, he was an animal. He'd run through a brick wall. He played hard, could shoot, and fought defensively. We knew there was something off, but we couldn't put a finger on it. He'd be talking about something, and the next thing you know, he'd be telling us all about cartoons.

Jefferson was cut from the same cloth. He was a man. I loved that guy. They'd just dump the ball to him in the post, and he'd go to work. He would have guys going one way and then he'd be going the other way up and down with his moves. I was like, "This guy is a beast! He's going to be here forever."

Eventually, Ainge used Jefferson to front a package to trade for Garnett. I was just heartbroken. I thought he was going to be the next Celtics great. My broadcast partner, Sean Grande, had covered KG in Minnesota and knew this was a great move by the Celtics. "I remember going on a talk show Max was co-hosting," Grande said. "I couldn't believe that Max's was the prevailing view. There was a poll in the *Boston*

Herald asking if you'd trade Al Jefferson for KG, and 80 percent of the people said no. Tommy Heinsohn said he'd quit if the trade happened... Fans thought, *He's a really good player.* They didn't understand this was franchise-altering."

Grande was right. We had no idea. And with KG as the centerpiece, it was time to welcome the new Big Three.

CHAPTER 21
THE BIG THREE REDUX AND RONDO

In the summer of 2007, Danny Ainge had put together some interesting pieces. There were good players, but the Boston Celtics were not yet a good team. There was still work to be done. Paul Pierce, of course, was in place. The All-Star was also a guy who was frustrated with losing. He had requested a trade but was willing to see what the team could pull off.

Boston was picking fifth in the draft, but adding another young player to the mix probably wouldn't move the needle. This was how our then-general manager became known as "Danny the Dealer." The Celtics took Jeff Green, a forward out of Georgetown with their selection. He wasn't *in* green for long, as Ainge traded him, Wally Szczerbiak, and Delonte West to the Seattle SuperSonics for Ray Allen, one of the best sharpshooters in the league.

Allen's obviously a great player, but even him and Pierce weren't going to be enough to really contend. I was on a radio talk show and spoke the truth about The Truth: having strong perimeter players is one thing, but we didn't really have a rim protector. Al Jefferson was more of an offensive threat, and Kendrick Perkins was still developing. Guys on the other team were just going to be running to the rim all game. I got heat for that, but I didn't know they were about to get Kevin Garnett, who is intensity personified.

When he visited the Milwaukee Bucks after high school, he worked out so hard he passed out. KG is one of the most loyal people you'll find. It was no easy task to convince him to give up on Minnesota. He'd grown up there, but even when the team made the playoffs, it was usually a quick exit. Boston wasn't his top choice. He wanted to play with Kobe Bryant on the Los Angeles Lakers. The only reason Ainge was able to make a deal was because he had more chips than the Lakers.

The biggest chip was my guy, Jefferson. Kevin McHale was the GM in Minnesota and he figured if the Timberwolves were going to lose anyway, they should lose with young players. If McHale was going to trade the best player in team history, he *had* to get something of value in return. Once Ainge and McHale agreed to the trade, Garnett still was not yet convinced. Ainge had flown down to recruit Garnett, but when he had left, Ainge still had no deal. That was when he made the deal for Allen. That's when Garnett got on board and thought with himself, Allen, and Pierce, there were the makings of something special. That's how I think it all transformed. Each player in his late prime needed to sacrifice some of the glory for the greater good.

I don't know that Pierce as the incumbent gets enough credit for accepting the other two guys. Much like I did when Larry Bird came to the team, Pierce was smart enough not to fight city hall and realize that with some help he was going to be much better. Gone were the days where Pierce would have to rebound every time or stop his man. He could funnel his guy to the middle, where Garnett was the last line of defense. And he wouldn't have to take every shot. Allen was one of the best shooters of all time and would relieve the pressure on offense.

When we got Garnett, I thought, yep, that's cool. I'd obviously seen him play before, but when a guy is on your team and you watch him day to day, it's different. And this cat was different. KG's first game as a Celtic came against the Washington Wizards, and he shimmied down the baseline, threw someone off of him, and then faded away with an impossible-to-block shot. I thought, *Okay, that's an NBA move right there. He'll be here for a while.* Even on that first night, I learned what Garnett is all about. He was out there pounding his chest like a crazy man. Not everything works here with Boston fans, but the first time they saw that, it was just electric. KG's pregame ritual became destination viewing.

His other routine was that he'd throw a rosin bag high in the sky as Sean Grande and I were preparing listeners for the game. That became an interesting conversation. I had a friend who worked in a local hospital, and he got me a gown like patients change into. So before the game, I'd have our engineer put the gown on me and get me a surgical mask so I wouldn't have rosin going all over me. Grande wasn't crazy about it because it took attention away from him and our job.

Acquiring Kevin Garnett (middle) and Ray Allen (right) in 2007 to go along with Paul Pierce ushered in a new era of greatness for the Boston Celtics.

Garnett, Allen, and Pierce would be the first to tell you the "Big Three" wouldn't have won anything without some really critical supporting guys, including Perkins and Tony Allen.

Everybody forgets about James Posey and just how good he was. He was a powerful guy who would come in, take charges, and dive into the stands. He was very quiet but understood the game at a really high level. He was also a three-point specialist.

Then you had Eddie House. This guy could and would shoot from anywhere. My line was: "Don't leave the damn House!" He was a good guy and one of the best open shooters I've seen.

Glen "Big Baby" Davis was someone who liked to have a good time. But he was also a sensitive type, who was just 20 years old when he came to Boston. There was one flight that illustrated his youth. We were on the plane, and Allen was just killing Baby, saying he didn't wear deodorant and smelled. Baby got so embarrassed and pissed that he was ready to fight. Garnett got up and told Baby to get his ass over there and Allen to go to the back of the plane. KG said, "We ain't doing this on the plane!" It's like Zeus had spoken! There were some sponsors and corporate folks on the flight, so KG came over to them and said, "I'm sorry about that, but this is what happens with family."

Grande and I looked at each other and said, "Okay, there's the leader of this team right there." Garnett sat with Baby, calming him down, and by the time we landed, everything was cool.

Despite his size—6'9", 290 pounds—Davis had surprisingly quick feet. He wasn't afraid to take a charge and had this little jump shot. I remember him talking about how great a running back he was. I was just thinking, *Damn, imagine trying to tackle him.* He must have looked like a buffalo coming. Baby was really athletic, but he was definitely on the wild side. Garnett and Pierce always shielded him like their little brother.

One of the guys who no one talks about is Leon Powe, who was a highly-ranked high school player and attended Cal. He blew out his knee in his sophomore year and wasn't really the same afterward. But he was a guy who certainly had some big moments. My favorite memory of Powe came when he and Perk were just killing each other in practice one day. Perk started yelling how he's going to kick Powe's ass. In his deep, Barry White voice, Powe turned and said, "I ain't going no place. I'll be right here." That group had some really cool moments.

* * *

Rajon Rondo was just 22 years old in the 2007–08 season, his second in the league. Being the point guard and trying to keep everyone happy was no easy task. But Rondo lived up to it. Even early in his career, Rondo was one of the most fascinating, complex people I've ever met. Guys would want to kill him, and then they'd sing his praises. I've always said he was the smartest dumb guy around. In a lot of ways, he was a genius on and off the court. He's always known how to push buttons. I could totally see him being a head coach when he's done. His brain works like that: manipulating people, like watching them play cards.

But even with that intelligence, he sometimes doesn't see the big picture. I remember one time when he and Kendrick Perkins came to me and said, "We're tired of this shit. We're starting just like those guys and we don't get the respect that Kevin, Paul, and Ray get." I talked them down and explained that it's like being in line at the movie theater. You don't get to just go to the front of the line. They'd get their opportunities.

When he wanted to play, there were times that he was on the floor with LeBron James, Dwyane Wade, Paul Pierce, Ray Allen, and Kevin Garnett, and Rondo was the best player on the floor. When the lights were the brightest, he played his best. They started calling that mode "Playoff Rondo." A triple-double was almost automatic. There were stretches where he could really do no wrong. He always had a lot of steals, and people thought he was a great defender. That wasn't the case. He was a great *anticipator*, and there were times when that paid off.

In his last year with the team, he was playing for Brad Stevens, who liked him. Rondo was working some real magic with Tyler Zeller and playing well after a torn ACL sidelined him. Zeller owes Rondo some money after the way he spoon fed the big guy. As well as he was playing, there were constant rumors that he wasn't going to be around for long. One night there was a Dallas Mavericks scout I knew, and he came up to me, saying he was checking out the Boston Celtics. He told me Dallas general manager Donnie Nelson wanted him to talk to me about Rondo because they were preparing to make a trade for Rondo and was interested in my take. "Wait a minute. I think you guy are getting confused," I told him. "I have no power here."

But they still wanted to hear my thoughts. At that point I felt like one of the Wallenda brothers, walking a tightrope. You want to get my thoughts on a trade that might not be happening? And if this trade doesn't go through because of what I said, and Ainge found out I'm the one who put the kibosh on it, wow. "Let me be as delicate as I can," I started. "There are times when Rondo can be the best player on the court. And then there are times that he can be the biggest asshole out there. There's going to be times when he's going to be just brilliant. But then there's going to be other times when he's just going to be asinine, and you're going to want to kill him."

And sure enough, it worked just like that in Dallas. It was funny. The trade went through, and I just laughed. In the days leading up to it, I was telling people what was going down, and they had him getting traded here or there. I just said, "He's going to Dallas."

He came back to Boston after they made the trade and made five three-pointers and went for 29 points in an easy win. Playoff Rondo had arrived because he was motivated to prove a point. He's probably got to be, I would say, the most competitive person out there. I mean, everybody talks about how Michael Jordan was legendary. But Rondo was just one of the most competitive, crafty, cold-blooded people that I had known.

You can say Rondo never reached his full potential, but he's made an impact just about everywhere he's been. Even in 2017 when he played for the Chicago Bulls, who were playing the Celtics. In the first two games of the playoffs, he was just carving our guys up, and Chicago won the first two games in Boston. Then he broke his wrist... and the Celtics won the next four games. He knew where everyone was supposed to be and was disruptive because he was calling all of Boston's plays.

Playoff Rondo appeared again during the 2020 playoffs in the bubble, as he came off the injured list to become the perfect complement to James and Anthony Davis, winning his second ring, and this one came with the Los Angeles Lakers. Never one to stay put, Rondo then signed with the Atlanta Hawks, but true to form, he was traded midseason to the Los Angeles Clippers. He's a person I say could have been more like me, or I could have been more like him. He could step up in those big moments, and that was what I did. We were both crafty, smart, and calculated. He was more like me than any other player I've seen.

CHAPTER 22
CELTICS–LAKERS (AGAIN)

There's no championship matchup that provides more hype and excitement than Celtics vs. Lakers. Think about the other sports, and it seems like all the great rivalries are in the same division, conference, or league: Red Sox/Yankees, Cowboys/49ers, Bruins/Canadiens. But they all meet *before* the title game. Celtics/Lakers is just different. When Boston's Big Three took on Kobe Bryant and company in the 2008 NBA Finals, it didn't take long for all of our previous matchups to get attention. The names had changed, but the interest sure didn't. My phone was ringing off the hook with two specific questions. "Do you have any tickets?" and "Can we interview you?"

I was very confident that the Boston Celtics would win banner No. 17. This was one of the most complete teams I've ever seen. Kevin Garnett was Don Corleone, and Paul Pierce and Ray Allen were brothers Michael and Sonny. We had great players coming off the bench. Bryant always said that Tony Allen was the toughest defender he'd gone against, and we had "Big Baby" Glen Davis and James Posey. Add in old pros like P.J. Brown and Sam Cassell, and we were stacked. My attitude was that Bryant alone wouldn't be able to beat KG, Pierce, and Allen. Sure, he had Pau Gasol, but at that time, KG just *owned* Gasol. He was in his jock in every one of those games.

As you can imagine with this being Garnett's first real shot at winning a championship, he was…intense. I've never heard the N-word used so often. Doc Rivers was definitely the coach, but KG was the henchman. Early in the season, we were on a flight, and Garnett began arm wrestling with Big Baby. Garnett was a couple of inches taller, but Davis had a good 50 pounds on him. They're going back and forth, and Garnett just wouldn't give up. Finally, he pinned Baby, jumped up, and said, "I'm the alpha male on this team!" Indeed he was.

I think the fact that Rivers hadn't been this far himself—as a player or a coach—helped because everyone was hungry. Rivers could say to his guys, "Hey, this is why you guys came here: to win a championship. This is your opportunity." It was that much easier to get his players to drink the Kool-Aid.

The NBA Finals series didn't exactly start as expected. About halfway through the third quarter of Game 1, Pierce went down with an apparent knee injury. He was writhing in pain and had to be taken out on a wheelchair. My thought was probably the same as everyone in the building: did our chance to win a championship just disappear?

Miraculously, just a couple of minutes later, Pierce came jogging onto the court. It was like watching Willis Reed back in 1970, hobbling out of the locker room before Game 7 vs. the Los Angeles Lakers. I remember watching that as a kid and hearing Marv Albert say, "And here comes Willis Reed!"

When Pierce came back, I remember seeing Cassell jumping up and down like a kid with new Christmas toys. The Boston Garden just erupted. This was right up there with Reed and with Larry Bird bouncing his head on the floor in the deciding Game 5 against the Indiana Pacers back in the 1991 playoffs and then coming back to lead the Celtics to victory. Yeah, it was just like that—or so we all thought.

It took 11 years, but Pierce came clean on what happened while working on ESPN. "I have a confession to make," he said. "I just had to go to the bathroom." Well, I'll be damned!

That was certainly one big memory from the series. The other came in Game 4, when the Lakers led by 24 points in L.A. I'll never forget watching the Celtics storm back and watching the Zen master, Phil Jackson, just have no answer at all as it happened. Mr. 11 Rings may be in the Hall of Fame, but Rivers totally outcoached him in this game. He mixed the lineup with Ray Allen and Eddie House in the backcourt and Pierce and James Posey up front along with Garnett playing center. L.A. couldn't leave anyone open. Bryant wasn't going to sag off Pierce obviously. House was hitting from downtown, and Posey was money from the corner. Then, when they needed defense, here came Tony Allen.

What a stroke of brilliance by Rivers! The Celtics were up 3–1 and were going back home to close it out.

Game 6 in Boston was one of the best sports moments I've experienced in my life. It's always cool to beat L.A.—and to do it by 39 points is something! It doesn't get any better than that. Former Lakers player (and current broadcaster) Mychal Thompson came in and was talking all kinds of noise before the game. Every time the Celtics hit a shot, I'd turn around and look at him; it was like we were playing again. As the lead hit 20, Bryant came out in the third quarter and hit two treys. Sean Grande was getting concerned but then came a barrage like I've never seen.

One of the guys I was happiest for was Ray Allen. He went off for 26 points in just 32 minutes. He's always been one of my favorites. I see a lot of myself in him and vice versa. We both would come to games dressed impeccably and at times we were both overlooked. When they talk about the Big Three of my era, it was really a Big Three and a Half or Four with Bird, Robert Parish, Kevin McHale, and myself. Even though Allen was included in the new Big Three, he usually gets the least credit of him, Pierce, and Garnett. But there's no way the Celtics win that championship without Allen. He helped set the culture, and that's why he should have his number retired in Boston. He just went about his job and didn't seek the glory. For him to be part of this moment was so cool.

Celebrating on the floor was wild. I was right in front of the scoreboard and saw Pierce come over to douse Rivers with the Gatorade. I actually had a parka on because I didn't want to get my suit wet. Then, the clock was winding down, and Big Baby threw the ball high up in the sky...and it landed right in my hands. Forrest Gump Max struck again; I was always in the right place in basketball history. Cassell came up and wanted the ball, but I held onto it. Then I thought about it and I couldn't be a Doug Mientkiewicz. He was the first baseman on the 2004 Boston Red Sox who didn't want to give up the ball from the last out in the curse-breaking World Series and got crushed for it. (He eventually gave it to the team.) I'm a team broadcaster. If I don't give up the ball, I don't have a job. I realized this and gave it to Cassell, who gave the ball to Garnett, who gave him a trip to Las Vegas in exchange. It was great for Cassell and Brown, two veterans who retired after the game. It's like how you want to leave life. I'd have the best meal ever and then keel over. Those guys clearly left on top.

* * *

If you told me after the Boston Celtics destroyed the Los Angeles Lakers that they wouldn't repeat as champions, I wouldn't have believed you. Sure, Kevin Garnett, Paul Pierce, and Ray Allen were 31, 30, and 33 years old, respectively, but they were playing the best basketball of their careers. James Posey left via free agency, and both Sam Cassell and P.J. Brown retired, but the bench was still solid. There's no question Boston was the team to beat.

It's never easy to repeat, but Doc Rivers had the team in a great mind-set, and the guys picked up right where they left off. Two days before Christmas, they were 27–2 with a 19-game winning streak. There's no doubt in my mind that if this team wanted to, the Celtics were going to win 70-plus games. On Christmas Day the Lakers got a small measure of revenge, ending the ride with a 92–83 win. The loss in L.A. took the 70 wins out of reach, as the Celtics went through a stretch, losing five out of seven. Still, on February 19, 2009, they were basically tied with LeBron James' Cleveland Cavaliers behind the Lakers in the race for the league's best record.

But on that night in Utah, the season changed forever. The Celtics lost to the Jazz 90–85, but the real loss came in the first half, when Garnett went up for an alley-oop. On the way up, he pulled up lame with a right knee injury. It didn't look good at the time. Always intense and emotional, Garnett started pounding the basket stanchion and grabbing his leg. I just got the worst feeling. It made me want to throw up. Superman doesn't go down. It just took the life out of our team. Seeing Superman get hurt just killed everyone. KG was limping badly onto the plane. If he was a racehorse, they'd have shot him. The whole scene was just so sad, seeing such greatness dissolve in a second. For me, it was a flashback to 1985 when I hurt my knee, which essentially ended my Celtics career.

Garnett missed 13 games and then tried to come back. That lasted just four games, and Garnett didn't play the rest of the season. Even without their spiritual leader, the Celtics won 62 games, finishing with the NBA's third best record. Their first playoff series was against the Chicago Bulls. This may have been a first-round matchup between the second and seventh seeds, but if you watched it, you would've thought it was the Eastern Conference Finals.

This might have been Allen's best stretch as a Celtic. He and Bulls guard Ben Gordon were just lobbing grenades at each other, bombing three-pointers, shooting darts. After losing the first game, the Celtics came back to even the series, and Allen's 30 points got the better of Gordon's 42. Game 4 went to the Bulls in double-overtime. Boston took a 3–2 series lead in Game 5 in overtime. Chicago forced a Game 7 in triple-overtime despite Allen dropping 51 points with nine three-pointers. Both guys were worn out, and the Celtics won by 10 to advance.

If anyone had forgotten just how great Allen was, this series was a terrific reminder. He was such a true professional. Allen was just going to do what he'd always done in this league. Of course, that meant shooting outside, but he also went to the basket. All of this happened with Garnett on the sidelines, trying to help his team, screaming, imploring, and talking shit. But as I learned more than 20 years earlier, you can only do so much without actually playing.

I was on WEEI radio, and people were asking if the Celtics could win without KG, and I said no. Team owner Wyc Grousbeck called in and said maybe the team didn't have the right broadcaster. I told him that we're speaking to the smartest fans around, and we have to be truthful. Maybe I could have said it a little differently, but it was pretty simple—no KG, no repeat. It was like having a car with a bad motor, and now you're going to try and drive in the Indy 500.

The championship reign came to an end in the next round to the Orlando Magic, when we lost a decisive Game 7 at home. There were rumors during the whole series that KG was coming back. Steve Burton of WBZ asked me, "Max, tell me—I heard Kevin had a secret operation." I told him it wasn't going to happen. Everyone wished it, but it wasn't meant to be.

After we lost Game 7 against the Magic 101–82, I appeared on Comcast Boston with Michael Felger, and he asked, "Aren't you ashamed of the way they played?" I responded that I had never been so proud of this team. They just didn't have enough without Garnett. I was actually even more proud of them than when they won the title. They'd lost their best player and still fought.

* * *

Doc Rivers used to say that the starting five of Kevin Garnett, Paul Pierce, Kendrick Perkins, Ray Allen, and Rajon Rondo had never lost a playoff series together. With Garnett back from injury, it seemed like the 2009–10 season had a chance to be special. This wasn't anything flashy. The team finished 50–32, third best in the conference.

Rivers still believed in them and put his (and their) money where his mouth was. During a February trip to Los Angeles, Rivers took $100 from each player, coach, and staff member and stuffed it into an envelope. Then he took the money and stuffed it into the ceiling in the locker room at the Staples Center. He told the team they'd come back during the NBA Finals and reclaim their cash. It was a classic Rivers move. He could sell ice to an Eskimo. He just has "it." Even during the civil unrest of 2020, he showed his leadership and charisma. He had a great line: "It's amazing why we keep loving this country, and this country does not love us back...It's really so sad." It made me think that I wish I had said it.

The next Celtics–Lakers showdown had a couple of new faces for the Green, most notably the additions of Rasheed Wallace and Nate Robinson. Wallace was one of my favorites, and it's because I got to know the man, not just the player. Everyone remembers him as the hothead, always getting technical fouls, getting arrested, and all of that, but that wasn't the real Rasheed Wallace.

From the very first time he came to Boston, we hit it off. He was driving a convertible and pulled up next to me outside the practice facility. He yelled, "It's Cornbread!" He talked about how much he'd heard about me from fellow Kinston native and his former North Carolina teammate Jerry Stackhouse, who was his homeboy. It was just really nice to be acknowledged by him in that way. Based on his reputation, I'd expected Wallace to be flamboyant, loud, all up in people's face, but he was just the opposite. Off the court, he was the quietest guy. He'd sit in front of me on the plane, watching cartoons, reading books. It wasn't the arrogant, cocky Wallace but really the quiet, almost Bambi-like Wallace that he was away from the game. He was really thoughtful, well-spoken, well-read. Just a cool guy. Given Wallace's background, you're thinking this guy was really going to be an asshole when Danny Ainge signed him. How's he going to fit in with these guys? But it was the exact opposite. He was like the low-maintenance girlfriend.

Robinson was a trip. He was a great athlete and actually played one season of college football at the University of Washington. Of course, everyone knows about him winning the NBA Slam Dunk Contest three times despite standing just 5'9". But this guy was a character. There were times where he'd put up these crazy shots, and my broadcast partner, Sean Grande, would say, "Let Nate be Nate!"

Once we were in Charlotte, staying in the Ritz-Carlton. Robinson went over to the epicenter across the street. He got an empty cup and started singing in front of Walgreens. He was so excited that he made $7. Of course, his signature moment on the court came in the 2010 Finals against L.A., when he was so excited that he jumped on Big Baby's back and was slobbering from his mouth. They called it Shrek and Donkey like in the animated movie.

The Lakers were the defending champions, looking for a repeat, and they were the favorite to do just that. But again Rivers' starting five had never lost a series. Probably the biggest difference from two years earlier was Pau Gasol. After just getting destroyed by KG in the Finals, he was playing with much more confidence. Still, the Celtics had overcome Kobe Bryant's 38 points in Game 5 for a six-point win in Boston. Now all they had to do was win one of two games in L.A., and they'd be champions again. Before that next game, I saw my old rival Mychal Thompson, watching them rope off the court to rehearse the trophy celebration. I crowed to Thompson, "Only one team can win the title tonight!"

I was extra excited because the league had told me that since I was the only Celtics legend in the building that they wanted me to present the team with the championship. How cool would that be? I had my speech all ready to go. I was going to get the trophy from the commissioner and say how great it is playing the Lakers, how they're still a great team, but how about those Celtics?

Unfortunately, disaster struck midway through the first quarter. Perkins was fighting for a rebound against Andrew Bynum. His right knee just gave out. Talk about taking the wind out of the team's sails. It was just like when KG went down the previous season, but this came when they were so close to another title. Talk about a devastating injury. Perk wasn't ever the guy who put up the huge stats, but he was a tough SOB, who did the dirty work that nobody else wanted to. The guys were so heartbroken that they got blown out 87–69.

That meant another Game 7 of Celtics–Lakers. It was what everyone wanted to see. This one wasn't a work of art, but it was a hard-fought battle as usual. Without Perkins L.A. could just throw the ball up against the backboard, knowing we couldn't rebound with them. (Not surprisingly, they had a 53–40 edge on the boards.) Wallace tried to fill in at center, playing a season-high 36 minutes. But this wasn't the Sheed of his prime. His job all year was to play a good, hard 20 minutes. After that you could tell his legs were shot. He was this team's P.J. Brown. Wallace just plain ran out of gas, and Bryant and Gasol took full advantage.

This wasn't a vintage shooting night for Bryant; he made just six of his 24 shots, and Boston led by four points heading into the fourth quarter. That's when Bryant showed everyone his famous Mamba Mentality, his will to win. He just wouldn't let his team lose. Bryant grabbed 15 rebounds and took 15 free throws. That's what great players do: he wasn't shooting well, so he did something positive to impact the stat sheet. This is where I hope Jayson Tatum gets as a player. Bryant basically said, "They'll have to carry me off on a stretcher. I'll be damned if I'm going to let the Celtics win on *my* floor."

Gasol grabbed 18 rebounds, and Metta World Peace hit the biggest three-pointer of his career, and just like that, L.A. repeated as champions. And in case it wasn't painful enough, the first person I saw after the game? Joe "Jellybean" Bryant, Kobe's dad, who I had played against. I had to extend my hand and say congratulations. It was like losing to them twice.

CHAPTER 23
BREAKING UP THE BAND

After the devastating loss to the Los Angeles Lakers, the Boston Celtics were at a crossroads. Danny Ainge knew time was running out on the new Big Three and he was also cognizant that Kendrick Perkins was going to miss a good chunk of the season, leaving the team thin in the middle. That's when Danny Ainge doubled down, signing two O'Neals—veteran big men Jermaine O'Neal and Shaquille O'Neal.

At this point, Shaq was 38 years old. After winning his fourth title with the Miami Heat, he'd bounced around, going from the Phoenix Suns to the Cleveland Cavaliers and now to Boston. Teams were still enamored with the dominant Shaq, who had won MVP awards and championships. He did have something left, but make no mistake: he wasn't Great Shaq anymore. It was more like Okay Shaq. To his credit, he seemed to be fine with his role. He'd still try different things, and you could see there were still some tools in his bag. For most of his career, he was the focal point, but now he was more of a contributor. We got along well. After all, we were both Omega Psi Phi fraternity brothers.

The other O'Neal "brother" was Jermaine, who'd carved out a really nice career, making six straight All-Star games in the early 2000s and three All-NBA teams. That's pretty good for a guy who didn't even average double figures until his fifth season. I really liked Jermaine. But like Shaq, he had a ton of miles on him by the time he came to Boston. He was heading into his 15th season that began at age 18. He brought some really good things I thought would help—namely defensive ability and attitude—but it was hard seeing the physical struggles he'd go through in Boston.

Perkins didn't return until late January, but with their new duo in the middle, the team was 34–10, including a 14-game winning streak. Still, when Perk came back for that game against Cleveland, the fans went bananas. As Doc Rivers had said, his starting five still had never lost a playoff series, and now they were back to full strength.

One of Ainge's best traits is that he's never satisfied. I'd heard some rumors that he might be looking to trade Perk because he didn't think the Celtics could afford to re-sign him. Perkins was not a guy whose contributions showed up on the stat sheet. His job was to be a big-ass man in the middle. He'd get the big rebound, set the huge pick, and protect his teammates. Just as importantly, he was the social policeman. He kept the guys in check, especially Rajon Rondo. I can still hear him saying, "That ain't right, [No.] 9!"

Even with the rumors, when the news came down that day in Denver that Perk was heading to the Oklahoma City Thunder, things changed with this team forever. Initially, I thought we got back good value in the deal. Jeff Green was a valuable part of the Thunder's Big Three with Kevin Durant and Russell Westbrook. I said to Ainge, "Pup, I think you might have something here."

There was one game where Green scored 43 against Miami. He was the best player on the floor—even with LeBron James, Dwyane Wade, and Chris Bosh. But he could never keep it up consistently; the next game he scored 13. Rivers really said it best: that great players believe they're great players. Green didn't believe he was a great player. It's too bad because he has the tools: big hands, good jumping ability, etc. Big man Nenad Krstic also came over in the deal and he had a nice little jumper, so it wasn't like we got nothing back. However, things could have been much different. Instead of Green, Ainge wanted another guy you may have heard of—James Harden.

Perk never wanted to leave Boston, but he did sign a $36 million extension with the Thunder and helped them get to the NBA Finals. That year the Celtics lost in the second round of the playoffs to Miami. We later learned that Shaq was playing with a torn Achilles tendon, and that was the end of his Hall of Fame career.

In the 2011–12 season, the Big Three had its last chance for greatness. The NBA's lockout-shortened campaign seemed to be tailor-made for an old team, trying to save themselves a bit, They had to play only 66 regular-season games. Sure enough, despite finishing 39–27, the team came alive in the playoffs and actually led James and the Heat 3–2 in the Eastern Conference Finals with Game 6 at home. The pressure on James was incredible. When he signed with Miami, he talked about "not one, not two, not three…" championships. But when they got to the Finals in his first season there, the Heat lost to a less talented Dallas Mavericks team, and James did not play well. Who knows what could happen with a loss to the Celtics? Pat Riley might have blown the team up.

James is an all-time great and he proved it beyond a shadow of a doubt in Game 6. He was *unreal*. This was a grown-ass man playing with kids. He was like, "This is what I'm gonna do." I was talking to Alonzo Mourning about it, and he said he knew James was going to have a monster game because when he came out of the tunnel he'd usually dab Zo and Riley. Instead, he just walked right by them. When the game started, he made a move in the first minute and hit a couple of jumpers, and it was over. It was like he was thinking, *No, not on my life, Celtics.*

That was really one of the all-time great games I ever saw a guy play on the road. It didn't matter who Rivers threw at him. James was going through them like a hot knife through butter. It was like watching Godzilla. When his team needed him the most, James played 45 minutes, scored 45 points, grabbed 15 rebounds, and threw in five assists for good measure. That meant we were heading back to Miami.

Game 7 was tied after three quarters, and once again being the only Celtics legend in the building, I was selected to present the Eastern Conference Championship trophy to the team. I was all set, speech ready to go…and then James (31 points and 12 rebounds), Wade (23 points), and Bosh (19 points) finished us off, and I was left holding the bag. The Heat beat Perk and OKC in the Finals, and James had his first championship.

After the 2011–12 season, Ray Allen had a decision to make. The Celtics were fading from dominance, and his situation was becoming uncomfortable. He'd been injured much of the season and essentially replaced by Avery Bradley. His 10.7 shots per game were the lowest of his career up to that point. Plus, it was well known that Ainge had at least explored trading him. In fact, there was a deal with the Memphis Grizzlies that was basically done: Allen would go to the Grizzlies, and guard O.J. Mayo would come to Boston. Fortunately for the Celtics, Mayo basically said, "Screw the banners," and the deal was off.

Allen felt disrespected, and that only got worse when Ainge signed free-agent guard Jason Terry. It was obvious to everyone that Jet was going to take Allen's minutes, so he signed a two-year deal with Miami—of all teams—reportedly for less than the C's were offering. As Allen told me on my podcast, "I left as a free agent. I left because there [were] so many unresolved issues that the team wasn't considering or willing to change."

And, of course, the season opener was what you'd expect—Celtics at Heat. Before the game Allen came over to the Boston bench and exchanged warm greetings with some of his former teammates and coaches. Those good feelings did not include Garnett. Upset that not only did Allen leave, but that he also went to the Celtics' rival, KG totally ignored his former "brother." On the one hand, I admire Garnett's sense of loyalty. Remember he always held out hope that he could stay with the Minnesota Timberwolves. It was only after 12 years of struggling that he agreed to be traded. (And he wanted to play in L.A., not Boston. It was only after Pierce worked on him that he consented to become a Celtic.) Garnett said he "lost" Allen's number.

Even with my love for Garnett, I don't like the way this feud has gone down. Garnett and Allen grew up together in South Carolina. They were homeboys. Then they won the title together in Boston. That bond is something they'll have for the rest of their lives. Allen made a business decision; Ainge didn't seem to want him, and Allen had a chance to compete for another championship, which he did, hitting one of the biggest shots in NBA history: the miraculous, game-tying three-pointer in Game 6 of the 2013 NBA Finals. So what exactly is the issue? I've always felt more akin to Allen than to any other player. When I got traded to the Los Angeles Clippers, Red Auerbach and others put out damaging information to Will McDonough of *The Boston Globe* that I didn't work hard enough to come back because I'd already received my money. Why couldn't they just wish me well?

It was the same thing with Allen and KG. If things were different, I think he would have stayed in Boston. I mean, he went to school less than two hours away at UConn. But with some people, it's out of sight, out of mind. It's like when Robert Parish reminds people that the original "Big Three" was actually the "Big Four" with himself, Larry Bird, Kevin McHale, and myself. People forget about me—just like KG eliminated Allen.

As you might expect, Celtics fans sided with the guys who were still on the team, which I get to a degree, but things got out of hand. "I've gotten so much hate, death threats, vitriol, from Boston fans," Allen said. "These guys have kind of removed me from the Big Three, said so many negative things about me. And I haven't had one negative thing to say about any of them...It hurt me...just to hear some of the things that have been said...We're supposed to be celebrating these times."

The next January, Miami came to Boston, and Allen got a nice ovation from the fans and a video tribute from the team. It was very well-deserved. Garnett may not agree with his business decision, but it's not so serious there should be that gap. It really pisses me off. That's one reason I've been openly campaigning for the team to retire Allen's uniform. There's no way banner No. 18 would be hanging without his shooting, his buying into the team, and his leadership.

Once Allen left for South Beach, the Big Three was down to the Not-As-Big Two. Garnett was 36 years old, Pierce was 35, and the team limped home with a 41–40 record. After a first-round playoff exit against the New York Knicks, there were about to be some big-time changes coming in Boston. In June of 2013, the team announced that Rivers was stepping down as head coach. On the one hand, the timing was strange, as he had just signed a contract extension the previous season. But Rivers knew the team was heading into a rebuild. Allen was already gone, and Pierce and Garnett weren't getting any younger. The days of challenging for a title were gone.

It really wasn't a surprise that Rivers would end up working amongst the beautiful people in Los Angeles. He's always been a Hollywood type with great charisma. The Clippers gave him the keys to the kingdom as both coach and the chief decision maker. There was no way he could turn that down. I know a lot of fans felt betrayed, but Rivers did was he was hired to do: win a championship and make the Celtics relevant again. Plus, Ainge was able to get a first-round pick for releasing Rivers from his contract. When was the last time you heard of a team getting a first rounder for a *coach*?

The fact is that Ainge and Rivers had a great working relationship. Even when things were seemingly hopeless, Ainge stood by his coach. But even when you're besties, sometimes one person gets tired and needs a change. I didn't have any issues toward Rivers leaving. Watching him rebuild the team was really cool to see. Compare it to how long it took for the Lakers to get back to the playoffs toward the end of Kobe Bryant's career and afterward.

Unlike when I left town, I really admired the way Ainge and the organization handled Rivers' departure. You never heard one bad word about him asking out of a contract or anything like that. You know that wasn't the case when I got traded. Even while people questioned my heart, don't forget I spent more than a month out in L.A., proving that my knees were healthy. Go ask my old coach, Don Chaney, if I worked hard. If I didn't bust my ass to get healthy, the Clippers would never have made the trade. If that happens, Bill Walton never comes to Boston and "the Greatest Team Ever" of 1986 may not have been. Did the Celtics sell their soul for one year of greatness? Kind of. They did win, but Walton never really played again.

Rivers will always be part of the Celtics. He helped us win a title. Going back to Allen, I want him to be celebrated like he deserves. It's been nice over the years that fans have always given Rivers a nice welcome when he comes back to town.

Allen was gone. Now it was time to say good-bye to the rest of the Big Three. Auerbach had a penchant for being loyal to his players (at least most of them). Bill Russell, John Havlicek, Tommy Heinsohn, K.C. and Sam Jones—they never played for anyone other than the Celtics. Bob Cousy and Dave Cowens only went elsewhere after they retired. After the '86 championship, the Celtics began to break down. Bird had heel and obviously back problems. McHale's ankle was never the same after breaking his foot in 1987. Ironically, it was Parish, the guy who was so out of shape when he came to Boston, who stayed healthy.

Bird and McHale were still good players and definitely had some market value. There were always rumors that the Indiana Pacers would try to bring Bird home for the end of his career. And the Mavericks offered Detlef Schrempf and Sam Perkins for Bird and McHale. But after everything those guys had done for the team: winning three titles, playing hurt, etc., Auerbach never pulled the trigger, and they kept aging, and the Celtics didn't recover for years. Auerbach told me it was always better to trade a guy a year too early than a year too late. "Don't fall in love with the product," he'd tell me.

Ainge learned that lesson better than Auerbach had practiced that in the late '80s and made sure he wasn't going to get burned. The Brooklyn Nets were desperate to make a big splash. Their Russian owner, Mikhail Prokhorov, had promised a championship when he bought the team in 2009, and five years later, it was time to put up or shut up. Ainge knew how much pressure was facing the Nets and took full advantage. He sent Garnett, Pierce, and Terry in exchange for Gerald Wallace, Kris Humphries, MarShon Brooks, Keith Bogans, and Kris Joseph. Oh, and *three* unprotected first-round draft picks.

My initial reaction was: how the hell did Ainge get this done? Of course, Garnett and Pierce were future Hall of Famers, but to use a golf analogy, they were on the 17th tee. KG just didn't have the same tools anymore. Pierce's quickness and elevation were gone. As you get older in this game, you just *know* when you don't have it anymore. It's like Superman not being able to use his X-ray vision. For me, it happened when I was in Houston. For all of my career, I always rode John Salley like a mule. Then on one night, I tried two moves on him, and he didn't bite. I was done. Garnett and Pierce were just about there, too.

Garnett was unsure of agreeing to the deal, but Pierce talked him into it. I remember talking to a couple of Celtics insiders, Gary Washburn and A. Sherrod Blakely, before it happened, telling them to mark my words: those guys were getting traded. They thought I was crazy. I don't know what the hell Nets GM Billy King was thinking, but they literally gave Ainge *everything* he wanted. The five players coming back were irrelevant; this was all about the picks, plus the right to switch first-round picks in 2017.

Celtics fans were disappointed. This was officially the closing of a championship window. Both guys were hugely popular. When the Nets came to Boston for the first time and they introduced Pierce in the starting lineup, there was a woman near me who was just bawling. After the game I introduced her to Pierce, and she went out of her mind.

In that same game, there was a cool moment for me as well. Everyone knows how intense Garnett was, and when he got locked in for a game, nothing else existed. Back on the night they beat L.A. for the championship, Russell asked Rajon Rondo to grab KG for him. Rondo said no way. Not many people said no to Mr. Russell. So that shows you just how reluctant people are to disturb Garnett. During warmups before his first game back, Garnett had that "If you bother me, I'll fuck you up" look. Naturally, I had to poke the bear. I came up to him and said, "And they say nobody can fucking talk to you!" We both just burst out laughing and shared the biggest hug. It was really special for me to have that relationship with a guy who played so many years after I was done.

As a result of one of the most lopsided deals in NBA history, the Celtics ended up with, among other players, Jaylen Brown and Jayson Tatum. By accelerating the rebuild, Ainge was able to set up his team for its next championship window. I've always said that if Ainge gets the right deal, his wife, Michelle, had better pack her bags.

CHAPTER 24
BRAD STEVENS
AND THE YOUNG GUNS

With Doc Rivers heading to coach the Los Angeles Clippers, Ray Allen in Miami, and Paul Pierce and Kevin Garnett both in Brooklyn, the Boston Celtics' rebuild was officially on. Danny Ainge needed to not only find a coach, but also find the *right* coach for a young team.

There were several names being floated around, and I thought Nate McMillan would be a great fit. After a solid playing career, McMillan coached the Seattle SuperSonics and Portland Trail Blazers and did a good job. At this time he was an assistant head coach for Frank Vogel on the Indiana Pacers. He dealt with all types of players, ranging from Hall of Famer Gary Payton to young guys like LaMarcus Aldridge and Brandon Roy.

There didn't seem to be a real favorite for the job, when Ainge pulled off a shocker, hiring Butler University coach Brad Stevens, who had taken Butler—a school many people had never even heard of—to consecutive appearances in the NCAA Finals. He helped a lightly-regarded high school tennis player named Gordon Hayward become a lottery pick and future NBA All-Star. Truth be told, I was surprised and confused by the decision because I really didn't know who Stevens was. I don't follow college basketball that closely, so Stevens was a mystery to me. The narrative had always been that college coaches would fail in the NBA. It happened to John Calipari, Jerry Tarkanian, Mike Montgomery, and, of course, Rick Pitino. But Stevens is *smart*. Ainge always wants to surround himself with people that are even smarter than he is, and that's one of his biggest strengths.

The best thing about Stevens is that he has no ego. This was a guy who was working as a pharmaceutical rep for Eli Lilly when he decided to try coaching. A lot of successful college coaches already have a rep by the time they come to the NBA. Because Stevens was so young, nobody knew him. He'd been around one coach who would yell and scream. Stevens thought, *This is okay, we're pretty successful, but there's another way.*

With his cerebral, low-key style, Stevens is the perfect guy for today's NBA. Players need to be pampered. He does that, but he also makes them accountable. He's not ranting and raving like Gregg Popovich. Stevens is more like the baby beach in Aruba—calm and tranquil.

I've been asked if Stevens would be able to coach in my era. In my opinion, he could, but he'd have to be a lot more vocal because we looked at our coaches to be like that. I think of guys like Pat Riley and Bill Fitch, who were intense. The only guy who seemed like he was on NyQuil was Phil Jackson. That guy was always acting like he was at a Grateful Dead concert.

Stevens was just steady, and it's made his players feel really comfortable. He's kind of like K.C. Jones. When Fitch yelled at me and told me that I'd be guarding the toughest players to protect Larry Bird, he scared the shit out of me. Jones would bring you to the side and kind of negotiate with you. When he got done being mad at you, it felt like you had been in a pillow fight.

In Stevens' first year, the Celtics only won 25 games. As usual, they got unlucky in the lottery and ended up with the sixth pick. This wasn't considered a deep draft, and the best player turned out to be Nikola Jokic, who went 41st overall. Ainge wanted to add grit to his team. Without Kevin Garnett around, who was going to make everyone else play harder, play better? He couldn't have found a better answer than Marcus Smart, a tough kid who grew up in Texas. He was so good as a freshman that had he left Oklahoma State he might have been the top overall pick. (Instead the Cleveland Cavaliers selected Anthony Bennett, who became one of the biggest flops in draft history.) Smart's sophomore year was good, but there were concerns after he got into a skirmish with a fan at Texas Tech during the game.

Offensively, he wasn't a great shooter. But what he brings to his team goes well beyond the stats. When I look at him, I say he's a guy who could have totally played in the 1980s, just like Jimmy Butler and Victor

Oladipo; they're old-school guys. Smart has that attitude where he's not going to let anyone talk junk to him. *You want to fight? Okay, that's what we need to do.* He can get into anyone's head. Just ask James Harden. In a 2017 game at Boston Garden, Smart just dogged Harden into shooting 7-for-27 from the floor and even drew two offensive fouls on "the Beard" in a dramatic come-from-behind win. Like Jackie MacMullan once said, watching him is one of the few experiences where you can go to a game and see something you've never seen—on the defensive end.

Here's how great Smart is: I believe he's the best defensive player under 6'8" (Bill Russell's height) the Celtics have ever had. And for me to say that didn't come easy given that the great Dennis Johnson was one of my best friends. After I made that statement, former player/coach and current ESPN broadcaster Mark Jackson told me he disagreed, saying "I'm taking D.J. because I played against him."

As I told Jackson, that's all well and good but I played *with* D.J. Smart can guard anyone, and I mean anyone, especially in today's NBA where big guys play on the perimeter. It's easy to see why Ainge loves Smart. He was the same type of irritant on the floor. The biggest difference is that Ainge would sometimes cross the line into dirty play like that Mario Elie incident I talked about. One of Smart's best techniques is when he does a puppet thing with his hand, basically mocking his opponent. I think it's hilarious. I'd love to get Smart and Toronto Raptors guard Kyle Lowry in a winner-take-all cage match. That would be a must-see.

Ainge did something really smart that not a lot of people noticed a few years ago. Smart's contract was up, and Ainge planned on paying him somewhere between $12 to $14 million per year. I thought that a team like the Pacers would come up with some crazy deal worth like $18 million. Smart went out on the market, and nobody was showing him the money. But when he came back to the Celtics, Ainge could have made him grovel and lowered the offer. They had Smart by the you-know-whats, and he would have had to take their revised deal. Instead,

Ainge honored his original offer, and Smart signed the contract. By not changing the offer, he allowed Smart to keep his pride and dignity.

The 2020 NBA bubble playoffs was kind of a coming out party for Smart. His entire game was on display. Defensively, he played like he always does. He was a first-team All-NBA defender, making a difference in just about every game. He played well offensively, but there are still times when you're watching him play and you yell, "No, no...*yes!*" Smart is like nuclear energy; he can kill millions or he can help people. Sure, there are times when he chucks up bad shots (though he's gotten much better in this regard), but that comes with the territory. He's the most creative point guard the Celtics have and did a terrific job getting the ball to guys like Daniel Theis. We also know that if Smart hits his first shot or two...there's more to come. But trust me: you want this guy on your team.

Smart reminds me of myself when it comes to playing better when the games mean the most. I always say—in a respectful way—that one thing I hated about Larry Bird is that whether the game was on October 28 or June 28 he played with the same intensity. People would always say to me that Bird played so much harder, was more consistent, and why couldn't I play like that? But when it mattered the most, like Game 7 of 1984, everyone knew what they were going to get from me.

The team sometimes has players dine with corporate sponsors as a perk for their support. Many times, I get asked to come along, basically to keep the conversation moving. I've been to several of these dinners with Smart and his girlfriend and really gotten to know the man off the court. Smart's upbringing really made him who he is today. Apparently, his neighborhood was so poor that they used to play the "Ghetto Olympics," including sports like stickball—with an actual stick, not a bat. And now you know why Smart plays hungry.

* * *

The 2016 NBA Draft was where Danny Ainge's Kevin Garnett/Paul Pierce deal to the Brooklyn Nets really started to pay off. Despite winning 48 games, the Boston Celtics had the Nets' first-round pick, which ended up being third overall. Not really following college basketball, I was unfamiliar with Jaylen Brown. He had spent one season at Cal and averaged around 15 points per game. We soon learned that he's a freakish athlete, but that's about it.

Like his partner in crime, Jayson Tatum, Brown is a quiet assassin. I think about when Paul Pierce came to town, and everyone was talking about him, including himself. People knew him from his three years at Kansas, where nearly every game was on TV. You can really see Brown's progression; he only played about 17 minutes a game as a rookie. When he made a mistake, Stevens would pull him out of the game. Usually when a kid gets picked that high, he's expected to put up big numbers immediately. But most of the time, those players are selected by lousy teams. Plus, there's been a disturbing trend where some high picks don't even play their rookie year—guys like Blake Griffin, Joel Embiid, and Ben Simmons, among others. Brown kept his head down, averaging 6.6 points. Remember he was 20 years old!

Each year Brown has improved his game and with that came more trust from Stevens. Although he did clash with Kyrie Irving in his third season, he came through it as a much better player. In the C's run to the Eastern Conference Finals, Brown was their most consistent player.

He's also one of the smartest guys in the NBA. I mean, how many 20 year olds get to lecture at Harvard? Brown has a terrific demeanor. He does get excited, but you can't tell. He's not one of those guys with a huge belly laugh but a quiet one. He likes to break everything down, and you can almost literally see the wheels turning.

And like a lot of guys from the South, he is extremely polite. When we were doing a postgame interview once, he called me "Sir." When we

The two young stars of the Boston Celtics, Jayson Tatum (left) and Jaylen Brown (right), celebrate during a win against the Brooklyn Nets in 2017.

finished I told him that he knew me, and there was definitely no need to call me "Sir." He answered by saying, "Yes, sir."

Since the time in the bubble, Brown has grown a lot. He's developed into a great defensive stopper and seems to have embraced the challenge on that side of the ball. Offensively, guys will do a move to make the defender back up and then they get a running start. Brown never lets the defense get comfortable; he's always attacking and has no fear. He's such a freakish athlete that it can get him in trouble. I'll never forget a night in March of 2018 when he threw down a dunk with so much authority that he flipped right on his neck and back. I mean, he could have easily been paralyzed. The medical staff wanted to take him out on a stretcher, but he jumped up and put his hand up to the crowd. He later told me that he wasn't about to let them carry him off.

Off the court, Brown is even more impressive. Some company came to me and said they were looking for player or two to do some commercials. The money was good, like $15,000 per man. I went to the Celtics media relations director to ask if he'd ask Brown to do it. He explained that money isn't a motivator for Brown; he's more interested in causes, things that will make changes. That's when I knew this was one different cat.

During the social unrest of 2020, Brown drove 15 hours to Atlanta to lend his support to the Black Lives Matter movement. Sometimes you hear a smart guy described as, "He's playing chess while everyone else is playing checkers." When you talk to Brown, you quickly realize there's a lot more to him than basketball. He's on a different plane. I can see him having an even bigger longtime effect after he leaves the game. Maybe he'll do something in politics, something that will help minorities. When you look at some players, they have their posse, wear huge bling, all of that. Not Brown. He's just a quiet guy who is into his music, and I can definitely see him becoming a captain of the Celtics. He's that kind of guy.

On a related note, I was really proud of how the NBA reacted during the BLM movement. It really showed how empowered today's athletes are. Back in my day, nobody got too involved with politics; it was too dangerous. Now guys are getting generational money, so they're not necessarily tied to the team like we were. I remember back in 1986, reading *The Sporting News'* top 100 highest-paid athletes. At No. 99 was yours truly, making like $800,000. Nowadays, these guys are conglomerates for themselves. Think about Steph Curry and how he's redefined Under Armor. You could see this type of thing developing back in the day. Michael Jordan, of course, took everything to a whole new level. Magic Johnson has made a huge impact in business. Guys like Junior Bridgeman, who bought more than 100 Wendy's franchises, or Dave Bing and his steel company—it's impressive. Back in the '80s, we were scrambling to get as much money as we could over a short period. Now, it's actually hard for these guys to go broke.

On the court, Brown has grown more in a short period of time than any player I've seen in a long time. One thing I really like is the way he and Tatum fit together. For all of the talent on today's team, there's no doubt that the guy with the highest ceiling is Tatum. Even this early in his career, I can tell he'll become one of the all-time great Celtics.

I struggled to figure out who he reminds me of, but I'd say the best guess is Grant Hill. Both guys went to Duke, where Hill was one of the greatest college players in the history of the game. As Jordan was winding down his career, everyone thought Hill would be the next great. He had it all: a great personality, super athleticism, and the right mind-set. His dad, former NFL player Calvin Hill, went to Yale. But, of course, he had those constant injuries to his ankle, and it never happened for him. I remember talking to Doc Rivers, who coached him with the Orlando Magic. They signed him and Tracy McGrady and tried for Tim Duncan. Rivers told me that if Hill was healthy, he would have changed Orlando forever.

Like it was for Hill, the world is Tatum's oyster. He's already being looked at as one of those faces of the game. He comes from an outstanding family, and his son, Deuce, became a celebrity during the bubble playoffs of 2020. I honestly don't see how this guy could fail. He's just starting to realize how good he can be. In the 2020 playoffs, he had a couple of games where he couldn't make a shot in the first half but ended up with a triple-double. Offensively, he's already a superstar. His college coach, the legendary Mike Krzyzewski, said he was the most ready player offensively that he's had. Now think about some of the great Dukies: Hill, Jay Williams, Elton Brand, and Irving, to name a few. That is some compliment.

There was a lot of talk that he might be the No. 1 pick after his single college season, but Ainge pulled off another incredible deal. He traded the top pick to the Philadelphia 76ers for the No. 3 pick *and* a first rounder the next year. The Sixers took Markelle Fultz, who barely even played for them and is now trying to carve out a career in Orlando, and the Celtics got Tatum (who they wanted all along) and selected Romeo Langford two drafts later.

Tatum's growth will come at the other end of the court with his defense and rebounding. Again, the playoffs in the bubble were a coming out party for him, as he showed us a peek of what he can be. This kid is so mature. It's really incredible. During those playoffs he wore a pair of sneakers with Lou Brock's name on them. Brock was a baseball Hall of Famer for the St. Louis Cardinals who passed away in 2020. Now granted, Tatum is from St. Louis, but I guarantee if you asked 95 percent of the NBA players who Brock was, they'd have no idea. Tatum is really an old soul.

When I say that, it's because Tatum respects history. During his first or second year in the league, I showed up at practice. Tatum and I had a good relationship, but it wasn't like we knew each other that well. The next thing I know, he starts shouting, "Cornbread, Cornbread," and I'm looking around and wondering what he's doing. He tells me how he saw the ESPN 30 for 30 *Best of Enemies* about the Celtics and Lakers. "You were a *bad* motherfucker!"

Shortly afterward, I had some of my fraternity brothers come to a game at the Boston Garden. Tatum hit the game-winning shot. My buddies decided that we should hit this club. I'm past the point of going out regularly, but I figured okay. We showed up at the place, and the music was blasting. I had no idea of what songs they were playing. I was just checking out the young folks. Then Tatum walked in, and I was like, "Check, please!" I'm 65 years old; he's 20. This is the last place for me to be.

The team was in Milwaukee when the COVID-19 pandemic hit and the NBA shut down. So the players had their own room in the hotel for meals and got their own chef to make whatever they want. This was off-limits to media, beat writers, broadcasters, etc. Someone with the team told me to come down to the dining room, so we could all hear what the instructions were. Our security guys, Johnny Joe and Phil Lynch, started busting my balls, saying "Look what happened—a former player is in our area. He must want a free meal!"

I didn't mind, but they kept going at me, and guys were starting to pay attention. Nobody knew that I was told to be there. I just turned around and let them know I wasn't *just* a former player. I said, "That would be Finals MVP!" I turned around and could see the whole team kind of stunned. "Has anyone here won a championship? Anyone?"

It was a like mic drop, but then one of our assistant coaches, Kara Lawson came up to me. "When you said that, I wanted to ask: does the WNBA count? You won two championships? How about the Olympics?"

They all count, but did she win a Finals MVP? Nope.

CHAPTER 25
I.T. AND KYRIE

One of Danny Ainge's greatest moves was getting a 5'9" shoot-first point guard who was the last pick of his NBA draft. In a three-way trade with the Phoenix Suns and Detroit Pistons, the Boston Celtics gave up Marcus Thornton, Tayshaun Prince, and a future first-round pick, and Ainge ended up with Isaiah Thomas. Nobody knew much about Thomas other than his name, which he shared with the former Pistons great, and that he attended University of Washington. But this Isaiah took over Boston like no one I'd ever seen, and that includes Larry Bird. He was a supernova: a brilliant light, and then it just faded, and he was gone.

You think about some of the smallest guys in league history, and very few have dominated the way he did. I always look at Tiny Archibald as the model; my guy is the only player in NBA history to lead the league in scoring and assists. The only knock on Thomas was his size. Fortunately for him in today's league, you can't touch the offensive player. Back in the '80s, we could get physical with hand checking. Thomas was already good, but the rules made him unstoppable. He'd get any big man on skates and then he was off. In the fourth quarter, he'd point to his wrist like it's "Isaiah time."

He was our David to everyone's Goliath, and the fans adopted him as one of their own. Thomas was the size of the average guy, so they could relate. In the post Big Three era, he took over. He did things I'd never seen a Celtics player do and did it with flair. I'll tell you what: I don't know if I've ever had so much fun broadcasting.

His moment of truth, however, was one of the biggest tragedies anyone could imagine: when his sister Chyna passed away during the 2017 playoffs. The Celtics had a game against the Chicago Bulls the next day, and, of course, the team gave him the option to go home to Seattle, but Thomas decided to play. That game was...well, the only thing I could really compare it to was the first game after the Boston Marathon bombing. It was just surreal. Everyone has seen that image of him sitting on the bench during shootaround with teammate Avery Bradley stroking his arm, trying to console his good friend. I don't know if I'd be able to play in a situation like that, but maybe the court was a place for him to escape for a moment. I've heard of guys' mothers dying, and they say basketball helped them heal.

Somehow, Thomas was able to score 33 points in 38 minutes of emotion-filled basketball. The Bulls actually won the game, but what Thomas did was absolutely magnificent. In the next round against the Washington Wizards, he dropped 53 points on what would have been his sister's birthday. Wow.

One of the craziest things about Thomas' run in Boston was how inexpensive it was. In two full seasons, he made two All-Star teams and finished fifth in the MVP voting—not bad value for a guy making less than $7 million a year. During that time Thomas made a comment about how the Celtics were going to have to "back up the Brink's truck" to pay him the maximum salary. On the way to the Eastern Conference Finals in 2017, Thomas' incredible postseason came to a screeching halt when he suffered a hip injury that just became too much to handle during a 44-point loss to the Cleveland Cavaliers in Game 2. Nobody had any idea it would be his last game as a Celtic.

After the season Ainge knew that he had a situation on his hands. Thomas was one year away from free agency, and as great as he was, there was no guarantee he could be the best player on a championship team. Add that to the fact he was coming off a hip injury that was more serious than anyone was aware. One night I was at the Boston Garden, attending a Mariah Carey/Lionel Richie concert, when people started coming up to me saying, "We got Kyrie! We got Kyrie!"

Now there had been some rumors that Ainge had his eye on Kyrie Irving, who wanted out of Cleveland, but nobody knew how close it was to happening. That night was the end of Thomas era in Boston. Ainge dealt him, Jae Crowder, the eighth pick in the draft (thanks again,

Brooklyn), and Ante Zizic to Cleveland for one of the best point guards in the whole NBA.

Some people thought it was cold to trade away a guy after he played so heroically through his sister's death and got hurt in the process. Plus, he was obviously the heart and soul of the team. Maybe it was cold, but I don't feel sad for Thomas. Here's why: what he experienced in Boston is something that 99.9 percent of people won't experience in their lives. He received such love; people even plastered his pictures on the subway and wore his jerseys. On a personal level, I won two championships, was a Finals MVP, and never felt love like he did. It certainly was unfortunate that Thomas was never the same player nor received his money. If there was ever a guy who deserved a payday, it was Thomas, but it never happened. It just goes to show that timing is everything.

Speaking of timing, it seemed to be perfect for Ainge to make perhaps his biggest move yet. Just one year after winning a championship with the biggest shot in Cavaliers' history, Irving wanted out of Cleveland. And the Celtics had the package to get him. Trading Thomas hurt, but this was a no-brainer. Ainge pulled the trigger *and* signed Gordon Hayward. With a starting five of All-Stars Irving, Hayward, Al Horford, and young guns Jaylen Brown and Jayson Tatum, the Celtics had a championship-level team. From a skill standpoint, I will say that there's nobody like Irving. Horford was just solid, a true vet you could count on. It's so sad that we never got to see the real Hayward. (He suffered a gruesome ankle injury five minutes into the opening game.) I sure thought this team would go on a run and win multiple championships.

But the key was Irving. He was the type of player who made me yell as a broadcaster. When a guy makes a great play, I like to watch how the bench reacts. They reacted a lot with Irving. He is the best finisher at 6'2" we've seen in a long time. He can hit the jumper and dribble through a screen door. When he's right, his brilliance is simply unmatched. When he'd come down on one-on-one or one-on-two situations, he could pull up beyond the three-point line or freeze the defender.

As talented is, he's also...different. Usually before and after the season, guys would sign 50 or 60 basketballs to give to needy kids. Everyone does it, but Irving wouldn't. He wasn't nasty about it; he just didn't want to do it. He said he wanted to get out of there, but everyone wants to go home. When your best player doesn't want to do something like that, it sets a bad example. On the court, Irving was great, but off the court, that was a different story. There were times during the Cavs' championship run when he went weeks without talking to anyone—and I'm talking about his teammates! Things weren't that extreme in Boston, but it was weird.

I was around Irving for two seasons, so he halfway knew me. And we met before he was even in the NBA. It was at an annual *Black Enterprise* magazine golf and tennis tournament down in Florida. I was working for Pepsi at the time. They'd bring in one of the best college basketball players for an appearance, and that year, it was Irving. He came up on the stage, and we started going back and forth. I said I was a two-time NBA champion, Finals MVP, etc. Irving was like, "Whatever." So I responded that we should settle this right here and now. Next thing I know, he's pulling his shit off, saying, "Let's do it."

Man, I was only joking. But he remembered it and brought it up on the bus once when he was on the Celtics. When the Celtics were in Cleveland before he joined us, he was injured. I saw him and said something like, "Stay healthy." Irving looked at me, and you could tell he was thinking, *Who is this dude?*

Irving was as cool as a cucumber, but I did get emotion out of him once. We were doing a postgame interview, something he always hated. But he came over, and my partner Sean Grande asked him a couple of questions. Then it was my turn. "I've got one last question," I began. "You've never been asked this question before. How was it the first time you beat your dad in one-on-one?"

Irving's response was awesome. "It was unbelievable," he said, "Man, when I beat my dad, I started crying." It was one of the best interviews that I've ever gotten from a player. His answer was so good. He said it was maybe the biggest win of his life. He was so excited that he ran around. It's a relatable experience. I remember playing my son in basketball. One time I beat him so bad that he started crying and I taunted him, "Go home and cry to your mom, okay?" Needless to say: when he finally beat me, he felt like he had just won the world championship. He was running around and talking trash.

In his first year with the Celtics, Irving played great, but he suffered a knee injury that kept him out of the playoffs. Shockingly, the undermanned Celtics made it all the way to Game 7 of the Eastern Conference Finals before losing to Cleveland.

The future still looked really bright for the 2018–19 season. Irving and Hayward were coming back from their injuries, Tatum had a huge coming out party against LeBron James and the Cavs, and Brown took some big steps as well. There was some concern, though, because Irving still had one year left on his contract and then would become a free agent. At an October preseason event for season-ticket holders at the Garden, Irving uttered the one sentence that soothed Celtics fans across New England: "If you guys will have me back, I plan on re-signing here next summer." Like everyone else, I took the man at his word: this was a done deal. Or so we thought.

Year Two with Irving didn't go as planned. Hayward had a tough time getting back to his former self, and the team struggled with championship expectations. Plus, everyone was walking on eggshells. Although Irving had pledged to re-sign, it wouldn't be a done deal until pen was put to paper after the season. From where I sat, there was just too much ass kissing with Irving. He could do whatever he wanted to, and that doesn't formulate well for a team. For example, we were at a gala before the season. All the players were there and mixed with sponsors and fans.

Irving actually had security around him. Nobody could talk to him or ask for autographs. It was clear that the team was giving too much power to one person. It was like the ball-signing incident all over again.

From there, the ball started rolling downhill. Guys in any pro sports know that great players are going to be treated differently, but it's not supposed to be to the detriment of the team. When your best players buy in, everybody else becomes comfortable. All I have to do is look back to our championship teams. One of the things that made me a valuable piece was that I was the perfect complimentary player. Before Bird came to town, I was the man, the high draft pick, scoring about 20 points a night. But as soon as we all saw how special Bird was, I could give up the reins and let him be him. That was a sacrifice I made for the team. Now in a big game, I could take over, control things, score, and defend like in Game 7 of '84.

Even 24 years later when Kevin Garnett and Ray Allen joined Paul Pierce, Doc Rivers told them that they were going to be the most important players on the team and had to act that way. Garnett became Doc's lieutenant, his godfather, and played that role perfectly. It didn't work that way with Irving. It kills me to think of what could have been because he's so talented and such a smart dude, but he just never bought in.

It was clear that his impending free agency was on everyone's mind. The security at the gala had to come from the top. Ainge's priority was making Irving as comfortable as he could. Did Ainge go overboard? Yes, but you're going to do that with your best player. But it allowed Irving to abuse his power, and it poisoned the team. And remember he was supposed to be the example with impressionable young guys like Brown (22 years old) and Tatum (20). When I'm asked who reminds me of Irving personality-wise, the guy I come up with is Quintin Dailey. He wasn't at Irving's talent level, but Q was a hell of a player. A star at the University of San Francisco and a high draft pick (seventh by the Bulls), he was forced out of Chicago when some guy named Michael Jordan came to town.

We played together with the Los Angeles Clippers. One day we were at practice, and he had his shirt on backward. I asked him why, and he said, "Because it fucks with people." Now how asinine can you be? But he stuck with it. That's all you need to know about Q. He was a great player who could shoot the lights out, but his attitude drove him out of the league.

In my opinion, Irving blew it in Boston. The most money he could get was from the Celtics. The best situation was right where he was, playing for a coach in Brad Stevens, who 100 percent believed in him, and with great teammates. But none of that was important to him. So he went to where he wanted to be: Brooklyn. And a buddy of mine saw it before I did.

Jim Chones played 10 years in the ABA and NBA mostly with Cleveland, where he now is the team's radio analyst. During the 2018–19 season, he told me Irving was leaving. This wasn't on any inside information, but after covering him with the Cavs, he just felt it. I thought Chones was crazy, but I was so emotionally invested in it that it blinded me.

Even until the end, I thought between the money and the team, Irving was going to stay. It turns out, of course, I was wrong. What really pissed me off is that not only did he sign with the Nets, but the very next day, a commercial came out with him on the Brooklyn Bridge. The next day! It was like when you're in grade school and go in for the last day. All you're thinking about is: "How quick can I get out of this bitch?"

Looking back, we heard things about Irving and how he'd leave town after practice and go to New York. Maybe the signs were there, and we all missed them. I'll just say this about Irving in Brooklyn: be careful what you ask for.

CHAPTER 26
WELCOME
TO THE BUBBLE

The year of 2020, of course, was the year of COVID-19. The world as everyone knew it was turned upside down. We were in Milwaukee when word came down that we were heading home and the NBA season was being suspended. Truth be told, we didn't think that it would start up again. But we didn't know about the bubble.

Commissioner Adam Silver was convinced that the league could finish the season. Everyone would be confined to a campus in Orlando with frequent testing and games all day for about two months. When the idea first came about, I didn't think there was any way it could work. But let me tell you something: whoever came up with the whole bubble idea should be working with congress on fixing the economy. It was magnificent, a total game-changer.

The NBA showed all sports teams how to do it. Silver picked the right place in Orlando, but this was really a story of commitment. Players, coaches, and everyone else realized they would be gone from their families and friends for two months. I mean, you're talking about a bunch of mostly 20-somethings with all kinds of money, and most of them aren't married. Get what I'm saying? I ask myself, *What the hell did they shoot these guys with?* Maybe it was tranquilizers because the overwhelming majority of guys behaved.

Sure, some guys left campus, but the only player we heard about having…well, extracurricular activities…was Rockets forward Danuel House Jr. Out of 18 teams, 270 players, that's incredible. I'll tell you right now, there's no way this confinement would have worked in the '80s. No way in hell. This thing had so many moving parts. It reminds me of when I was younger and was into building model airplanes. I'd put together the frame and the wings, and that was about it; I didn't drop in the pilot, put on the wheels, or any of that. Again, too many moving parts and not enough patience. And that was just with one person!

These players wanted to finish the season and crown a champion: they'd already been paid for most of the season, so it wasn't about money.

That's why I laugh when people try to tarnish the Los Angeles Lakers' title. All of the teams were forced to travel a path that nobody ever had. What looked like surefire failure provided some great basketball, a good schedule, and a worthy champion. (And yes, it hurts to give the Lakers any credit.)

* * *

The 2020 season also represented the end of the line for Gordon Hayward in Boston. He came in with great fanfare, but things never worked out for Hayward and the Boston Celtics. Every year it was something. Five minutes into his Celtics career, he dislocated his ankle and missed the rest of the season.

In his second year, he returned to the starting lineup, but he wasn't ready physically or mentally and struggled before returning to the bench. His relationship with his coach at Butler, Brad Stevens, seemed to create friction with Kyrie Irving and some of the other guys. As is the case in life, it was all about timing. When he first came to Boston, he was going to be the No. 2 option to Irving. Once he suffered that injury, Hayward never recovered that position of value. By the time he came back, Jaylen Brown has passed him, as did Jayson Tatum.

For the team it was a good thing, as the young guys' growth was accelerated out of necessity. They were put on a faster learning curve. Had Hayward stayed in the lineup, their opportunities wouldn't have been as many. Good for the team but hard on him. When he came here, he was great player who could defend, facilitate, shoot. He had a lot of clubs in the bag. Because of the injury, he never regained his footing, so to speak. Given my experience with my knee in 1985, I could definitely relate.

A lot of so-called experts thought it was a mistake for Stevens to force Hayward in the starting lineup that first year back. I disagree. This guy was a great player. Eventually, he was going to have to jump in the water and see what he had. And there were moments; in our two games against the Minnesota Timberwolves, he went for 30 and 35 points. Plus, the guy was making more than $30 million. He wasn't brought here to be the sixth man. Eventually, in almost everyone's career, they evolve into something else. A great example was Kareem Abdul-Jabbar. The guy is the all-time leading scorer in NBA history. But when the Los Angeles Lakers got Magic Johnson, Abdul-Jabbar's role changed. It's not always easy. Even as Bird got older, Reggie Lewis developed into a great player, and his role was different. Before that there was a point when Kevin McHale became just unstoppable, and Bird had to adjust.

I do think that Stevens maybe could have put Hayward in the role of initiating the offense. Too often he looked like he was in a track meet, just running down the court and back. His best role could have been bringing the ball up court like Denver Nuggets big man Nikola Jokic. I hate the word because it's so millennial, but it would have given Hayward more *touches*.

Hayward actually played well in the 2019–20 season, resembling the player Danny Ainge thought he was signing when he gave him that max contract. But then he got hurt again. First, it was a broken hand trying to steal the ball against the San Antonio Spurs. That cost him 13 games. Then he had inflammation in his ankle. The last injury really hurt him and the team. It was toward the end of Game 1 of the bubble play-offs. The Celtics were wrapping up an easy win against the Philadelphia 76ers, and Hayward sprained his ankle. He'd miss the next 12 games before returning for Game 3 of the Eastern Conference Finals against the Miami Heat. Hayward provided a temporary boost but clearly wasn't himself, and the Heat won in six games.

Celtics fans were frustrated because the team was paying him $34 million a year, and it was just a series of starts and stops. But I always felt that was unfair. These were all fluke injuries that weren't at all his fault. Then during Heat series, his wife Robyn Hayward gave birth to their fourth child. The original plan was for him to fly home to welcome his son. If he did so, he'd have to self-quarantine upon returning to Orlando, surely missing another game or two.

Hayward showed me something, some real sacrifice, by staying in the bubble, trying to make up for the time he missed and skipping the birth. When he didn't play well, I thought it was unfair to criticize him, but everyone did.

Little did the Celtics know the drama was only getting started. Hayward's contract had a player option for the fourth year at $34 million. Given the pandemic it seemed like a no-brainer that he'd opt into the contract; it appeared there was no way he'd get that money on the open market. The deadline for his decision was the day before the NBA draft. Both sides agreed to push it back 48 hours. The plan was that he'd opt out, and Ainge would try to work out a sign-and-trade, giving Hayward his money and a fresh start and the Celtics a player or two in return.

Once he officially opted out of the contract, everyone thought he was heading to the Indiana Pacers. Hayward is from Indiana and had already enrolled his kids in school there. According to reports, the Pacers offered center Myles Turner and sharpshooter Doug McDermott.

Ainge reportedly wanted Turner and either Victor Oladipo or T.J. Warren. While the two sides wrangled, Michael Jordan swooped in with a four-year, $120 million deal. Hayward signed, and that was that. Boston figured it would get some compensation, as the Charlotte Hornets didn't have sufficient room under the salary cap. But Charlotte general manager (and former Lakers forward) Mitch Kupchak decided to stretch out the contract of Nicolas Batum, creating cap room for the deal, and the Celtics received nothing. Ainge quickly pivoted to sign veteran center Tristan Thompson, but the damage was done.

The fact is that Hayward got more than a fair shot. The team was very cautious and let him play when he felt he was ready. I don't think they babied him. They let him go at his pace, which is what any player would want. Hayward was gone, and all kinds of venom was pointed at him for taking the money. Let me tell you something: he got offered $120 *million*! If he turned that money down, I would have slapped the taste out of his mouth.

* * *

The other big story of 2020 besides the coronavirus was the Black Lives Matter movement. Racism, of course, has been around longer than anyone can remember. But when a man named George Floyd died from a Minneapolis police officer kneeling on his neck, it ignited a fire that hadn't been seen across this country in many years. Although Floyd died in May, the bodycam video surfaced in August.

The NBA was early in the bubble playoffs, but the Milwaukee Bucks decided they didn't want to play against the Orlando Magic as a result of the Jacob Blake shooting. This situation—and really the whole bubble—showed a huge difference between Commissioner Silver and his predecessor, David Stern. Don't get me wrong, Commissioner Stern did an enormous amount in building the NBA, but he was a dictator. He set the rules, and everyone had to follow—whether it was dress codes or changing the basketballs themselves. There was no question of who was in charge.

Silver has much more of a partnership with the players. He's done whatever he can to allow freedom of expression. When the players showed up in Orlando, many of them wanted to wear social messages on the backs of their uniforms. In my day we wore whatever the league gave us and didn't ask questions. Silver worked with them to come up with a plan, and that was that. He also had "Black Lives Matter" painted on the court. And keep in mind this was all happening during a season that saw Houston Rockets general manager Daryl Morey enrage China with a tweet, Stern and Kobe Bryant pass away in January, and COVID-19.

So when the Bucks decided they weren't playing, it was just the latest lightning bolt to the league. But Silver understood their outrage and canceled the rest of the games for a couple of days until he was able to work something out with the players. The boycott is another thing that wouldn't have happened in the 1980s. We just weren't strong enough financially. Nowadays guys could sit out a full season and still be set for life. That's what happens when the average salary is close to $8 million. Plus, what players make from their teams is just a fraction of their income. I mean, Steph Curry makes more than $20 million a year from Under Armor. James Harden's deal with Adidas is for 13 years and more than $200 million. Shit, the best endorsement deal I ever got was $125,000 from Pony.

Racism certainly came to the forefront in 2020, but as someone who grew up near a segregated beach in Kinston, North Carolina, I can tell you it's been around for a long time. It's just that with cell phones and the 24-hour news cycle, now everyone can see it in front of their own eyes. When I came to Boston, I was unaware of the racial problems the city was known for. Boston doesn't have a monopoly on racism—not even close. Back home crazy stuff was routine.

We'd hear about people that all of a sudden went missing. One guy allegedly resisted arrest and got shot eight times. Another guy was shot while he was in handcuffs. When I'd return home from school, I passed this place called Smithfield. Until 1977 they had a billboard saying, "Help fight communism and integration. Join and support the United Klans of America, Inc. KKK welcomes you to Smithfield." And of course, there was a drawing of a klansman riding a horse with a burning cross.

Back in the '70s, with all the Black players on New York, they weren't called the Knickerbockers, but the "N-----bockers." When I was playing for the Los Angeles Clippers, a buddy and I were meeting for lunch. I was driving a nice Volvo and was sitting outside the restaurant in my car, waiting for my guy. Suddenly, I heard someone shouting through a bullhorn, "Put your hands on the dashboard." I had no idea who they were talking to. Then the person shouted, "You in the blue car, put your hands on the dashboard!"

That's when I realized he was talking to me! Apparently, there was a report of a stolen car in the area. As you can imagine, I was more than a little nervous, even though obviously I hadn't done anything wrong. Then he asked for my license. When he saw it, he said, "Cedric Maxwell! Oh my God, yeah, I loved you when you played for the Celtics!"

Now having said all of that, Boston does have its problems like anyplace else. When I first came to town, everyone told me whatever you do: make sure you don't go to South Boston. I was told to stay in places like Roxbury and Dorchester, which were predominantly Black areas.

But now things have changed. South Boston now has a lot of people of color, and many White people came back and moved into the projects in Dorchester and Roxbury. There used to be townhouses there that sold for like $35,000. Now, those homes are going for billions. So yes, things can change. In 2020 I was out on Cape Cod and couldn't believe how many Biden/Harris campaign signs there were right next to Black Lives Matters signs. I'm just very proud of our players and society in general with the changes that have happened.

Whatever racism is still there today pales in comparison to the '50s and '60s. I've spoken with Tom "Satch" Sanders quite a bit about that, and to hear the stories about what he and Bill Russell dealt with is just incredible. When Russell came to Boston, he lived in a town called Reading about 15 miles outside the city. When he was traveling once, he came back, and someone had broken into his house...and defecated on his bed. "Boston is just a hardworking, tough town that loves their sports," Larry Bird told the Undefeated. "I know how Bill Russell was treated when he was there, and it gives you a feeling in your stomach. It makes you want to throw up."

Back in 1990 a rookie named Dee Brown moved into Wellesley, a suburb about 20 minutes outside of Boston. One day he was forced from his car at gunpoint by police and thrown on the ground—only to find out it was a case of mistaken identity. But nobody had it worse than Russell. As the best player on the best team in the NBA, he was an easy target. Fortunately, he had the perfect champion in Red Auerbach, who always had his back. The relationship between Auerbach and Russell was remarkable, especially for the times. The Celtics knew what they had in Russell, a guy who was so competitive that he used to throw up before nearly every game. Once when he hadn't puked, Auerbach looked at him and said, "Hey, go throw up so we can get this thing started."

Russell was born in Louisiana, then went to the University of San Francisco, where he won two NCAA championships. He also won a gold medal at the Olympics. When he joined the Celtics, he instantly became the best player on the team, a guy who was just obsessed with winning. He didn't care about scoring points. It was always: "What can I do to help the team?"

Maybe more important than his skill (and will), Russell allowed himself to be coached. And Auerbach coached him hard. But unlike some guys who'd have their feelings hurt, Russell just took whatever Auerbach dished out. Now Auerbach was always respectful, which was critical because of Russell's enormous pride, but it showed the rest of the guys that if the top player on the team could be coached this way, then nobody else had the right to complain. Russell knew what Auerbach was up to and went along for the good of the team. I could certainly relate. When Bill Fitch was pissed, he wasn't yelling at Bird. He'd go after Robert Parish, Kevin McHale, and myself. I remember Bird missing an assignment on defense, and Fitch screamed...at me!

Russell had really strong beliefs during his career. For example, he never signed autographs. He just didn't get why that was such a big deal to people. He's always been just an ornery guy about some things. Satch told me once he asked Russell to sign an autograph for his mother's birthday or some other occasion. "Satch," Russell responded, "You know

I don't sign autographs." It was just like that. No anger, no animosity, just a matter of fact.

But at least now, he can laugh at himself a little bit. Whenever I see Russell, he has all types of security around him. Obviously, they know me and aren't going to stop me from paying my respects to the man. So I sneak up behind him and poke him in the back, and say, "Excuse me, Mr. Russell, would you sign…" And Russell whips around like he's going to snap someone's head off. Then he sees that it's me and breaks out that awesome smile…and gives me the finger. He did that every season when we saw each other; it's all in good fun. But that's because we're friends.

Not everyone can get away with things like that. When Russell used to do NBA games on CBS, he was working in Game 5 of the 1981 Finals with fellow Hall of Famer Rick Barry and Gary Bender. They showed a shot of Russell celebrating from the 1956 Olympics. Bender asked Barry if he knew who the guy was, and Barry said, "I don't know. It looks like some fool with that watermelon grin."

The camera pulled out to a shot of Russell, and let's just say he wasn't pleased. Oh, and it wasn't even him! They showed another picture which was him, but Russell was steaming. When they showed the last photo, Russell had to tell them it was actually K.C. Jones, not him. Bender added, "Well it looks a lot like you."

The person in the picture was drinking beer; Russell never drank beer. He didn't have much to say the rest of the game. Russell doesn't suffer fools gladly, especially after what he's gone through. Satch talked about how Black players couldn't eat in certain places in the South and how they'd eat at each other's homes. Think about that: intense competitors like Russell and Wilt Chamberlain eating together because they were being discriminated against. As a kid I saw Russell on stage with Muhammad Ali, Joe Louis, Jim Brown, and others talking about the civil rights movement. Without guys like that, things never would have changed.

Russell is just an amazing guy—not only as a player and a competitor, but also as a thinker. He'd challenge his teammates to be better and wasn't afraid to ask for help. I think that's what made him so good. Take a second and contemplate how many championships he won as a player and coach. Plus, he was a player/coach for three seasons and won two titles. In my second year, when Satch was fired, Dave Cowens took over as player/coach for half a season and he'd be so exhausted from playing that he could barely draw up a play. But Russell did that for three years in a row. In the spring of 2021, Russell was elected into the Hall of Fame again—this time as a coach.

During the recent civil right protests, there was a lot of debate about the national anthem. One question I get asked a lot from my playing days is why I never stood with my teammates for it. Time to set the record straight. It was just nerves. Honestly, standing there, I got all fidgety, started shuffling, and didn't want to be disrespectful and become a distraction. So I'd use that time to run into the locker room, get a drink, use the facilities, and then return to the floor. Unfortunately, my timing wasn't always great. One of my favorite singers, Charlie Wilson of the Gap Band, sang the anthem one time, and I got stuck there watching.

About 10 years ago, a Celtics fan came up to me, and said, "I remember you. You were a Muslim."

That one caught me off guard. I told him I am not Muslim and asked why he thought that. He assumed I was leaving the floor during the anthem as a protest. I had to explain that I'd never do that—not with my father being in the military. As I've often said, don't let the facts get in the way of a good story.

CHAPTER 27

LARRY BIRD
AND THE LEGENDS

There's no question that over the years, the relationship I get asked the most about is between Larry Bird and myself. Well…it's complicated. He contributed to Jackie MacMullan's book, *When the Game Was Ours* and he came after me pretty good. "He got his money and he quit," he said.

When he was asked about that by *The Boston Globe*'s Dan Shaughnessy, he stood by what he wrote. "He did quit on us…You can ask everybody. Everybody was mad at Max in the Finals that year. It was disruptive. You get a chance to win a championship," Bird said. "It was about him not wanting to play more, more than anything else. I like Max. But he quit. I've said it to him a million times. He quit on us. He says I quit on him, but that trade—I didn't have nothing to do with it."

What hurt me the most was people questioning my competitiveness, my heart. Of course, I heard what Bird said, but it's always been secondhand. To hear him use those words was a slap in the face, being I was first guy he played with. For him to think or insinuate I quit or wasn't trying, well, that did hurt. I guess it was partly my fault because of my attitude. I just was acting happy all the time and then I got hurt. But I was still the same person even when I couldn't come back and play. I think that pissed Bird off. There wasn't a lack of effort, but there was a lack of communication and understanding between us regarding my situation.

Let me say this: Bird and I have never really had an argument. And I've never had a disparaging remark about him. Some people thought when I said Kevin Garnett is the best all-around player the Celtics have ever had that it was a shot at Bird, but that couldn't be further from the truth. KG wasn't as good as Bird offensively, but he wasn't far off. He wasn't as great as Bill Russell on the defensive end, but he wasn't far off there either. That's all I was saying.

So it was important for me to have a conversation with Bird. I've had a great relationship with nearly all the guys I ever played with.

When Bird and then Robert Parish and Kevin McHale came to town, I changed more than anyone on that team because Bill Fitch wanted me to take another role. On offense I went from the first option to fourth or fifth. So yes, after hearing about my lack of desire, it bothered me.

I called Bird in October of 2020. We'd never really had a long one-on-one conversation. There were a couple of times a bunch of us went to his house for Christmas, but that was about it. I used to go out to dinner with M.L. Carr, Parish, and Danny Ainge, but Bird didn't come along. He was a beer drinker, and his guys were Rick Robey and Quinn Buckner—though Buckner and I were good friends, too—but we came from different worlds. That makes it hard to really build an off-the-court relationship.

When Bird returned my call, I saw the Indiana number and was pleasantly surprised. It was mostly light shop talk. We discussed things like the zone defense the Miami Heat was employing to give the Boston Celtics trouble during the bubble playoffs. But there was not a lot more than that. There was nothing that made the Earth move or anything like that. I've always felt like it's important to maintain relationships. Listen: Bird was the greatest player I ever played with. He and I were one of the best forward combinations in the NBA. We weren't the best of friends, but we were basketball friends; that's the best way I can put it. We loved the game, and our competitive juices made each other better.

I couldn't help but admire how Bird went all out every time he took the court. I've never seen anyone who could play like that all the time. But I despised that at the same time because there were nights when guys like Chief, McHale, and I just didn't have that drive. It certainly wasn't a surprise to see Bird break down toward the end of his career. Bird was so competitive with Magic Johnson that he 100 percent dedicated himself to become better physically. I remember him running a 5K before a game once. That's what made him Bird. He was always trying to refine his game and he wanted his teammates to be all in like he was.

A lot of people have talked about how Larry Bird and I got along, but he was truly one of the greats—as evidenced by him winning the NBA's MVP award in 1986 for the third consecutive year.

It's strange to think that Bird has actually spent more time with the Indiana Pacers organization—as coach, general manager, president, and consultant—than he did with the Celtics. Obviously, he's a legend in Boston, but I don't think former owner Don Gaston was necessarily his favorite, and once Rick Pitino came to town, that might have been the last straw for Bird.

* * *

The Boston Celtics were in New Orleans in January of 2020, getting ready to take on the Pelicans. I had taken a nap and then woke up to a text that Kobe Bryant had been killed in a helicopter crash. It was like someone taking your Christmas presents away. The world was in slow motion. Bryant and his daughter Gianna both perished. There were a few other families onboard, as they were heading to a basketball tournament. Bryant was just 41 years old and a couple of seasons into his retirement. Obviously, you never expect something like this—and certainly not to him.

Then my mind went to the personal side, the dad side. That probably hurt me more than anything else, thinking about having my daughters with me on the helicopter. When I hear stories about how he tried to protect her, how he grabbed her, that probably resonated with me more than anything.

I knew Bryant personally. It's not like I had his number or anything like that, but he'd always speak to me when we saw each other. Even today, I still have a picture up in my townhouse of the two of us.

In our little Celtics circle, we didn't know if we were going to play the game, which sure didn't seem important at the time. I was on the bus, talking to Jaylen Brown, and he told me how sad he was that he'd never met Bryant. The previous summer Jayson Tatum had worked out with Bryant. He was learning the Mamba Mentality and honing his footwork. That mentality was something. To honor him our home crowd even started chanting "M-V-P" for him. Boston Celtics fans have always appreciated greatness.

Because of who Bryant was and the circumstances of how he passed, I can't say I was surprised at the reaction. But the way it affected people did take me aback. We were in Los Angeles the day before his memorial service and played a great game, losing to the Lakers by two. Fittingly, Tatum erupted for 41 points.

I wasn't sure if I was going to be able to go to the service. Tickets were extremely limited, as everyone wanted to go. But since the Celtics were in L.A., I ended up with a ticket, and on the way there, the streets were just lined with fans, paying their respects. I'm not sure how, but I ended up with great seats. Bill Russell was in front of me, James Harden was with Russell Westbrook next to him, and Kyrie Irving and Steph Curry were to my left. There were all kinds of celebrities from Jay-Z and Beyonce to Queen Latifah and Samuel L. Jackson. When they introduced Michael Jordan, I realized he was sitting eight seats away. I remember passing him on the way out and complimenting him on his speech, saying, "Not bad for a country boy."

When it comes to great opponents in Celtics history, Bryant was definitely in the mix. So was LeBron James. As he showed in Game 6 of 2012—going for 45 points, 15 rebounds, and five assists—he is a grown-ass man.

I would rank James in my all-time top five, maybe the top three of players to ever play the game. The 2020 championship really elevated him to a new level. He definitely has his haters, but I like him as much as a basketball player as for what he does with social issues. Jordan didn't want to be in the limelight that way; he just wanted to play basketball, which is okay. James has stepped up in the social arena. Whether you're a fan of his or not, I always ask this: when was the last time you've heard anything bad he's done? And on the court, he's a facilitator, a scorer, and a defender—and tremendous at all of it. Nobody has ever come into the league with so much pressure.

For him to win his fourth title at the age of 35—in a bubble—as the best player on the court was just incredible. The guy has been the Finals MVP on three different teams. I asked Kendrick Perkins and some other folks about how James has been able to be so dominant even after coming into the league at 18 years old. Apparently, James spends $1 million on his body per year. He gets his rest, doesn't party, and sits in a tub of ice after each game to get rid of some of that trauma to his body. He's got a trainer who stretches him out before each game.

I've been saying for the last couple of years that Father Time is going to catch up to him and knock him out. But you know what? He keeps going. He may not be quite as explosive as he once was, but he's still unstoppable. People ask me if I can still dunk at my age. I probably could. The getting up part wouldn't be the issue; the coming down would be. That would be like a car crash on my knees and back. But James just keeps getting it done.

James is a man among boys. Celtics fans will always remember Tatum's rookie year, when he posterized him with a massive dunk in Game 7 of the Eastern Conference Finals. It was certainly a great moment, but what people tend to forget is that James played 46 minutes in the previous game (when the Cleveland Cavaliers were down 3–2) and put up 46 points, 11 rebounds, and nine assists. In that Game 7? Sure, he got dunked on, but the King played *the entire game* with 35 points, 15 rebounds, and nine dimes. After the game I wanted to cut him and see if he actually had any blood in his body.

CHAPTER 28

ON THE COURT,
OFF THE COURT,
AND BEHIND THE MIC

One of the most enjoyable parts of my game was trash talking. It's the way the game should be played. Basketball is a psychological game. When you get into a guy's head, he's done. I always went up against guys who were more physically talented than I was, but I always knew that they couldn't beat me because I was smarter. The key to trash talking is to go right up to that line and get to the guy's intellect, right to his brain. Do that, get inside his head, and he'll forget his assignments because he's so pissed at you. One of my favorite lines was asking my opponent, "Your coach doesn't like you?" He'd look at me, not sure what I was talking about. That's when I'd tell him: "because he's making you guard me! Are you on some type of punishment?"

Growing up in Kinston, North Carolina, you had to be able to talk shit to your opponents. We'd play at the Holloway Center, where the court was pretty small, so the games would be three on three. From a skills standpoint, that was great because everyone would have to handle the ball, and the games were intense. You'd hear the noise the entire time. Guys would be talking junk, whether they were playing or waiting for the next game. And it wasn't just basketball either. People would be up in your face if you were playing Ping-Pong, bumper pool, hell—even swimming.

If you thought I'd get a break from trash talking when I got home, you are wrong. You've got to remember my mother was a baller. She played at North Carolina Central. When I was 13, we'd go at each other in the backyard, and she wasn't afraid to let me know she could take me. Bessie Maxwell took things to a whole new level. When my father went to Vietnam, I was basically Mom's best friend. So we'd play cards. She even taught me how to play canasta. Yeah, she taught me how to play so she could talk trash the entire game. We'd play Sorry, Monopoly, etc., and it was always loud.

I hate that trash talking isn't a big part of the NBA anymore. I don't know how I'd last in the league. A few years ago, Milwaukee

Bucks star Giannis Antetokounmpo wound up and did this left-handed hook dunk over Jaylen Brown. The "Greek Freak" looked at Brown, raised up his muscles, and just flexed. The refs gave him a technical foul. Man, if I'd done that dunk, I'd have been doing the moonwalk across the floor. They would have thought something was wrong with me, like I was having a seizure. To me that's part of the game, and when I played, it was.

In 1981 we took on the Chicago Bulls in the second round of the playoffs. Ricky Sobers was their starting shooting guard and he was a pretty good player, scoring about 14 points per game. We were cruising along, up 3–0 in the series. Apparently, nobody told Sobers. He started chirping about how we're going to be playing next week, meaning that they'd win a couple of games off us. I told him, "If you're playing next week, it'll be by yourself, and it won't be an NBA game because we're going to the conference finals!" We ended up sweeping the series. I didn't hear much from Sobers after that one.

I could effectively trash talk against good players like Sobers or Hall of Famers like James Worthy. I flashed the choke sign to him while he was shooting free throws and, of course, told him, "You can't fucking guard me."

It's no wonder that Worthy said his toughest matchup was me. "That damn Cedric Maxwell. Cornbread? Man, I used to dream about playing him," he said. "I'd have damn nightmares planning for the matchup." Yup, I was in his head before we even played the game.

If you wore purple and gold, you felt my wrath and you didn't have to be an All-Star or Hall of Famer. At the end of the Los Angeles Lakers bench was a player named Larry Spriggs, and he was talking all kinds of shit to me. It was time for me to put them in his place. There was a dead ball, and I was getting ready to take it out of bounds. I was like three feet away from Pat Riley. The ref handed me the ball, and I said, "Hold up for a minute."

Riley and the ref both look at me like, *What are you talking about?* I said to Riley: "Do me a favor: put one of those motherfuckers on the bench into the game."

Considered a master of the mind game, Riley obliged and put Spriggs in to guard me. Big mistake. Spriggs came in, and oh my God, I tore him a new asshole, just destroyed him. In case he didn't get the point, I told him, "Hey, real players are right here on the court, playing. And you've got a free seat. Maybe you'll just shut the fuck up. Okay? How about doing that?"

Riley just stood there, fuming. He got his ass toasted and he knew it.

The one thing about talking junk, though, is that you'd better back it up. That's why Game 7 in 1984 against L.A. was the highlight of my career—even more than winning the Finals MVP in 1981. I said, "Don't worry about this. You bitches climb on my back, and I'm going to carry you hoes to the championship." That put me on edge that much more because I knew if I didn't back it up, I'd be the buffoon. Yes, there are levels of shit talking, and I happen to be on the top rung.

* * *

As a professional athlete, I spent more time with my teammates than with my own family. Between training camp, the regular season, and the playoffs, I'd see Larry Bird, Robert Parish, Kevin McHale, and the guys nonstop from September into June. And when I say nonstop, I mean *every* day. Now that I'm broadcasting for the team, it's not quite the same, but I see my play-by-play partner Sean Grande almost as frequently. To make a successful radio team, there needs to be a certain chemistry. I feel like I can work with just about anyone, but over time Grande and I have really found our groove.

I broadcast a Boston Celtics game in 2007. I have truly enjoyed my second basketball career.

It's funny, but the first time we actually worked together was by accident. It was December 23, 1997, and my regular partner, Howard David, who also did college football games, was stuck in a snowstorm. They called Grande, and we did our first Boston Celtics game together with no advanced warning. The broadcast was fine, and Grande was able to hook up a gig doing Minnesota Timberwolves games the next season. Eventually, he came to Boston, working as the program director at WEEI. By 2001 he replaced David and was my new cohort on Celtics games. The station's general manager worked at the same station where I did some stuff at in North Carolina. So we knew each other. He asked me to reach out to Grande. We had a good talk, and I said we'd love to have you, and that was that.

Grande knew his stuff, but at that time, hoops wasn't his passion. "I was an NBA fan, but basketball was my No. 4 sport, which comes from where I grew up. If you're a big hockey fan, it's hard to be a hard-core basketball fan because you sort of have to choose," he said. "I knew a lot about Max, but I wasn't a Celtics fan. Put it that way. I knew about Game 7, 'Climb on my back,' but I hated Bird, hated McHale. I didn't hate Max because he didn't stay after 1985."

We're a bit of an odd couple. "He's the African American guy in North Carolina who likes James Taylor. And I'm the younger guy from New York City who likes Jay-Z," Grande said.

Grande is a 5'8" New York City-bred White guy. He has that edge to him; I'm a 6'8" laid-back brother from North Carolina. I'm 17 years older than him, and it can show, like when he's into rap music before the game, and I'm asking for Nat King Cole singing "Chestnuts roasting on an open fire." Back during his high school days, Grande was known as DJ White. (Yes, I'm serious.) He was all about the rap.

Over the years we've come to appreciate each other in different ways. I was one of the people who spent a lot of time around him when he was going through his divorce and the typical ups and downs of life. It's like the yin and the yang. We come at things from different perspectives. Grande once put it perfectly. He said, "I haven't been there before. You have. You've been a Finals MVP, a two-time champion, you can't get any bigger than that. That's why I do all the other sports. You're on the plateau; where else are you going to go?"

Our different experiences make us a good team. We don't agree on everything, so it stays interesting. "I realized something we didn't work on was sort of arguing about things," Grande said. "We would argue about, say, Michael Jordan coming back. He hated that Jordan had joined back with Washington. I loved it because I thought: one, he's still one of the better players in the league, so he deserves to be playing. Two, from the selfish standpoint, we'd get [to do] the games."

It's been quite the ride with Grande. "The things we've been through in our lives—in my case, a divorce, a second marriage, a child custody case…and he's become a grandfather," he said. "These people in front of you, I don't think that anyone could have imagined that with his background in life, my background in life, we would have become what we've become. That doesn't happen if we didn't love each other."

* * *

One thing I know is how blessed I've been and I've done my best to really enjoy life to its fullest. My NBA career was more than I could have ever hoped for after growing up in a small town. Two championships, Finals MVP, my number retired—it's been one hell of a ride. Along the way, there have been some pretty crazy times. I like to call them Max being Max.

I loved baseball as a kid. We used to go to minor league games all the time. You never knew who you might see. I remember watching a guy named Dock Ellis. He was one of the few Black pitchers of his generation who made it to the big leagues. Ellis won nearly 150 games and is best known for two things: starting for the National League in the 1971 All-Star Game (where he gave up a titanic home run to Reggie Jackson at Tigers Stadium) and, of course, throwing a no-hitter…which he did while on LSD! Seeing this guy in Kinston, North Carolina, was cool. Not only did he pitch, but he also played basketball at the local youth center.

There, of course, have been times where I'm the one who gets recognized. We were in New York once, and I was leaving my hotel for Madison Square Garden to broadcast the game. As I passed by the Four Seasons, I saw actor Mark Curry from *Hangin' with Mr. Cooper*, a great TV show from the '90s. A small group of fans had cornered him and asked for his autograph, which he provided. He looked up for a second and spotted me. Curry left the crowd, and said, "Oh my God, man, I was a huge fan when I was in high school. I wore your number." At the time I didn't think it was a big deal, but thinking back on it, that was pretty exciting to have that type of impact on a famous actor.

There have been times where my Forrest Gump-like existence of being at the right place during major historical events has been downright scary. I was standing at the finish line of the 2013 Boston Marathon, watching the runners as I'd done several times before. It was a long day, and I was getting tired. So I walked down the street to Nordstrom Rack and bought a pair of shoes. Suddenly, I heard an explosion and then a second. I had no idea what was going on. So I left the store. Next thing I knew there were like 10,000 people storming at me. So I ran back into Nordstrom because I thought someone was chasing them. I eventually got out onto the street, and a police officer told me to go home because there was an explosion. I asked if anyone was hurt, and he said yes and that it was bad. Eventually, I got back home, turned on the TV, and realized that I'd been standing exactly where the bombs went off.

When one of my college teammates, a guy named Lew Massey, died in 2014, it really hit me. We were the one-two punch that led our team to the Final Four. I showed up at his funeral and was a bit better known than most of the folks there. We all started talking about the good old days and the "M&M Boys." I began to speak, and Lew's wife came up to me and said, "No, no, no. I don't want you to talk." I didn't understand what the problem was. "No," she said, "I don't want you to talk now. You're in the program! You're talking at the funeral." Sure enough, I read the program, and there I was. Good thing I didn't use up all my material.

And then there was the memorial service for my good friend, Dennis Johnson. D.J. and I were extremely close, and losing him in 2007 was just devastating. Doc Rivers and a couple of other guys and I flew out for it. When we got there, D.J.'s wife, Donna, asked if I'd be able to say a few words, which was such an honor. Apparently, she was debating between myself and Bill Walton, who was also close with him. I got up, talked about what D.J. meant to me, and how I loved him. Then I had to say one more thing to try and lift people's spirits with a joke. I said, "I'm sure Dennis is looking down on us, saying, 'Damn, I'm sure happy Max is speaking and not Bill Walton!'"

Ain't that the truth. If Walton spoke, it would have been a three-hour service. "I absolutely loved Dennis. He was the quintessential Celtic," he would've said. "It reminds me of a Grateful Dead concert."

As a Boston Celtics broadcaster, I fly on the charters with the team—unlike how we used to fly commercial during my playing day. Anyway, we were flying somewhere over Cincinnati. Sean Grande wasn't on the trip because he had some other obligation. So Jon Wallach filled in. Soon, he'd be sorry he did. We landed on a remote runway, and all of these police cars came speeding up to us. I was wondering, *What the hell happened?*

The pilot came over the loudspeaker and said he didn't want to let us know, but there was a bomb threat called in on the plane. They thought it was a fake, so didn't want to alarm us. If he thought it was fake, why were 85 trucks coming up here? Why were there 20 FBI agents taking us to a remote area? In the end there was no harm, but maybe they should have let us know.

We also had some great times in the sky. We had little fun with our Hall of Fame radio broadcaster, Johnny Most, who was a legendary smoker. "We were heading out on the West Coast, and Cedric and Danny Ainge tied his shoelaces together," Robert Parish said. "Then they got his cigarette tips and replaced them with those exploding cigarettes. And Johnny lights one up, and it goes, 'Pop!' Johnny was like, 'What the fuck?' Then he lit up another one, and it happened again. He didn't realize his laces were tied together and he was falling all over everyone. It was one of the funniest moments of my playing career, and nobody said a word about who did it."

* * *

You've probably heard the old saying that nothing good happens when you go out after midnight. Well, a few years ago in Indianapolis, I proved that to be true. Some of the guys on the team were going to a strip club during the exhibition season. Paul Pierce was the leader, and a few of his teammates were trying to talk me into joining them. At first, I resisted. I mean, these are guys who were in their 20s and I was well past that stage in my life, but I agreed to meet them there.

I got to the club at like 12:30 or 1:00 AM, which was late, considering that Rick Pitino for some reason had a curfew for the guys, but that's a whole other story. The boys decided to take off so they wouldn't get in trouble for being out late, but I decided to stay for a bit since I'd just gotten there. About half an hour later, I decide to go back to the hotel and called a cab. It was pouring outside, and when I got in the back of the taxi, I felt like something was just off. It had a peculiar smell. (Remember, these were the days before Lyft or Uber, so smelly old cabs were kind of normal.)

When I returned the lobby was empty except for one other gentleman, and we shared the elevator to our rooms. On the way up, I couldn't shake this smell. I didn't know if it was him or me. I couldn't identify it. He got off at his floor, and I eventually reached mine. Something just didn't seem right. I reached to the back of the trench coat I was wearing and I felt something. I pulled my hand forward and saw that it was brown. Still, I couldn't process what it was—until I brought my hand to my nose and took a whiff. I ran to my room and took my coat off in the bathroom, and there it was: there was shit all over the back of my coat!

I replayed the events in my head to try and piece together what the hell had happened. It couldn't have been in the club. I realized I must have sat in feces during my taxi ride. When we returned from the trip, I still had the receipt from the ride and called the company to tell them someone had taken a dump in their cab. The guy I spoke with just kept saying, "No sir."

I said, "I sat in shit in your cab!"

Finally, he said he'd check the taxi's log (no pun intended) to try and track down the driver and car. I gave him all the details of when I was picked up and where I was dropped off. He called me back and said, yes, there was shit in the cab and that they'd suspended the driver. He then asked if I wanted them to clean my coat. Did he think I actually kept the coat and flew back to Boston with shit on it?

. My crazy stories extend to stories of misidentification as well. When I first moved back to Boston, Renee and I were divorced, and I was dating a woman named Valerie Diamond. M.L. Carr's wife, Sylvia, was friends with Renee and Valerie. One Saturday morning Valerie called me, asking, "Are you okay? Are you sure? Would you tell me?"

She explained that Renee had told Sylvia I was in jail for not paying child support. I called my daughter Morgan, and she'd heard the same thing. That was enough for me. I needed to call Renee's ass to straighten this out. She told me that it was on the radio that I was in jail. This didn't make any sense; I always paid the support on time. I called the radio station to find out what was going on. Turns out it was *Vernon* Maxwell, the former NBA guard, who had been arrested on a weapons charge. You'd think that when you were married to someone and had children with that person, you might call that person if you heard something was wrong. But I guess you'd be wrong.

Misidentification got me in trouble again. Like a lot of NBA players, I've got big feet: size 15. I'll never forget the time I inserted that big-ass foot, right in my mouth—and in front of one of my idols. I was at a celebrity event in Las Vegas. It was a softball game, and there was some gambling as well. There were a lot of guys there, including Julius Erving. I had heard his wife, Turquoise, was having a baby. So naturally, I asked Mrs. Erving when she was expecting. Turquoise then explained that they'd already had the baby. I'm 6'8" but felt about two feet tall! I mean, where do you go from there? Suffice it to say, I've never asked a woman—any woman—if she's pregnant ever since that night.

Whether they're stars like Dr. J or just ordinary players, a lot of players have summer basketball camps to teach kids how to play the game. Danny Ainge had one in Utah and asked me to come out to give him a hand. Since he's one of my closest friends, I, of course, made the trip. I know there's not a lot of brothers in that part of the country, but I was not ready for what happened next. "We're out before my camp starts, and I take him to the middle of nowhere, and we're driving along this dirt road in a pickup truck," Ainge said. "We stop and go for a beautiful walk along the river way out in the mountains of Utah, and I'm a few steps ahead of him. We see a pickup truck come by, and Max notices the guns in the back window of the truck. All I hear is Max yelling at the top of his lungs, 'I'm with Ainge! I'm with Ainge!' I sprinted back to him. He thought we were heading into some trouble."

* * *

I'll bet you didn't know that I could have been Oprah Winfrey's BFF. About 20 years ago, I was at this tennis and golf event for *Black Enterprise* magazine. It was a big deal. There were a lot of celebrities and influential African Americans were there. (It was actually the event where I first met Kyrie Irving.) I was hanging out at the pool and looking pretty good (about 60 pounds ago). I looked up, and there was Gayle King, the broadcaster and bestie of Winfrey. We started chatting. It was nothing serious, just a casual conversation.

That night there was a pre-concert reception. I was all "Max-ed" out, very dapper. King stopped for a few minutes, told me I cleaned up pretty well, and then moved on to mingle with some other folks. In fact, this young woman—probably in her 20s—came up to me and started talking. King walked up behind me and whispered, "Do you want me to kick her ass?"

When I got home, I wanted to track King down and take her out. I have a friend who makes fancy baskets, so I sent one to her. King thanked me and mentioned that she was coming to Boston to visit her daughter at Harvard. She mentioned that she was staying at the Ritz-Carlton, which was like a block from my house. We went to the Capital Grille for dinner and had some great conversation. It was one of the few times that I actually felt inferior to the person I was sitting with. She was a big deal!

Then we passed the subway system called the MBTA. I was showing her how my daughter was using it to get around the city. Then she got on the train and left. My big chance with King, and I put her on the subway! I must have left *some* impression though. A few years later, we were flying somewhere, and I passed Doc Rivers on the plane. He said he had seen King, and she asked about me.

Not all of my dating experiences ended so well. Back in the day, we used to play exhibitions all over the country. One time we were in Seattle, and I met up with this woman named Carolyn. On this afternoon, she came by the hotel, and, well, we did what adults sometimes do. She was cool. So I told her to go back home, get dressed up, and we'd go out for a nice dinner. All was good…or so I thought.

As soon as she left, my teammate, Eric Fernsten, called me up and said he had tickets to The Rolling Stones concert and asked if I wanted to come. Hell yeah I did! I'd never seen The Stones, and they were playing at the Kingdome with like 200,000 people. I was all pumped up to see the spectacle. I called Carolyn and explained that I couldn't make dinner, I was going to see Mick Jagger. That didn't go well. She said, "Oh, no, you aren't going to come here, fuck me, then do me like that. Uh-uh, you ain't gonna do this shit to me."

Fifteen minutes later, there was a knock on my hotel room door. I had the chain on, and she asked to come in. I knew this wasn't going to be fun, but then she said, "You owe it to me to speak to me."

I took the chain off, and she kicked the door open like she was part of a SWAT team. Keep in mind: she was 5'2", maybe 125 pounds. She screamed, "I'll have to kick your ass for what you did to me!"

I knew I couldn't be in the room with her alone, so I walked out. I didn't grab my wallet, my room key, or anything. I walked down the hall to Fernsten's room, and she's right behind me. She then said quietly, "If I was you, I wouldn't walk too fast. This gun might go off." Carolyn was swearing so much that a sailor would blush.

I got to Fernsten's room, and she followed me right in there. Because Fernsten was there, Carolyn stopped cussing me out for the moment. I told Fernsten that I needed to get my key but didn't have any ID with me and asked if he could go to the front desk and get it for me. The second he got on the elevator, it was back on. Carolyn saw The Rolling Stones tickets on his nightstand. She grabbed them, ripped them in half, and flushed them down the toilet. She told me, "I'm not done with your ass!"

When Fernsten returned, I let him know the tickets were gone. He was like, "We need to call the cops!" I talked him off that ledge and told him I had good news and bad news. The bad news was that the tickets were gone. The good news was that if he went to the show, he could surely scalp tickets and I'd give him the money for them. I was just trying to defuse the situation. Fernsten went to the concert, and I finally made it back to my room. I was exhausted because I was still on East Coast time. It was 10:00 PM, but my body felt like it was 1:00 AM. An hour later I get a call. "Max, are you okay?" It was Bill Fitch.

I told him I was fine and asked what's wrong

"Are you sure you're okay? Two minutes ago, this girl called here and said you raped her!"

I let Fitch know that never happened, and she was 100 percent making it up. Man, was he furious with me over the next couple of days. He scolded the team, "You fucking guys go out and deal with these women!" Of course, he was looking directly at me.

I guess the fortunate part is that if this had happened today, I'd probably be trying to find my way out of jail because we did have sex, but it was consensual. It sure wasn't rape. The postscript to this was our next game was in Vancouver, and who do you think was sitting in the lobby? Yep, it was Carolyn, begging for my forgiveness. That was my Mick Jagger experience, and no, I still haven't seen The Rolling Stones.

CHAPTER 29
PRESIDENTIAL HONORS

I've had a chance to meet a couple of presidents. It's pretty cool to be with the commander in chief. The first was Jimmy Carter. It was my junior year in college, and he was on a campaign stop. We had just got finished as the runner-up in the NIT. When we returned to Charlotte, there were like 5,000 fans at the airport. They took us downtown for a celebration, and there was President Carter. Someone introduced us, and Mr. Carter said, "You know I love me some Cornbread!"

I don't remember why I skipred the White House after we won the title in 1981. But president Ronald Reagan made sure I wasn't forgotten. He said, "Well, Cedric Maxwell put it quite simply last night: 'How could anyone have thought we'd lose? We are the Celtics, you know.' Well, you are the Celtics, and like the original Celtics, the great Irish warriors in olden times, you have fought for and won great victories and great glory." Then Mr. Reagan showed his trademark sense of humor. "Well, yours is a tradition of hard work, of teamwork, of dedication, a tradition of Celtics Pride. But aren't you afraid you might be getting in a rut?"

In 1984 I didn't make the trip because I was exhausted after beating the Los Angeles Lakers in Game 7 and was getting married in a few days.

A few years ago, we were in Milwaukee for a playoff game, and our broadcast position was pretty high up off the court. Before the game I saw a huge crowd gathering around this guy on the floor, but I couldn't see who it was. The guy took a couple of steps, and I realized it's Bill Clinton! Well, you know I had to get down to meet the prez. So I walked down through all the people and introduced myself to him. "Oh yeah, I know you. I used to cheer for you," Clinton said.

That was cool. So I asked if we could get a picture together, which was fine with him. I pulled out my phone and handed it to a guy, asking if he could take the shot. He looked at me 100 percent serious and said

K.C. Jones, Red Auerbach, and Dennis Johnson present President Reagan with an autographed ball in 1984. Though my wedding prevented me from going to the White House that year, I've been fortunate to meet several presidents.

no. I then realized he was in the Secret Service. I found someone else to take the photo.

What happened in 2004 was a case of my impatience getting the best of me. The Democratic National Convention was being held at the Fleet Center (now the Boston Garden), which was fitting, since Massachusetts senator John Kerry was the nominee. I had tickets for one day and went to the festivities. As you can imagine, these things take forever. So at one point, I decided it was getting late and decided to skip the next speaker. No big deal, right? What was I going to miss: some boring keynote speech? Well, it turns out it was a guy you may have heard of. His name is Barack Obama.

Back in 2019 we were in New York, getting ready for a game with the Knicks. I looked down on their bench and spotted a familiar-looking guy. I walked over and said, "How's your brother-in-law doing?"

He responded, "Pretty well...for an ex-president!" The man was Craig Robinson, a former college basketball coach who now works for the Knicks and, yes, is the brother of Michelle Obama. I told him that I still have the ticket from the DNC and hope that one day I can meet President Obama and have him sign it.

Hall of Fame Worthy?

One question people ask me a lot is whether I think I should be in the Basketball Hall of Fame. What you have to remember is that the Hall of Fame isn't for everyone. There are nearly 5,000 guys who have played in the NBA and fewer than 200 are in the Hall of Fame. It is for the elite of the elite. There were times that I was on that level, but I didn't do it on a consistent basis.

The fact is that I was never an All-Star, so I think I'm just on the outside looking in. Did I have moments that were All-Star worthy? You bet. When I think back on being the NBA Finals MVP in 1981, the floor was full of future Hall of Famers (Larry Bird, Kevin McHale, Robert Parish, and Nate "Tiny" Archibald for us and Moses Malone, Calvin Murphy, and Rudy Tomjanovich for the Houston Rockets), and I swell up with pride. It's the same thing looking back at Game 7 in 1984, when I was the best player on the floor with Bird, McHale, Parish, and Dennis Johnson on my team and Magic Johnson, Kareem Abdul-Jabbar, James Worthy, and Jamaal Wilkes on the Los Angeles Lakers. I carried our guys to the championship.

It boggles my mind that I actually helped change NBA history. Our era was so important, and I was a big part of that. I get a huge thrill when a dad walks up to me and tells his son the impact I had.

(That is actually how I met my co-author.) Having said all that, I had a reaction when former Boston Celtics big man Dino Radja was voted into the Hall of Fame in 2018 (as an international player). I mean, Radja was a good player, but he was only in the league for four years.

My guy, Parish, who is in the Hall of Fame, was a little less diplomatic. "Max should be there for sure. Someone told me that Dino Radja was in the Hall," Parish said. "Get the fuck out…you're going to tell me Cedric can't get a nod? They put Dino Radja in, then Cedric Maxwell needs to be in the Hall of Fame. [Radja] wasn't that good, but he's in the Hall of Fame, so I'm just going to leave that alone."

It's always a hot debate when you're talking about such a prestigious honor. I remember arguing with Doc Rivers about whether Dennis Rodman should be in. I didn't think so, but Rivers was dead set in his corner. Later that night Rivers was doing a pregame press conference, and I walked by. In the middle of whatever he was talking about, he said—loud enough for me to hear—"So yes, Dennis Rodman should be in the Hall of Fame." I believe I jokingly called him an asshole right in the hallway.

I'm actually in a more exclusive club. As of 2020 there only have been 31 men who have won NBA Finals MVPs, and No. 31 was one of the 31.

ACKNOWLEDGMENTS

Writing a book like this is an all-encompassing project. There are so many people to thank, too many to mention. *But* Jeff Twiss, the vice president of media services for the Boston Celtics, was an enormous resource. His 40-plus years with the team provide incredible institutional knowledge, and he was more than willing to share that.

As a huge Celtics fan growing up in Sudbury, Massachusetts, the chance to interview guys like Robert Parish, Kevin McHale, Danny Ainge, M.L. Carr, Don Chaney, among others, was the thrill of a lifetime. When you find out that the players you idolized growing up are even better people, that's an incredible feeling.

One thing that really hit me in researching this book is the positivity and loyalty that Cedric Maxwell inspires from his friends, former teammates, and anyone that comes into contact with him. To hear hardened newspaper reporters like Dan Shaughnessy and Bob Ryan of *The Boston Globe* talk about what Max has meant to Boston ever since his arrival in 1977 was telling.

Speaking with CNN's John Berman—a Massachusetts native and huge Celtics fan of about the same age—was a great experience. It's cool to hear how Max's popularity is national.

I also want to mention several resources, which were helpful during the writing of this book, including Basketball-Reference.com, NBA TV, *The Washington Post*, the *Locked on Celtics* podcast, and ESPN's *Get Up!*

Lastly, I want to thank Max himself. He'd been approached several times about writing a book and always declined. This time he acquiesced, and I am so grateful. The first time I met Max was in the fall of 2007, which I thought was cool. To count him as a friend all these later, is mind-blowing to me.

—*M.I.*

ABOUT THE AUTHORS

CEDRIC MAXWELL is a two-time NBA champion and was named the Most Valuable Player in the 1981 NBA Finals with the Boston Celtics. He is the only forward in NBA history to lead the league in field-goal percentage twice. After his playing career, the team honored him by retiring his No. 31 in a ceremony at the Boston Garden. He has served as the Celtics radio analyst since 1995. "Cornbread" lives in the Boston area and has four adult children: Shemeka, Madison, Devin, and Dr. Morgan Maxwell, along with grandchildren Giga and Acacio.

MIKE ISENBERG is a TV talent agent at Napoli Management Group. He lives in Michigan with his wife Katie and "dog children" Vinnie, Barkley, and Toby. His son Zachary attends Michigan State University's business program, and his daughter Alexandra (aka "Cookie") studies theater. A lifelong Celtics fan, Mike grew up in Sudbury, Massachusetts. During his basketball career at Emerson College, he wore No. 31 as a tribute to his favorite player. Mike has worked at ESPN and FOX Sports Detroit and has earned 11 Michigan Emmy awards.